Taking Stock

Taking Stock

The Writing Process Movement in the '90s

Edited by
Lad Tobin
Boston College

&

Thomas Newkirk
The University of New Hampshire

Boynton/Cook Publishers
HEINEMANN
Portsmouth, NH

Boynton/Cook Publishers, Inc.
A subsidiary of Reed Elsevier Inc.
361 Hanover Street
Portsmouth, NH 03801-3912
Offices and agents throughout the world

The authors and publisher wish to thank those who have generously given permission to reprint borrowed material:

"To Juan at the Winter Solstice" (1st verse). From *Collected Poems 1975* by Robert Graves. Copyright © 1975 by Robert Graves. Reprinted with permission of Oxford University Press, Inc.

Library of Congress Cataloging-in-Publication Data
Taking Stock : the writing process movement in the 90s / edited by Lad Tobin and Thomas Newkirk.
p. cm.
Includes bibliographical references.
ISBN 0-86709-346-3 (acid-free paper)
1. English language—Rhetoric—Study and teaching. I. Tobin, Lad. II. Newkirk, Thomas.
PE1404.T25 1994
808'.042'07—dc20 94-20470
CIP

Editor: Peter R. Stillman
Production: Melissa L. Inglis

Printed in the United States of America on acid free paper
99 98 97 96 95 94 EB 1 2 3 4 5 6 7 8 9

Dedicated to
James Britton (1908–1994)

Contents

Section Three
Institutionalizing the Writing Process

Section Four
Deconstructing the Writing Process

Section Five
Narrating the Writing Process

Acknowledgments

Most of the papers in this collection are versions of presentations from the University of New Hampshire's 1992 conference, "The Writing Process: Retrospect and Prospect." The original idea for the conference came from Bob Connors, who worked with Pat Sullivan and John Lofty to develop the program. Chris Ransom did heroic work to oversee advance registration, meals, housing, and dozens of other details. She also helped with the final stages of manuscript preparation. We are also grateful to Jason Anthony, Dot Kasik, and Tammy Niedzolkowski for their help with sound equipment, on-site registration, and meal arrangements.

The conference was underwritten, in part, by grants from the Humanities Center, the College of Liberal Arts, and the Office of the Vice President for Academic Affairs. We are thankful to Burt Feintuch, Stuart Palmer, and Walter Eggers for their consistent support for our conferences.

We appreciate the help we had from the readers of individual chapters—Bob Connors, Eileen Donovan, and June Roberts. We all benefited from the two readers who responded to the entire collection and pushed us to improve it—John Lofty and Libby Rankin. We also appreciate the encouragement given us by Peter Stillman at Boynton/Cook Heinemann.

As we were completing the final editing of this manuscript we learned of Jim Berlin's untimely death. He is clearly a presence in this collection, with many authors arguing against his reading of composition history. We suspect, though, that Jim would have enjoyed these debates he helped initiate. We will certainly miss him and the uncomfortable questions he would ask about the field.

Finally, we want to acknowledge the contribution of the late James Britton to this collection and, more importantly, to the field. Though posthumous publications are always bittersweet, we are consoled by our confidence that James Britton's voice and wisdom will continue to guide and inspire teachers and scholars.

Introduction: How the Writing Process Was Born—and Other Conversion Narratives

Lad Tobin
Boston College

In spite of all the scholarly talk about protocol analyses, paradigm shifts, and the making of knowledge, the history of composition is still written primarily through the stories we tell. Stories about the dreadful ways writing was taught—or not taught—when "we were in school"; stories about the miraculous changes brought about by the writing process movement, and, lately, stories about how some of those changes may not have been so miraculous after all.

My own version usually begins with the late '60s or early '70s, not because those were the years in which the first manifestos of the writing process movement were published[1], but because that was when I was a student in a composition class. Or I begin with 1977, talking about the first writing course I ever taught. In either case, my narrative begins with self-irony and apology. It has the sort of form and tone that recovering addicts use when they describe the first throes of their addiction. I admit to certain self-destructive behaviors—writing from outlines, writing for grades—and I confess that the problem only got worse as I moved on in school.

I tell about the time Mrs. Palmer, after thirteen weeks and thirteen five-paragraph themes, finally announced, "For this final essay, you still must provide three supporting statements for your thesis,

BUT this time you do not necessarily have to provide three supporting details for each of those statements. You may decide that you can actually provide four details, or [and here she paused to let us know just how much she was giving up] . . . that you only need two." Sometimes I tell about my first days as a high school English teacher—about requiring three supporting statements and three supporting details from my own students, about shining hot lights in my students' faces until they confessed to plagiarism, and about how I got some strange pleasure from circling student errors in red ink and writing AWK! and SOURCE? and VAGUE!!! in the margins.

I will confess that I usually present these stories not just as vignettes of one miserable writing student and teacher but rather as examples of how writing was typically taught in the old days. That way they fit nicely with the following story which I tell about all life before the writing process movement:

> Once upon a time, in an age of disciplinary darkness and desolation, say about 1965 or so, writing students were subjected to cruel and inhuman punishments. They were assigned topics like "Compare Henry Fleming from *The Red Badge of Courage* to one of the characters in the *Iliad;* make sure to consider the definition of an anti-hero" or "Describe your shoelaces in great detail" or "Write about your most humiliating moment (excluding the experience of writing this essay)." They were told, with a straight face, that no decent person ever wrote without outlining first, that talking about how all cats have four legs would actually help them write a persuasive essay; that there is a clear distinction between description, definition, narrative, and argument; that grammatical errors were moral and mortal sins; and that teachers' evaluations of student essays were always objective, accurate, and fair.
>
> Sometimes they were assigned term papers on topics such as the causes of the civil war—a very dangerous procedure in those days (the term paper, not the Civil War). Not only did all of the information have to be put on special 3" x 5" cards, which were easy to misplace, mislabel, and even lose, but also although it was crystal clear that the lines separating scholarly citation from effective paraphrase from outright plagiarism must never, ever be crossed, no teacher would or perhaps could effectively explain exactly where those lines stopped and started.
>
> In fact, teachers in that dark period of our disciplinary history rarely explained anything about the *process* of writing (unless you count "outline, write, proofread, hand in" as the student's process or "assign, collect, grade" as the teacher's). Instead they would hold up products that were meant to be models—maybe a Shakespeare play or a Yeats' poem, perhaps an essay by Forster, Orwell, White, or Woolf (though probably not Woolf; after all this was still 1965)—so that students having now been exposed to great writing

could produce some of it themselves. Or they would explain some of the rules governing good writing: they might spend as much as a whole week of class on the benefits of brevity. But they would say nothing about invention, about how to get started, what to do in the middle, what to do when the middle turned back into the start, and so on.

But, remember, these were also dark days for teachers. They were the ones who had to read the summer vacation vapidities, the weekly themes on dearly departed dogs, the melodramas on "the day I won the big game." They were the ones who demanded 750 words and then had to read essays that started out:

> Gerard Manly Hopkins is a very great poet. That fact cannot be denied. In fact, he may have been one of the greatest poets of the 19th century. If he was not such a great poet, he never could have produced such an excellent poem as "God's Grandeur." In fact, his greatness is revealed in every single line of that poem. The speaker in that poem, which by the way uses an "abba" rhyme scheme, could also be called the narrator if it was a short story, but since it is, in fact, a poem, it is better to refer to him as the persona.

Here I usually pause to make sure my listener understands how miserably traditional writing instruction had failed and how desperately the times cried out for change—and for heroes. And here my version of the narrative usually shifts to quick images (like *The Dirty Dozen* or some other hokey adventure movie) where one by one the leaders of the process movement are introduced:

> There was Don Murray in the woods of New Hampshire, drawing on his experience as a REAL writer, developing one-to-one conferences, writing to learn, and the revolutionary slogans "Teach writing as a process, not a product!" and "Maybe the teacher should cut class!" . . . Ken Macrorie in Michigan railing against dishonest writing, Engfish, and weasel words and proving what students can produce when they are trusted and pushed. . . . Janet Emig at Harvard and the University of Chicago identifying previously undiscovered phenomena—that a student writer actually has an unconscious, a clue, and a composing process. . . . James Britton in Britian talking about the narrowness of school writing and the possibilities of expressivism. . . . James Moffett at Exeter Academy placing the process movement in perspective, that is, in the whole universe of discourse. . . . Peter Elbow, at MIT and then out in the woods in Washington, somehow combining a background in medieval literature and an interest in group therapy to come up with freewriting, the doubting and believing game, and Writing Without Teachers . . . and then Don Graves, Nancie Atwell, and Lucy Calkins bringing the movement to the elementary and middle schools. . . .

Somewhere along the line my story about this random collection of pioneering theorists turns into a full-fledged conversion narrative:

> Suddenly all over the country, students were told from the very first day of class that they were writers and they were treated like it: they were allowed to choose their own topics and to write in their own voices. Writing teachers, realizing, finally, that less is often more, began throwing things overboard—grammar lessons, lectures on usage, old chestnut assignments, the modes of discourse sequence, prose models, grades, rules, prescriptions. And they began experimenting with exciting new techniques—freewriting, mapping, peer editing groups, one-to-one conferences, writing workshops, portfolios. Students began to write essays that other humans might actually want to read. And, not coincidentally, teachers began to think that composition wasn't just a service course, a burden, a dues-paying debt on the way to real teaching, but actually a real field in its own right and, for some, even a calling.

I know, even while I tell it, that this story presents, first, a caricature of life before the writing process movement and, second, a misleading image of unity and coherence during it. But in spite of its excesses, I keep telling it because I believe that it conforms in some sense to a narrative or psychological (if not historical) reality of that period.

I know, of course, that there are those who would deny that the philosophies of, say, Murray, Elbow, Emig, Macrorie, Moffett, Britton, Graves, Atwell, Brannon and Knoblauch, and Calkins were ever similar enough to constitute a particular approach, let alone a coherent educational movement. And I know that there are others who would argue that these contemporary composition scholars came up with nothing new, that the roots of the process movement are really found in the approaches of early composition teachers such as Fred Newton Scott or Barret Wendell; or in the educational theories of William James, John Dewey, Sylvia Ashton-Warner, Paulo Friere, and A. S. Neill; or the psychology of Freud or Vygotsky; or the essays of Woolf, Coleridge, and Montaigne; or the philosophy of Rousseau, Plato, Aristotle.

But while writing process pedagogy clearly is indebted to all sorts of earlier theories and philosophies, it is impossible to deny its own powerful legacy: over the past thirty years or so the whole nature of the way we think about and teach writing in schools has changed. And most of us who have established careers during this period have changed along with it. I suppose that's the other reason I keep telling stories about the life before and during the process movement: it serves my own political agenda as a supporter of this particular pedagogical approach.

It also serves my agenda as a critic of traditional teaching. The writing process movement began, after all, as a critique and an alternative. In many ways, then, the term *the writing process* has always been misleading, suggesting both more and less than what the movement has come to represent. Every single written product is the result of *some* process—and almost every process leads to some sort of product. But in the composition world, the term has come to mean something else: an *emphasis* on the process, student choice and voice, revision, self-expression. But most of all it has come to mean a critique (or even outright rejection) of traditional, product-driven, rules-based, correctness-obsessed writing instruction. The process movement, then, has been a rejection of a particular kind of product—the superficial, packaged, formulaic essays that most of us grew up writing and teaching—and a particular kind of process—write, proofread, hand in, and then move on to next week's assignment.

In the old days, say the mid-80s, those of us who supported writing process pedagogy could tell stories about bad writing classes and bad writing teachers and then prescribe an antidote: change everything. And while we advocated such radical change, we were comforted by the knowledge that we occupied the higher moral ground. After all, we were speaking up against rigidity, legalism, authoritarianism, fuddy-duddyism. We were speaking up for students, freedom, innovation, creativity, and change. As long as we could characterize our opponents as old fogeys, too tired to change, we were in a pretty comfortable position.

But, like rock music, free love, political protests, and other trends that flourished in the late 60s, the writing process movement has begun to get squeezed by the past and the future, by the right and the left. The critique from traditionalists, including many administrators, teachers, and parents, was expected: the writing process was just another fad, a product of its time—interesting and maybe even understandable in its way, but, in the end, excessive, soft-headed, and irresponsible. Now, traditional opponents of process pedagogy argue, is the time to get back to basics; that is, back to grammar, usage, logic, argumentation, belles lettres, great literature. Back to standards and models. In other words, back, once again, to solving the literacy crisis in America.

Proponents of process are, of course, used to these arguments. What they are not used to is what happened next: somewhere along the line, the followers of Murray, Macrorie, Macrimmon, and Moffett, still struggling to convince the establishment, somehow became the establishment. And to their surprise and horror they suddenly found themselves exposed on their left flank (the military metaphors unfortunately seem to fit the spirit of the debate).

The leftist or cultural critique of the writing process movement starts from a different point than the back-to-basics one, but ends up, ironically, in many of the same places—with an attack on the writing process movement's radical support for student writing and student freedom. In fact, it has become increasingly difficult to distinguish between traditional and cultural critiques of process pedagogy. At a recent conference I heard progressive composition theorists—that is, theorists committed to cultural studies, social construction, oppositional politics—make statements that sound eerily similar to those made twenty years ago by traditionalists:

> "Students should not be allowed to write about themselves; we should not be afraid to assign topics."
>
> "Writing courses shouldn't focus on self-expression; they should focus on the conventions of academic discourse."
>
> "I don't see any role for personal writing in an academic setting; I'm not interested in reading an essay about some guy's pregnant girlfriend or some girl's homesickness."
>
> "We need to start focusing more on rhetoric and less on composition."
>
> "Students learn to write by reading great writing."
>
> "First year writing courses should be organized around content."

If the emphasis on material culture in literary studies is the "comeback of history," then this movement in composition is the "comeback of content." According to this argument, we need to restore real content (in this case, Supreme Court cases or advertisements or historical documents and artifacts); to move students away from thinking and writing about their own individual ethnocentric experiences and feelings; to teach the secret tropes and conventions of academic discourse; and to emphasize cultural studies, situatedness, and critique.

Where the social constructivists and cultural critics come together with the traditionalists, then, is in their criticism of expressivism and personal writing, and so that is where the critique of the writing process movement has been strongest. Though there is not a necessary connection between process pedagogy and personal writing, that is a teacher could assign a personal essay but ignore the writing process or assign a critical analysis yet nurture the process, the two have often been linked in practice and perception. From this perspective, the writing process founders are seen as terribly déclassé and outmoded: they are entrepreneurial (for emphasizing the commodification of the individual writer's assets); evangelical (for refusing to provide hard evidence, definitions, research); bourgeois (for treating students as writers or artists or free agents rather than as workers, citizens, and culturally situated beings); and, worst of all for an academic, naive (for not knowing there is no authentic voice, no single-authored text, no self).

The fact is that in the 90s, advocates of writing process pedagogy are now being caught between conservative teachers, parents, and administrators who never liked the movement in the first place and contemporary composition critics who, interested in separating themselves from the previous generation, believe they have moved beyond it. And yet in spite of these attacks, many of the fundamental beliefs of the writing process movement—that writing should be taught as a process, that writing can generate as well as record thought, that students write best when they care about and choose their topics, that good writing is strongly voiced, that a premature emphasis on correctness can be counterproductive, and so on—continue to hold power for most writing teachers and students. In fact, these ideas continue to be revolutionary to teachers and students who have always worked within a system that insisted upon a five-paragraph theme per week in which the writer could never use *I*, never write about her own experiences, and never stop thinking about grammar, usage, and the correct answer.

The result is an odd though not unusual discontinuity between theory and practice in which the writing process movement, and particularly its emphasis on expressivism, is frequently dismissed in contemporary scholarly books, journal articles, and conference papers, while it is still embraced by huge numbers of classroom teachers. (In many ways, this gap between theory and practice in composition studies is not unlike the gap that still exists in literary studies a decade after New Criticism has been dissected and dissed by high-powered literary theorists; the simple fact is that, despite the reader-respondents, post-structuralists, feminists, deconstructivists, and cultural critics, a huge percentage of literature teachers on the high school and college level continue to teach from a new critical perspective.)

This gap between theory and practice—the fact that the approaches of, say, Elbow, Murray, Macrorie, and Moffett continue to exert a powerful influence on our classrooms, textbooks, and teaching methods, even as they fall further out of favor with theorists pushing for back-to-basics on the one hand or social construction and cultural studies on the other—is one reason that the time is right to reassess the writing process movement. But there is another compelling reason: many of the current criticisms are fair, valid, and useful.

For example, contemporary composition critics are right when they point out that early writing process advocates did not pay much attention to the larger cultural and social influences on individual authors; that the movement has, for the most part, posited "the writer" in a way that erases differences of race, class, gender, personality; and, finally, that in some cases writing process pedagogy has simply replaced one mechanistic process with another: "First you brainstorm, then freewrite, then draft, revise, edit."

I think that it is fair to say that as advocates of process pedagogy many of us have often spoken about process pedagogy in inflated terms, as if it were a panacea, and have reified many of the materials and methods of our approach. Worrying too much about protecting our own turf and selling our own products—journal articles, workshops, conference papers, curriculums—we have often been guilty of oversimplifying traditional writing instructors (see my earlier caricatures) and of overselling ideas that needed more nuance and depth.

And so while I often find myself complaining about what I see as the many distortions, oversimplifications, even demonizations of process pedagogy, I suppose, in some sense, that the legend had it coming. After all, in order to critique what had become a dominant paradigm and to create space for themselves, the first generation of process theorists posited a traditional teacher who may have been something of a straw man or woman. And so it is only fair (or equally unfair) that traditionalists and leftists now tell stories in which process classrooms sound like sensitivity groups, EST meetings, Grateful Dead concerts, Zen retreats.

The problem is that the writing process has become an entity, even an industry, with a life of its own, certainly a life apart from its first theorists. Don Graves often tells the story of his shock and dismay when he first overheard two teachers discussing the differences between what they described as "the three-step and the four-step Graves writing process." And Peter Elbow, in writing about all the criticism he has received as a proponent of "expressivism," explains, "I rarely see the term used except by people who identify themselves as *not* expressive. I don't think I used the term until I began to reply to its hostile uses" (See page 200 in this volume).

But once an intellectual idea and an academic movement are established, those hostile uses are inevitable. And given how quickly and far the process movement has carried our field, I suppose we should not be surprised by the powerful backlash against it. What *is* surprising is that many contemporary theorists continue to practice process pedagogy while at the same time announcing the death of the movement. People are quick to say that we have moved beyond

Murray and Macrorie, Emig, and Elbow—and then continue to assign freewriting and multiple drafts and conferences and peer response groups. It's a little like people who tell you glibly that Freudian theory has now been proven as outmoded as Lamarcke's theory of evolution but who still acknowledge the unconscious, the significance of slips and dreams, and the value of psychotherapy—or people who say that Communism is finally dead but who see no irony that profit-sharing, socialized medicine, and social services exist in most industrialized nations. My point here is simply this: recent reports of the death of the writing process movement have been greatly exaggerated.

At the same time I will acknowlege that the movement is at a crossroads. Twenty to twenty-five years after the appearance of the primary manifestos of the process movement and ten to fifteen years after those ideas gained widespread acceptance, the field seems on the verge of another major shift. Not a shift away from the premises and pedagogies of process, necessarily, but a reconceptualization of those premises. This book grew out of our recognition, then, that the time was right and ripe for a book reassessing the ways that the writing process has been taught, institutionalized, researched, and theorized. That recognition was fostered by a national conference at the University of New Hampshire in the fall of 1992, "The Writing Process: Prospect and Retrospect." The conference brought together many of the major early and contemporary theorists of the movement. The keynote speakers were Peter Elbow, Donald Murray, Janet Emig, James Britton, James Moffett, Ken Macrorie, Lil Brannon, and Lisa Ede, while concurrent session presenters included Donald Graves, Toby Fulwiler, Andrea Lunsford, Lynn Bloom, and Richard Larsen, among many others.

In spite of this Woodstock-like lineup, the conference was not simply a feel-good, retro event; instead it was a rigorous reassessment of the movement's past and a provocative preview of its future. Almost all of the conference papers integrated the past and the present, the personal and the theoretical. In almost every case, the speakers were offering some sort of critique of process pedagogy, but it was not a critique that called for a complete rejection or overhaul. Rather it was an inside critique that called for maintaining the fundamental strengths of the approach, retrieving some valuable assets, that were thrown overboard in the first wave of excitement about process pedagogy (for example, an emphasis on reading and research), and factoring in new perspectives gained from contemporary research and theory.

While most of the contributors to this collection seek to reassess the past in terms of the present, it is these new perspectives that hold their interest. And, while none of these authors offers a horoscope for the writing process movement in the 21st century, each hints at problems and possibilities that we should anticipate in the teaching of writing. Let me suggest just three new trends or stories that lurk behind many of the chapters in this book and that, it seems to me, writing process theorists will need to follow into the next century:

The Influence of Gender, Race, Class, and Culture

Most early process theory and pedagogy paid remarkably little attention to students on the margins; to differences in race, class, and gender; or to the ways in which our goals, methods, and standards are culturally determined. As a result, the implication seemed to be that this method would work equally well for all students, or perhaps, that differences in race, gender, class, or culture were not particularly relevant or significant in this case.

Fortunately, awareness of these issues is quickly rising in scholarship and in the classroom. For example, dozens of scholars have extended our understanding of the roles gender plays in writing, reading, and learning; other scholars, such as Lisa Delpit, Denny Taylor, and Catherine Dorsey-Gaines have suggested new ways for process practitioners to think about the influence of race on writing; Mike Rose, Gordon Wells, Shirley Brice Heath, and others have examined the influence of social class on the process of literacy; Nancie Atwell demonstrated how a process approach can work with special needs students; etc. For the movement to continue, these sorts of beginnings will need to be developed.

The Effect of New Technologies

The most obvious new technology shaping the writing process is the computer. But the PC is not the first—just as the interactive network is not the last—technological development that has shaped writing theory and pedagogy. In fact, Paul Doherty has suggested that all new theories and approaches in composition have grown in part out of changing technologies: the printing press made textbooks available; slate and chalk made large-class instruction possible; affordable paper led to daily themes; and so on. To understand the new conditions facing writing students, teachers, and programs, we need to consider not only new computer technologies (such as multimedia workstations, notepads that can transform written notes or spoken words to word-processed text, new software for long-distance collaborative writing) but also the way that the popular media (such as television, rock music, and movies) continues to transform and shape contemporary American culture.

The Teacher's Reading Process

Since the process movement has always placed such a strong emphasis on student choice and on decentered authority, we have not looked closely enough at our own role. We need to look much more closely at the process we use when we read student writing. Too often we have failed to understand the complex, symbiotic relationship between a student's writing process and a teacher's reading process. In fact, too often we continue to read student essays in very traditional ways—focusing on error, acting as if we are dealing with "finished" products, isolating ourselves from other readers. A positive development would be to look more carefully at applying what we have learned about the student's writing process to our own reading process—to think, for example, about "freereading," about the recursive and revisionary nature of our interpretations, about how important our unconscious associations are when we read, about reading collaboratively with other teachers, and, finally, about how the teacher-student relationship shapes interpretation, response, and assessment.

All three of these trends build on process theory but problematize its focus on individual writers in isolation by more fully acknowledging the influence of context on content. This is a process we have tried to continue with the articles in this book. Almost all of these articles start—but don't end—with an understanding and acceptance of basic process philosophy. We were not interested in gathering together a mutual admiration society of authors who would simply extol the virtues of process pedagogy, but rather in looking critically at the past and imaginatively at the future. These articles, which speak for themselves, also speak eloquently for a new writing process movement, one that more fully integrates abstract theory and down-to-earth practice. In each section of this book, there is an attempt to locate and re-locate writing process pedagogy in terms of both contemporary theory and the author's own experiences.

In the first section, for example, each of the four contributors reads the writing process movement through personal as well as political and institutional histories. James Moffett, drawing on his own experiences as a freshman composition student at Harvard, high school English teacher at Exeter, and freelance educational consultant all over the country, explains what took the writing process movement so long to arrive, and then looks to the future by reasserting the role of self-realization in any writing course or program. Lisa Ede, while acknowledging the tremendous contributions of process theory on a personal and professional level, suggests that contemporary conditions now call on us to revise our assumptions, research strategies, pedagogical approaches, even fundamental goals. James Marshall, after establishing that the process movement grew out of the particular political climate of the early 70s, suggests that since "now we are in charge, and we cannot pretend otherwise," it is time to move beyond our sense of ourselves as rebellious outsiders. "Thus, I wonder," Marshall asks, "if it isn't time to undertake a middle-aged enterprise—to take stock, to examine what we've built, to ask with a critical eye, is this enough after all?" Finally, Don Murray suggests that it is the acceptance and even celebration of mystery, of discovery, of *not* knowing, that has been at the center of the writing process movement—and at the center of his own experiences as a writer, teacher, and researcher.

In the section on teaching the writing process, each of the contributors reexamines a fundamental relationship in the classroom. Ken Macrorie puts a new spin on the relationship between product and process, arguing that, in spite of some misunderstandings of early process theory, the quality of the product *does* matter and that certain teaching strategies, including the creation of peer-edited magazines, foster high-quality products. Daniel Reagan shows how playing with lyric poetry can reinvigorate the relationship between composition and literature by defamiliarizing language and empowering student writers. Michelle Payne, in an essay on the relationship between gender and authority, explains how the non-directive, decentered stance of process teaching can be particularly difficult and unsettling for women teachers.

The authors in the section on institutionalizing the writing process seek to put the movement into new historical perspectives. Tom Newkirk's "The Politics of Intimacy" and Charles Moran's "How the Writing Process Came to UMass/Amherst" are paired as institutional case studies of process pedagogy. Newkirk, going beyond what he demonstrates to be misinterpretations of Barrett Wendell's writing program at Harvard and of nineteenth-century American writing instruction in general, shows how an early attempt to establish a process program was thwarted by institutional biases and constraints. Though Moran claims to be telling the story of just one institution, he describes a series of changes that occurred in almost every university in the country. In the final chapter in this section, Mary Minock suggests that writing programs in the country have taken an unproven hypothesis—that expressive writing leads naturally to effective academic writing—and, given an American mythological belief in progress, made it the unquestioned cornerstone of an entire curriculum.

Each of the chapters in the first three sections attempt to show how certain theoretical principles have been played out within and around the writing process movement. In the section "Deconstructing the Writing Process," those theoretical principles are examined more directly. Peter Elbow reassesses and extends his earlier work on the uses and abuses of binary thinking about writing, teaching, and learning. Robert Yagelski responds to the postmodern critique of expressivism by showing how these seemingly different theories of meaning-making are—in theory and practice—actually quite compatible. And Thomas Recchio posits a theory of "essaying" that integrates self with culture, or in this case, that integrates his own experiences as a Marine and a literature teacher with theories of Adorno, Bakhtin, and Rorty.

In the final section, "Narrating the Writing Process," the contributors look at the ways process theorists talk and some new ways to talk about the process. Susan Wall, for example, shows how the differences in the language that classroom teachers and university theorists use about the writing process can be explained, in part, by differences in the material conditions in which they work. Wendy Bishop, in "The Perils, Pleasures, and Process of Ethnographic Writing Research," shows why the writing process and ethnographic methods are particularly well suited to each other. And, finally, James Britton discusses the relationship between story and philosophy which, not coincidentally, is where my introduction to this book began.

But it is not, we hope, where this discussion will end. Like all good stories, the pieces in this collection invite response, reflection, and, if we're lucky, other stories.

Note

1. *A Writer Teaches Writing* by Don Murray, *The Composing Process of 12th Graders* by Janet Amig, *Writing Without Teachers* by Peter Elbow, *Teaching the Universe of Discourse* by James Moffett, and *Telling Writing* by Ken Macrorie were all published between 1968 and 1973.

Works Cited

Atwell, Nancie. 1988. "A Special Writer at Work." In *Understanding Writing: Ways of Learning, Observing, and Teaching K–8.* 2nd ed. Edited by Thomas Newkirk and Nancie Atwell. Portsmouth, NH: Heinemann.

Britton, James. 1975. *The Development of Writing Abilities (11–18).* London: Macmillan.

Delpit, Lisa. 1988. "The Silenced Dialogue: Power and Pedagogy in Educating Other People's Children." *Harvard Educational Review* 58:280–98.

Doherty, Paul C. 1993. "Belles Lettres, Belles Lettres!" (presentation) *Conference on College Compostion and Communication.* San Diego.

Elbow Peter. 1973. *Writing Without Teachers.* New York: Oxford University Press.

Emig, Janet. 1971. *The Composing Process in 12th Graders.* Urbana IL: National Council of Teachers of English.

Heath, Shirley Brice. 1983. *Ways with Words: Langauge, Life, and Work in Communities and Classrooms.* New York: Cambridge University Press.

Macrorie, Ken. 1970. *Telling Writing.* Rochelle Park, NJ: Hayden.

Moffett, James. 1968. *Teaching the Universe of Discourse.* Boston: Houghton Mifflin.

Murray, Donald M. 1968. *A Writer Teaches Writing.* Boston: Houghton Mifflin. 2nd ed. 1985.

Rose, Mike. 1989. *Lives on the Boundary: The Struggles and Achievements of America's Underprepared.* New York: Free Press.

Taylor, Denny and Catherine Dorsey-Gaines. 1988. *Growing Up Literate: Learning from Inner-City Families.* Portsmouth, NH: Heinemann.

Wells, Gordon. 1986. *The Meaning Makers: Children Learning Language and Using Language to Learn.* Portsmouth, NH: Heineman

Section One

Reading the Writing Process Movement

1

Coming Out Right

James Moffett
Mariposa, California

I got all A's in English during high school and flunked my first theme in college. My high school English teachers loved my highfalutin' vocabulary, complex sentences, solid paragraphs, and clear organization. They didn't care much about what I might be saying, but they wanted me to say it right. To them composing was like carpentering or tailoring. You cut and fit until things came out right.

After all, what different students thought about one of those canned topics wasn't likely to vary much. Originality was valued precisely because unusual ingenuity was required to write something unique in these circumstances. But if you merely refurbished what you'd heard and read about the topic in the adult world, that was all right. You sounded grown up, and the purpose of education was to prepare for adulthood. Anyway, content was mainly just fodder for form, because teachers responded to student papers by pointing out faults in phrasing, sentence construction, paragraphing, and organization. Correcting of this sort went more easily the more teachers held content constant across students, who ideally would all write about the same thing. The deeper and more original the thinking, the harder it was for teachers to determine when students were saying what they didn't mean, organizing poorly, failing to document their points, contradicting themselves, or concluding inappropriately.

I fell from A to E because my freshmen composition course differed from this. My first theme there, on the open topic of "my home town," was clear, coherent, and well organized. The vocabulary was top-dollar, the sentences scanned, the paragraphs did what they said they would, and the continuity ran fluently from a beginning through a middle to a conclusion. Everything came out right. But it was ghost-written in the sense that I wasn't there. It was a vacuous tourist brochure. Harvard's old English A instructors had been as well trained to pillory formulas and drivel as my high school teachers had been to pounce on malformed sentences and meandering paragraphs. Granted a second chance to write that first week's theme, I reversed the grade and my perspective in the process. The main thing I revised was my notion of making things come out right.

But some of Harvard's subject-matter courses cast me back into high school. In general-ed science, students did a glorified sort of book reporting. That is, for our term papers we plagiarized three or four assigned texts to show that we had read and understood them. I got A's on those. Likewise, the topics of essay exams invited us only to pull together the information and concepts presented through lectures and labs. As today, writing in the subject areas was mainly a form of testing. The Shakespeare course was not the exception that one might expect. When I argued with my section man about a final exam I had written, he said that he and his colleagues in that huge course had listed eight main points that they would look for in grading that essay question on *Othello,* and that I had come up with only six of them.

When I was a kid in Jackson, Mississippi, males who dressed up carried two handkerchiefs—"one for show and one for blow," that is, one folded with a flourish into the upper jacket pocket to look sharp with a tie and another stashed in the hip pocket for real use. Consequently I now distinguish between writing to know and writing to show what you know. Writing to know is real authoring. I regard writing to show what you know—term papers and essay exams—at worst as an emetic to make students throw up what they have learned so instructors can check it out, and at best as a study aid that may help students assimilate and consolidate the content of a course. Trying to do justice to the facts and concepts of a discipline constitutes a legitimate if limited way of making things come out right. Some essay exams and term papers I wrote in some courses turned into writing to know, but only when I had so much choice, among such open topics, that I could use the material of the course to pursue the building of my own knowledge structures.

After English A, I took a creative writing course because I wanted to use writing, at last, for my own purposes. I thought I wanted to be a famous novelist, but I really wanted to understand what had happened to me as a child and to heal from it. I was writing to know. To the extent that my family trauma was available to my awareness, I fictionalized it directly. The deepest part I unconsciously allegorized through stories about other people, some drawn from the military service that I underwent between graduate school and my first teaching job, which was at Exeter.

There my continued efforts to know and heal through writing taught me a lot about literature and composition that I in turn taught my students. In trying to render how my father's alcoholism had sobered me for life, I experimented with the gamut of techniques for fiction and theatre, including converting a novel into a play. For teaching purposes I arrayed these techniques into a spectrum of first- and third-person story-telling that spanned from the infra range of interior and dramatic monolgue to the ultra range of folk tales. This spectrum became part of the structure of my courses through which my hapless students read and wrote their way. It also became an anthology of short stories called *Points of View*, compiled with a colleague, Ken McElheny.[1]

My own writing gave me insights into literature beyond what my professors had taught me, because in putting myself through what novelists and playwrights go through I became more of an insider to this great game. I tried to help my students know literature in this way also, not just as consumers but as creators. When you have tried writing fiction, plays, or poems yourself you understand more readily, without needing explanation and analysis, what professional authors are doing. You understand their options and their choices and how these relate to their subjects and their intents. My students wrote in the genres and forms they read in.

And of course telling stories leads into other kinds of discourse—making statements, some factual, some poetic. The more I wrote about the narrative spectrum, and illustrated it with professional and student samples, the more I expanded it across the whole universe of discourse, into the range of exposition and essay. As my professional life supplanted my early family trauma as something I needed to probe, my own writing was shifting from narrative to essay. (We have to change traumas from time to time.) I was now more intent to discover how to proceed with these adolescent boys whose emotional, extracurricular, and intellectual life was my job. As I wrote less to know the past than to know the present and future, I stopped writing fiction and began writing essays and books on education and on discourse itself. No doubt I was influenced too by the fact that, by more frequently publishing this work, society positively reinforced the new behavior more than it had the old. In any case, I felt that writing to know and grow professionally formed part of the same impetus toward self-realization as the writing to heal.

I often joke that although writing may have been *invented* some five thousand years ago it was *discovered* only about twenty years ago, at least in American public schools. But this was not true of

Exeter, where writing to know was thriving long before I arrived there in 1955. Oh, they assigned more lit crit papers than they should have, and kept students writing in a narrower range than they read, but some English teachers there understood that self-development is central and that the best way to achieve good exposition and essay is to cultivate personal writing first. So some of them pioneered in teaching autobiographical and investigative writing along with creative writing, not as specialities or electives but as staples. When I left Exeter after ten years to work with public schools, it was very much because I couldn't bear that such a small portion of American youth should get educational opportunities that all ought to have.

You can't separate writing from the rest of the curriculum. What I learned in my own classroom about teaching writing concerned verbal growth as a whole and teaching as a general activity. No one ever told me at Exeter what to teach or how to teach. This is what the teachers mired in public school bureaucacy who wrote to us for our secret couldn't believe. No grammar or composition books, no syllabus or canon, no set curriculum. I was never credentialed, never even took an education course, and Exeter probably wouldn't have hired me if I had. It gambled on personal qualifications and qualities. In this double-edged freedom I had to learn quickly and had to take full responsiblity for results. Free to try anything with America's best students, some of whom I knew were brighter than I was, I ran through a lot of bad ideas fast. I realized that if an activity didn't work with them, you could forget it. No better student population existed somewhere else who might make your pet idea work. On the other hand, with such high performing students you might be a terrible teacher and never know it. (The real secret of a place like Exeter is "send us winners and we'll make winners out of them.")

In those favored circumstances of a dozen learners seated around an oval table I learned student-centering, in a double sense. I could focus on individuals, and they could interact with each other. Learning could be both more personal and more social than ordinarily possible in public school. This meant I could conference with individuals and turn classes into workshops. For tighter interaction I sometimes broke even this dozen or so down into trios and quartets. To facilitate conferences and workshops, I created a folder for each student to keep his writing in (*his* because Exeter was not then co-ed).

For my own growth I was interested in group dynamics and participated in a variety of small awareness and therapeutic groups, which were first being tried at the National Training Laboratory in Bethel, Maine, and in pre-Esalen, General Semantics groups in Calfornia, where I went on sabbatical. Trying to write my family drama as a play engaged me in the group dynamics of the theater. I took courses in improvisation and thought about using small-group discussion and improvisation as ways to further academic, esthetic, and practical learning all at once. For me drama took on a broad sense that encompassed theater and therapy, dialogue and dialectic.

As a research associate at the Harvard Graduate School of Education, I spent the three years following Exeter experimenting with and writing up an innovative language arts curriculum for public schools. While this university environment sponsored very effectively my efforts to bring to public schooling what I thought I had learned about teaching, I began to see how academe itself was a major stumbling block to improving education. The more I read about and discussed the scholarship and research influencing schools, the more university disciplines like rhetoric, linguistics, and literary criticism appeared to me as culprits rather than saviors. Often I felt that what I was trying to replace in public schools had been imposed in the first place by university people allowed to pull rank because of their position at the top of the educational hierarchy. Thus not only were colleges pressing hard on schools to sacrifice the individual uses of writing to their institutional uses for evaluation, but also some scholars and educators were causing schools to misconceive what they were doing by misapplying specialists' formulations to learning processes.

Like structural grammar before it, for example, the new transformational grammar seemed to justify prolonging a fanatical focus on the isolated sentence, a focus that translated into the classroom as drills and exercises. What may be a properly narrow or specialized arena for investigation can become a crippling compass for learning. I found interesting the work of Francis Christensen on levels and direction of sentence modifiers,[2] of my friend John Mellon on sentence combining (which he himself never pursued beyond research),[3] and of the tagmemics people, who, God bless them, managed to haul themselves up from the sentence to the paragraph and perhaps eventually beyond.[4] But I deplored converting this research directly into school activities that were billed new but that perpetuated a major cause of school ineptitude—stripping away contexts and zooming in on artificial particles. It has taken many years for what is now called the whole language movement to even begin to offset the atomistic exercises engendered from the subfields of linguistics like lexicon and syntax. American linguistics left its mark on education before it began to expand into psycholinguistics and sociolinguistics, which have restored those realistic personal and cultural contexts of language that accommodate human learning processes.

The discipline of rhetoric provided a larger purview, but again, concepts intended to describe, classify, and analyze for other purposes were peddled as pedagogy. In keeping with medieval and renaissance traditions, we presented students with rhetorical ideals but not with the practical means of attaining them, because the logical is not the psychological, and taxonomy tends toward taxidermy. Teachers were trained to prescribe all sorts of good things like unity and coherence, consistency and harmony, clarity, vividness, proportion, and so on but were never shown how human beings really achieve these when authoring from authentic subjects and for authentic audiences. True, rhetoric had inherited a whole arsenal of *devices* such as topic sentences and transitional phrases, paradox and parallelism, foreshadowing and incremental repetition. But these could only come across to students as a bag of mechanical tricks. What was missing were the circumstances of some actual practitioners. The upshot of offering only ideals of good composition on the one hand and only isolated techniques on the other, without situations to join and vitalize these within the student, was to create a pedagogy of nagging—of admonishing before writing and scolding after: "I *told* you to be clear, cogent, and coherent, but, you see, you didn't heed me." The problem was not that psychological theories of rhetoric like Kenneth Burke's didn't exist,[5] but that, unless mediated considerably for education, scholarship ends up mangled and mangling.

Writing suffered, like literature, from the whole effort to make English look like school content subjects instead of construing discourse as a set of activities to be practiced. Since most English teachers majored in literature, they tried to draw on it for help in teaching writing. But literary criticism has tended to historicize and scientize literature. "Study it but don't practice it." Like the other arts, literature has been objectified as a corpus of facts and concepts—romanticism and onomatopeia—and formated to fit the pedagogy of academic courses. The imperative to cover it and conceptualize it prevented teachers from offering literature as a live tradition that all students may participate in. The change came, symbolically, when we turned to the *Paris Review* interviews with professional writers and inaugurated the writers-in-the-schools programs.

The teaching of writing improved only after we quit looking to linguistics, rhetoric, and literary criticism for guidance and turned instead to actual practice outside of classrooms. The so-called process approach amounts to no more than teaching writing as adult practitioners go about it. It is phasing composition into the recursive stages of mulling, looking around, conferring, drafting, seeking feedback, revising, and polishing that people who write for real purposes have always found themselves doing. Implementing the practitioner's way into schools did not depend on new research or new theory. The process approach was always there waiting for us. It was what we should have been doing all along and would have had we not confused the basic human act of discoursing with the kind of knowledge you can store in vaults, just because they were both being taught in the same buildings.

It was also only when we looked beyond academic walls that we began to open up the range of discourse that students might write in. Journalism and creative writing had been offered but mainly only as electives, which is to say they were put up on a shelf out of reach of most students. Teachers constantly ask how to get students from personal experience writing to exposition and argumentation, and I say one of the best ways is through investigative writing, staring us in the face as one of the most commonly practiced and highly developed sorts of discourse in our society but one of the least practiced in schools. When I tried during the 80s to anthologize student samples of investigative writing from schools and colleges, I had a terrible time locating enough even though I searched across the whole country and called on the National Writing Project network.

The problem of the narrow range of writing is twofold. Writing has for generations been usurped as an instrument for evaluating reading, starting with the book reports in grade school, continuing through essay exams and term papers in high school and college, and culminating in the doctoral dissertation, which with its opening "survey of the literature" and its following references and concluding bibliography served as the model of writing to show what you know. This is why even grade-schoolers have had to make heavy weather out of the format for footnotes and citations, a piece of trivia that varies according to style sheet anyway. Under one guise or another, schools and colleges make you write after you read.

Couple this with the fact that most English teachers were taught to write critiques of literature and you get a writing program that services the reading program, that kills two birds with one stone. This seems to make things come out right. The false problem of what students should write *about,* which has hounded writing pedagogy to this day, stems from an insistence on teacher control. The problem arises when teachers want to standardize subject matter and limit it to what they are familiar with in order to facilitate "correcting" papers. The excuse is that kids don't *know* what they want to write about, which is true if they haven't experienced choice before. A critical part of the process approach concerns how authors come up with their own subject matter.

The second main reason for the narrow range of writing arises from the fact that teachers were once students. So most English teachers themselves have never done any kind of writing except writing to show what you know, or at a bit more elevated level, literary criticism. Writing about books is a narrow specialty in the world out of school and represents only a small band of the discourse spectrum. And even when teachers learn to do other sorts of writing in Writing Project institutes and when the profession *talks* a lot about broadening the writing repertory, I find that even the best writing teachers settle into a relatively narrow range of discourse that they prefer and have become familiar with. And many good teachers still have their students spend an inordinate amount of their writing about books. At Exeter I did too, because the math and history and science and foreign language teachers were testing constantly, so that if I did not make students write something on the reading, they would punt it and spend their time on the tougher courses. This problem is not likely to go away until schooling is placed on another footing than compulsion and testing, and writing is honored as a humanistic activity in its own right.

The university's implication in the very problems of schooling that it later set about trying to rectify merely echoed, I found, the implication of the whole society in the poor education that the public doublemindedly thought it wanted reformed. Experimenting in schools around Boston while at the Harvard Ed School showed me a brutal truth that twenty-five years of consulting around the continent since have only confirmed in harrowing detail. Changes in education would not happen through dynamic new understanding about learning, because the conditions of learning were determined by noneducational factors. I discovered that futile sentence exercises were masquerading as composition because the public had a grammar mystique that no school superintendent dared cross, no matter what educators thought; that schools *bought* their curriculum in a box in which writing had small place and teachers little voice; that standardized testing not only drove the curriculum but set *teaching* models, as in the fraudulent College Board "composition" exam, which required no writing; that the sheer bureaucratic institutionalism of schooling left little room for writing and militated against the personal and interactive approaches it needed.

The fractionation of discourse that characterized university disciplines meshed only too well with the meaningless breakdowns that suited multiple-choice testing, the commercial programs geared to them, the mechanistic and manipulative managerial systems installed in classrooms over the heads of teachers, the generally splintered and depersonalized effects of managing schools like factories, and the public's pressure to keep schooling innocuous by sanitizing it.

I became a free-lancer eventually who worked with schools and colleges but avoided permanent institutional affiliations. "Self-unemployed," I think the term is. The reason I did this was that I could see no other way to stay focussed full-time on how to change public education. This specialization put me in a position to troubleshoot *why* schooling was the way it was and why it was so hard to change. The reasons are intricate of course, but the single most powerful block to improving schools has been this fortuitous match-up between the penchants of academic disciplines to break down and depersonalize subjects in order to study them and the corresponding societal penchants to break down and depersonalize education in order to institutionalize it according to our political, commercial, and cultural imperatives. This is why the movement that has tried most to remove this block in English education has had to stress whole language for whole people.

In looking to the future it's important to acknowledge that desirable change does not, as I began my career believing, await insightful new research findings nor brilliant new conceptions about teaching and learning. I've come to believe instead that if we actually implemented the best that we already know, we could have a splendid writing program in a splendid total curriculum.

Many people have known for a long time what English education needs now and in the future, because society has had a long practical experience with literacy. The more we look to this experience the more we realize that the main problem is to reorganize schooling for it. I have never regarded my own proposals for teaching English as new ideas but rather as sensible things others proposed before me that would have been implemented a long time ago had public education not been forced to accommodate business other than its own. Academic people seem bowled over by research telling us that the language of many school children is different from that of the classroom, or that people have multiple intelligences, or that writing requires a mental organization that is less difficult for narrative than for exposition. The people whose language or learning modality was discriminated against knew these so-called *findings* all along, as did no doubt many of the people who lived or worked with them. Maybe some *university* people did not know these things. Likewise, people who had done both narrative and expository writing knew bloody well which might require more difficult mental organization. Much research strikes me as one class of people finding out at last how another class lives. That's fine, but let's don't pretend nobody knows the things we need to know to improve the teaching of writing until formal research rends the veil.

A kind of research, however, that helps bring on change—well exemplified by some work here at UNH—demonstrates that some activity not common in school works and works perhaps better than another that no longer deserves a berth aboard. To this we may add another positive kind of research that consists, precisely, of observing or interviewing practitioners out of school as they go about or talk about a target activity such as writing.

Public education has to move in the future, I believe, toward increasing control of learning by learners. Truly individualizing would overcome most school problems, because it could accommodate a great variety of issues usually considered separately, from apathy and boredom to those cases of speaking a nonstandard dialect or favoring a nonverbal modality. Most school problems come from standardizing activities—making everybody read the same text or write in a certain genre or on a certain topic at the same time, or read and write for the same assumed motivation in the same stipulated conditions. It is the particularity of circumstances that makes learning happen, along with feeling in control of what you do. Students should be constantly making decisions about everything from the genre and subject and audience of their writing down to phrasing and punctuating.

But individualizing does not obviate social interaction, which is in fact essential to writing. Decisions about what to write and how to go about it can be made with partners or in workshops or under the influence of mid-composition conferences with teachers or others. And other people, after all, afford the motives and audiences for most writing. Drop composition texts, which are not needed when you quit standardizing, and use the money for desktop publishing, which will foster dissemination and exchange. Workshops can allow for individualizing by letting students bring to their group not only papers they have written in a common genre but kinds of writing they have elected to do independently.

Letting individual students write different things at the same time can alleviate a major unsolved problem that gets worse as students progress through school and into college. At a given moment classmates don't all need experience in the same kind of writing. Some may have done a lot of personal narrative and some little or none. Or some may master or tire of it sooner than others. Some simply want to do a kind that others don't at the moment. Readiness is all in these matters. Teachers should use portfolios and conferences to find out which kinds of writing might be best next for an individual. When students see others doing kinds of writing they haven't, they get inspired or intrigued to try them also. This is one reason why we shouldn't *want* students to be doing the same thing at the same time except as small working parties elect to write in common.

College composition courses will benefit most of all from individualizing because virtually no incoming students have written their way developmentally up to the kind of abstract and analytical writing colleges want. A semester or even a full-year course is not long enough to bring a class to this point *evenly*, because putting everyone through the same sequence of assignments is terribly inefficient when some need only certain kinds of writing and some need others. I would counsel students about this individually according to their particular experience and problems or motives. This means that any given workshop session may be dealing with somewhat mixed kinds of writing, but this will further the aim of filling in everyone's writing experience.

For purposes of individualizing, I have long worked at arraying a repertory of discourse and illustrating it with anthologies of professional and student writing. If student decision-making lies at the heart of individualizing, what are the choices? Students and teachers can work together in such a repertory to understand what all the kinds of writing are and to discover how they relate to each other. Authors choose subject matter from experience, investigation, or imagination according to authentic personal intentions. From the repertory authors choose the kind of discourse—poem, editorial, memoir, factual article, fable, how-to directions, and so on. What to write about becomes a chronic problem of head-scratching and staring at blank paper only because unrealistic composition conditions do not permit student authors to choose subject matter befitting the circumstances of their inner and outer life.

What I've suggested so far for the future assumes courses, classes, subjects, and schools more or less as we have known them. But in ten to twenty years these will of necessity evolve into something very different. Learning will not primarily be organized around disciplines but around projects cutting across subjects and resembling activities now going on out of school to make something, investigate something, or improve something. Some projects will be individual, some group, but all designed by learners with the help of teachers and other specialists. Ages will become mixed as this school-based projects curriculum evolves into a total community learning network for everybody all the time.[6]

Learning sites and opportunities will then be located all over a community and include apprenticeships, tutoring, and other arrangements. Learners may choose not just a specialized site, as now proposed through magnet schools, but may put together their own programs, availing themselves at any time of any learning resources across the whole network. For a good example of a school interdisciplinary projects curriculum on its way to being a community learning network, look at the McFarland Model being tried in Wisconsin under the name of Project 2061 and under the sponsorhip of the American Association for the Advancement of Science.[7]

Both the projects curriculum in schools of the current sort and its eventual evolution into the community learning network will change drastically not how we think today about learning to write but how we may organize for it. Actually, projects supply precisely the realistic writing circumstances schools have lacked—the motives and the processes and the total repertory of discourse that the infinite variety of projects entails. In parallel with the International Reading Association's position that reading comprehension should not be taught as a separate subject but through the other subjects, projects will ensure that writing not remain a separate course with only reading or trumped up topics for subjects but will be distributed across all subject matters and endeavors that call for it. Projects will consumate our positive trend to base the teaching of writing on what practitioners do in real life. It will consumate "writing across the curriculum," "whole language," and the "process approach."

But where will the writing teacher be in all this? All teachers will obviously be reassigned in some way and will feed in their expertise differently than now. Projects require teams of specialists either directly involved or immediately on tap. Something like the writing process and writing workshop would have to become a familiar part of the educational culture so that older learners could initiate younger in them as they worked together, and everyone grew up knowing how to do these. Though their role will change, experts in writing and discourse will be needed to prime and maintain this rippling process, to help learners familiarize themselves with the discourse repertory, to advise on particular projects, and generally to bring their special knowledge of language and literature to bear on this new organization of learning. Personal counseling will be at a premium, because as an extension of individualization over a broader environment, this sort of future will work only if educators constantly help learners connect with the right activities, people, sites, and materials at the right times. If this sounds disquieting, consider that today's English teachers will probably be readier for all this than most other teachers.

If this doesn't sound disquieting *enough*, let me throw in one final possibility. A major reason it has been so difficult to sponsor writing in schools and colleges is that they in effect barred at the outset two of the main reasons why people may choose to write on their own. I alluded to one in speaking of my own writing to heal. Any successful writing program has to allow, and allow for, therapy. The other writing motive that institutions haven't welcomed aims beyond healing toward a spiritual sort of personal development—self-realization at whatever depth one understands the self. Contrary to the criticism, by the way, that a personal approach to writing is narcissistic or asocial, fostering this sort of self-development makes people more empathic and more moral. Social relationship is part of the humanity that develops as a person grows. Everything that rises must converge. Can you imagine self-realization that did not include relations with other people? Can you imagine any kind of social ill that greater personal maturity will not be required to solve?

I was helped to understand the chasm between these basic writing motives and present educational institutions by a session at the 1992 Conference on College Composition and Communication called "Spiritual Sites of Composing"[8] The three presenters, all women, gave examples of writing groups that participants chose to join for purposes of healing and personal growth in a spiritual direction. All of their examples, and ones I could think of, take place off-campus. Schools and colleges feel that therapy and spirituality are not their business. "You can heal and grow on your own time. We're not shrinks and priests." But you don't have to be to include these motives in writing programs, now or in the future.

Actually, projects and a community network should be able to accommodate healing and spirituality far more easily than today's institutions. Authors will do their own healing and growing for themselves when licensed to utilize writing for personal motives and to frame it in projects involving others. Individualized writing teaches learners to determine, and be responsible for, their own subjects, genres, and audiences according to their needs and purposes. Some writing under these circumstances will always be therapeutic and spiritual, as it currently is in voluntary, adult, off-campus classes and workshops. Teachers help authors to know what the writing repertory consists of and to find the partners and other means to accomplish what they have in mind. When requested, you respond as you deem useful to everything from exploratory and interim talking-out to written drafts. Given this teaching situation, motives and subjects make no difference, since your job is to facilitate any emerging discursive experience. Whether you distinguish writing to heal or grow from other composition depends on your judgment in a given instance as to whether such identifying will further your student's education. Individualization is nothing if not playing case by case.

In this way you can sponsor writing to heal and grow and remain just a writing teacher, not become a shrink or priest, but you understand that two such powerful reasons to write must be acccommodated for a writing program to succeed. If education is supposed to help people get better, that's not only in the sense of "get better *at* something," like writing, but in a second sense of "get well" and in a third sense of "become a better person." People want to *get better* in all senses at once. We don't just want our *writing* to come out right, *we* want to come out right.

Notes

1. A thoroughly revised version is scheduled for publication in early 1995 by NAL/Dutton (New York).

2. Francis Chistensen. 1967. *Notes Toward a New Rhetoric.* New York: Harper and Row.

3. John Mellon. 1969. *Transformational Sentence-Combining.* Urbana, IL: National Council of Teachers of English, Research Report 10.

4. Richard Young, Alton Becker, and Kenneth Pike. 1970. *Rhetoric: Discovery and Change.* New York: Harcourt Brace.

5. Kenneth Burke. [1945] 1962. *A Grammar of Motives and a Rhetoric of Motives.* New York: World Publishing Company.

6. This concept is the subject of *The Universal Schoolhouse: Spiritual Awakening Through Education* (San Francisco: Jossey-Bass, 1994), where I have developed it in some detail within a universalist kind of spirituality.

7. *Project 2061: Education for a Changing Future: McFarland Model.* 1991. Washington D.C.: American Association for the Advancement of Science.

8. Published as a symposium in *College Compostion and Communication* (May 1994, pp. 237–63).

2

Reading the Writing Process

Lisa Ede
Oregon State University

This chapter represents my effort to "read" the writing process movement—and to do so in a particular way. Rather than asking whether the writing process movement as it was constituted and practiced during the last twenty years is good or bad, conservative or progressive, theoretically and pedagogically sound or flawed, I wish instead to consider a different series of questions. What function, for instance, has the writing process movement played in the disciplinary and institutional formation of the field of composition studies? What discursive practices helped constitute the writing process movement as a movement, and what disciplinary desires might this constitution reflect? What can a reading of the writing process movement tell us about the relationship between theory and practice as it has been both textually and materially inscribed in our field?

This essay thus attempts to investigate how the writing process movement has been both "written" and "read" in the field of composition studies. But what of my own role in this analysis? (There is, we have come to understand, no innocent reading or writing of texts or practices.) I write this as one whose early years in our field not only coincided with the ascendancy of the writing process movement but who has had considerable theoretical, pedagogical, and personal identification with it. I also write as one concerned (as many are) about the future of composition studies, one interested in considering whether there might be different and more productive ways of constituting ourselves and our field. And I write as one increasingly influenced by feminist theories and practices, one interested in exploring alternatives to traditional academic argument, which so often relies on totalizing and oppositionalizing strategies. Later I will suggest that arguments for what has come to be called writing as a *social* process have at times depended upon just such strategies to justify their own revolutionary rhetoric. For the moment I would simply note how seldom academic arguments make space for appreciation, for acknowledgement of the ways in which current intellectual projects depend upon those which they critique.

I wish to begin this "reading" of the writing process movement, then, by acknowledging the impact that research on the writing process has had on my development as a writer, teacher, and scholar. I do so knowing that some readers may construct such a reflection as confessional (a term used by an anonymous reviewer of this manuscript), as an inappropriate eruption of the personal into the scholarly. I do so nevertheless because I am acutely aware of the extent to which my current understanding of the writing process movement grows out of previous experiences of and identifications with it.

When I think back to my years as an undergraduate and graduate student, I realize that in an important sense I didn't *have* a writing process. What I did (or didn't) have was luck—luck and rituals and the sense that writing had a force and logic of its own, a force and logic that I couldn't understand, much less employ for my own purposes. At my very best I composed slowly, painfully, revising each sentence as I wrote, spending hours on an introductory paragraph that might well be—and often was—discarded. Because I was willing to spend not just hours but days working on even brief papers, I was generally able to write essays that pleased my instructors. But the cost was high.

Too high to continue paying as a new assistant professor. The pressures in my early years of teaching were substantial. A literature "retread" attempting to pass myself off as an expert in composition studies (my Ph.D. is in Victorian literature), I needed to teach three classes a semester, direct a writing program, and publish—all while attempting to educate myself about my new field of study. I couldn't afford to continue my slow, halting writing process. Sometime during my first few years of teaching it occurred to me that I should do more than study the theoretical and pedagogical implications of the writing process studies that I was beginning to read in the journals—I should *learn* from them.

This was no academic interest. If I was to survive professionally—to get tenure—I needed to become a more efficient and productive writer. And so, influenced by early process research, I began to study myself; I became my own laboratory rat. In an informal but systematic manner I observed myself, taking notes on my own writing process during and, especially, at the end of drafting sessions. And learn I did. I learned that I needed to resist my tendency to fiddle endlessly with sentences, that I needed to focus on developing my ideas and to forestall concern with style until later in the process. I learned that I could actually work too hard and long on my writing, that I could often be more productive if I stopped writing while I was still fresh enough to articulate questions and problems for the next day's work. I learned that, yes, I had to trust that revision would help clarify my ideas. (I *didn't* learn how much others could help me by responding to work in progress, or how rewarding writing with another can be. This understanding came later, primarily as a result of my collaboration with Andrea Lunsford, my friend and coauthor.)

I know from my own experience, then, that thinking about and attending to the writing process can help a motivated writer, if not all writers, become more productive and efficient. And as a teacher I have seen what it can mean to students when they understand, really understand, that writers are made, not born, that writing is not an inherently magical or mysterious activity. In my twenty years of teaching I have watched students who felt defeated by language discover, as I discovered, that they could analyze—and change—their writing behaviors. And I have seen students who had written only to be tested understand that they can use language not only to express ideas of genuine importance to them but to learn new concepts, to understand that which had previously been murky and unclear.

The writing process movement has had a significant impact upon my own writing and teaching. But I wish to acknowledge also the impact that research on the writing process has had upon my scholarly work. Many of the early studies of the writing process evoked in me that "eureka" or "aha" response that hits when we suddenly see that which our common sense understanding—of writing, of our students, of our role as teachers—has kept hidden from us. *Of course* student errors aren't perverse and random manifestations of ignorance but rather "traces of the different pressures and codes and confusions that have gone to make up 'English'" (Shaughnessy 1977, 10) as they have experienced it. *Of course* writing is not a rigid, sterile filling in of forms but a recursive process requiring writers to attend to, and value, their "felt sense" as they compose (Perl 1980, 115). The studies of such scholars as Mina Shaughnessey and Sondra Perl are essential features of my intellectual landscape. My own research has been stimulated and nurtured by these efforts.

My current effort to "read" the writing process movement is grounded, then, in a deep appreciation of the contributions of a number of scholars whose work in the sixties and seventies helped define the initial theoretical and pedagogical projects of our field—scholars like Ken Macrorie, Peter Elbow, James Britton, Donald Murray, James Moffett, and Janet Emig. I want to acknowledge the achievements of these and other scholars and the impact that this admittedly broad and diverse movement has had on our field. But what is, and should be, the status of the writing process movement in the *contemporary* disciplinary scene?

In considering this question, it is important to remember that the writing process movement—like all scholarly and pedagogical movements—developed in response to specific disciplinary and institutional conditions. Like all texts, the essays and books that most clearly defined the writing process movement were rhetorically situated; they were composed at a particular time and in a particular (disciplinary and institutional) place. Of particular consequence in this regard is what was then termed the literacy crisis of the early seventies. In response to cries that "Johnny Can't Write," scholars such as Shaughnessy, Emig, and Flower and Hayes argued that Johnny—and Jane—could write if we better understood the strategies they brought to bear when faced with the task of composing. It was also in the early seventies that composition studies began to assert itself as an academic discipline, not just the service wing of the English department. Many of the studies from this period conveyed an implicit as well as explicit message—that scholars in the newly-minted field of composition studies were better prepared than others in the education establishment to respond to the needs of students and that they had their own disciplinary enterprise and scholarly contribution to make.

The writing process movement thus helped to create and to legitimate the field of composition studies. It did so both by responding to a crisis, the literacy crisis, and by in effect creating a theoretical crisis of its own. In 1970, for instance, Janice Lauer began an essay on "Heuristics and Composition" as follows: "Freshman English will never reach the status of a respectable intellectual discipline until both its theorizers and its practitioners break out of the ghetto" (80). Writing in 1978, after the "writing as process" movement was well established, Richard Young similarly posited a crisis in composition. For too long, Young asserted, teachers of writing have been committed to a "current-traditional paradigm" (30), one that emphasizes, among other things, "the composed product rather than the composing process" (31). If we recognize that teachers' commitment to this paradigm comprises a "crisis in our discipline," we can, Young argues, "make a kind of sense out of the recent and rapidly growing interest in the composing process and the numerous proposals for controlling it. And we can also construct a rationale for a program of research" (35). Continuing Lauer's and Young's rhetoric of crisis and revolution, in 1982 Maxine Hairston proclaimed that the "move to a process-centered theory of teaching writing indicates that our profession is probably in the first stages of a [Kuhnian] paradigm shift" (77).

More than a decade later, Hairston's proclamation that composition studies was in the first stage of a "paradigm shift" can seem both hasty and naive. Indeed, with the 20/20 vision of hindsight we can now see that which the terminological screen of the times kept hidden. Should we be so surprised that some of those aspects of the writing process movement that seemed most valuable at the time now seem, if not most problematic, then most in need of re-visioning?

Consider, for instance, the writing process and the student writer. Any consideration of this issue must confirm, as Lester Faigley has noted, that process theory and pedagogy gave "student writing a value and authority absent in current-traditional approaches" (1986, 537). Most process theory did not, however, acknowledge the extent to which both its methods and its conclusions depended upon the reduction of students, in all their diversity, into a construct called the student writer, and of writing, with its rich multiplicity, into student writing. (Another obvious issue here is the process movement's unquestioned acceptance of the "the" in "*the* student writer.")

Similarly, process theory did both students and teachers a great service by challenging rigid and formalistic stage-model pedagogies. But the concept of "process" governing its own theory and practice was seldom scrutinized. Recent arguments about cognitive-based research in general, and protocol studies in particular, have reminded us of the potentially mechanistic, and even industrial, connotations of this term. To the extent that this mechanistic conception of process has literally and metaphorically informed both the teaching of and research on writing, it has inevitably oversimplified and distorted a phenomenon whose richness and complexity we have yet adequately to acknowledge.

A similar tension might be noted when considering the role the writing process movement has played in catalyzing institutional change. That it played such a role seems clear: research on the writing process, particularly as articulated and embodied in the Bay Area (and, later, National) Writing Project, influenced not only the way that teachers at all levels went about the business of teaching writing but also its curricular and institutional context. Particularly important in this regard are the Project's non-hierarchical, collaborative, decentralized structure and its respect for the capabilities, and professionalism, of teachers. But any consideration of the role that the writing process movement has played in effecting institutional change must also acknowledge the ease with which these changes not only can be but at times have been coopted and commodified—by textbooks that oversimplified and rigidified a complex phenomenon, by overzealous language arts coordinators and writing program administrators who assumed that the process approach to teaching could be "taught" in one or two in-service sessions, by all those who (myself included) forgot that the very term "writing process movement" refers not to a concrete and material reality but to an ideologically-charged construct.

And perhaps this is the moment to acknowledge the substantial diversity of the activities that are often lumped together under the rubric of the writing process movement. Janet Emig's, Donald Graves', Peter Elbow's, and Linda Flower's research projects differ in as many ways as they are similar, for instance, yet all have been cited as examples of process research. Such diversity is also evident in the disparate, and at times even contradictory, pedagogical activities that teachers have cited as evidence of their commitment to a process approach to writing. A class structured around freewriting and personal narration differs substantially from one that emphasizes structured heuristics and academic writing, for instance, yet both approaches have been cited as examples of "process" teaching. Given this diversity, we might well consider the extent to which the teaching and research activities that have characterized this orientation justify the term "movement" at all.

As Susan Miller observes in *Textual Carnivals*, there are indeed "many slips between [announcements of paradigm shifts] and the lips of the majority of teachers and students" (1991, 105). Changes in approach and curricula that take hold in universities and model public school programs don't necessarily circulate through all of our educational institutions as fully as we might prefer to think—and what does circulate can be considerably altered in the process. We need to at least acknowledge the possibility, then, that in an important sense the writing process movement has existed more strongly in the discursive practice that we call theory than in the theoretical enactments that take place daily in our classrooms. But such is also the case, I would argue, with this movement's announced successor project, the writing as a social process movement. As James Reither and Douglas Vipond note in "Writing as Collaboration," writing as a social process has "become [such a] dominant strand in our literature and at our conferences. . .[as to constitute] a kind of revolution in composition theory" (855). Despite its theoretical impact, there has not, they argue, been "a corresponding transformation in the ways writing is conceived and dealt with in our classrooms" (1989, 855). Collaborative writing activities, for instance, are still very much the exception in most composition classrooms—including those taught by advocates of writing as a social process.

For all its valuing of the social, the writing as a social process movement has valued some forms of socially-generated knowledge more than others. Consider that form of socially-generated knowledge that we term student resistance. Only recently have researchers begun to investigate the nature and implications of student resistance—despite the fact that such resistance is surely one of the most salient features of the pedagogical scene. Furthermore, as any language arts curriculum coordinator or director of composition knows, students are not alone in maintaining an active "underlife" (to use Robert Brooke's [1987] term); teachers can be equally adept at finding ways to enact their resistance to discourses that oppress them. For many classroom teachers, theory is such a discourse. And yet until recently teachers' resistance to theory has most often been treated as a problem—a sign of teachers' anti-intellectualism or of the need for more theoretical training—rather than, as Louise Phelps notes in *Composition as a Human Science*, an "arguable issue" that is one of our "constitutive problems" as a field (1988, 207).

Despite their differences, then, the writing as a process and writing as a social process movements have thus shared in the academy's general devaluation of practice. As feminists have helped us to see, this disvaluation is gendered—and in more ways than the obvious. Our assumption that theory should inform and guide practice, for instance, reflects the western tradition's positivistic claims for reason. These claims situate the "man of reason" above and beyond the buzzing and blooming multiplicity of everyday life. Like the patriarchal father, the man of reason in his abstract and decontextualized wisdom sees the unvarying and universal "laws" that women and children (and teachers), caught up as they are in the daily and the contingent—or so the familiar western narrative of reason goes—cannot see. So powerful has this conception of reason (and of theory) been that only now are we beginning to see through its claims to question the rejection of the particular and the situated—of, for instance, the knowledge required to interpret and act upon the "teachable moment"—upon which it depends.

I have just argued that research on writing as process and as social process share central epistemological assumptions about knowledge and its relationship to practice. These two movements also have relied, I believe, upon similar foundational principles and strategies. Each, for instance, in effect constituted itself through a denial of origins that involves creating that which it wishes to oppose and then erasing the shared ground that made the original construction of the other possible. In an important sense current-traditional rhetoric did not exist until advocates of writing as a process created it; similarly, the writing as a social process movement can exist only in opposition to—and thus in dependence upon—a consolidated and reified writing as a process movement. This strategy is, as deconstruction has taught us to see, a characteristic move of the western intellectual project. The same move both constitutes "woman" as Other while denying the extent to which privileged "man" depends upon the maintenance of that very construct. It also discourages individuals of both sexes from critiquing those shared assumptions—such as the assumption that humans are coherent, autonomous individuals—upon which *both* constructs depend.

There are a number of problems with this general approach to constructing and maintaining intellectual projects. Feminist theorists, for instance, have begun to recognize the counterproductiveness of recent debates over what have been termed essentialist and poststructuralist theories of gender. As Diana Fuss (1989) notes in *Essentially Speaking*, arguments about essentialism have resulted in a theoretical impasse that threatens to derail feminism's political (and thus also pedagogical) goals. Fuss goes on to argue that rather than being oppositional binaries, essentialism and poststructuralism (or, in her terms, constructionism) in fact depend upon each other. The tension created by this binary opposition has, she argues, been responsible for "some of feminist theory's greatest insights" (1).

We need to consider, I believe, whether our own field (which in terms of its origin and situation in the academy has so much in common with feminist studies) might be in a similarly unproductive theoretical, political, and pedagogical place. I believe that this may at least in part be the case. I suggest this not to discredit or disvalue earlier research that has in fact helped bring me to my current understanding—I hope it is clear that I want to resist this argumentative strategy. I also do not see myself as arguing for yet another theoretical revolution in our field. Indeed, I wish to challenge the very idea of theoretical revolutions, with its concommitant hierarchized theory-practice binary. Rather, I raise this issue because I am concerned that our own pedagogical and political project may be at risk.

I wish to suggest, then, that it is perhaps time to call an end to arguments about whether the writing process movement has been good or bad, progressive or reactionary. These arguments—which have often relied upon the taxonomizing and categorizing of theories and theorists and the consolidating and reifying of diverse activities and approaches into movements—have served a purpose. (Jim Berlin's [1987] taxonomies in *Rhetoric and Reality: Writing Instruction in American Colleges, 1900-1985* helped us make sense, for instance, of what at the time seemed like a bewildering array of competing theories and practices.) But perhaps as a field we are established enough—and have learned enough from the poststructuralist critique—that we can acknowledge that the same assumptions and practices that enable us to see some realities inevitably blind us to others—and that this blindness is in many cases not accidental but reflects our own desire (however unconscious) *not* to see.

We have not always wanted to see, for instance, the extent to which our field has been constituted as a site where our culture's deep anxieties and ambivalences about literacy are situated. We have not always wanted to see that as a field formed in response to a perceived literacy crisis we have had—and perhaps *can* have—less of an impact than we once anticipated on student literacy. We have not always wanted to see that our own understanding of the "problem" of student literacy may in fact itself be a theoretical and pedagogical problem for our field. We have not always wanted to see (and I hope you understand how clearly I include myself as part of this "we") the contradictory nature of our own positioning in the academy and the ways in which we are consequently "written" as professionals. And we have not always wanted to see the ways in which we as writing teachers have, without really intending to, based many of our assumptions and practices on our own predilections as writers and on the forms of writing that we most often read and write.

Lest I seem too pessimistic, I want to mention what I believe we as a field have seen or are beginning to see. We are beginning to understand, I think—thanks to the work of Steven North, Louise Phelps, Susan Miller, Andrea Lunsford, and others—that reenvisioning the nature of and relationship between theory and practice represents one of our most pressing tasks. It is not a rejection of theory to observe that theory's privileged position in our field and in the academy is hegemonic and that we need radically to reconceptualize what we do when we "do" theory. Can we acknowledge that writing, theorizing, and teaching are *all* discursive practices, rhetorical acts, language arts?

We are also beginning to see that little real progress in the teaching of writing can occur without substantial changes in the material conditions that characterize this teaching in North America today. The Wyoming Conference Resolution is a visible sign of this understanding, one which provides at least a potential mechanism for change (CCCC Committee On Professional Standards for Quality Education). I'm not sure, however, that we have adequately considered the assumptions about theory and practice that inform this document. Does the Wyoming Resolution's recommendation that all teachers of writing should have Ph.D's in composition studies unintentionally further the hegemony of theory over practice in our field? We have always understood that the question "What do teachers of writing need to know?" raises difficult issues. In the past, however, our response has focused on *what* teachers of writing need to know—theories of the composing process, for instance, or the history of rhetoric. But doesn't this question also require us to consider our assumptions about the nature of pedagogical power and authority?

To consider issues such as this is, as Susan Miller pointedly observes in *Textual Carnivals*, to rethink the narratives that have thus far constructed our field. Such a reconsideration also challenges us to redefine our disciplinary ambitions and, perhaps, to be both more modest and more accepting of the tensions that animate not only our field but writing itself. What do I mean when I refer to the tensions that animate writing itself? An illustration may clarify my point.

Last summer I listened to an interview on National Public Radio's program "Fresh Air" with AIDS activist and author Paul Monette. Several years ago Monette wrote *Borrowed Time: An AIDS Memoir*, a moving account of the death of his partner from AIDS. Monette, who is himself HIV positive, recently published a new book, *Becoming A Man: Half a Life Story*, in which he reflects on his experiences as a gay man in America. At one point the interviewer, Terry Gross, asked Monette the more-or-less standard question about future projects: "What do you want to write about next?" Monette spoke at length about the "terrible sense of urgency" he felt to write about his own life, and that of other gay men.

I believe that Paul Monette's urgent need to write—and his sense that he could write—his life challenges the dichotomies that our theories have tended to construct about writing. Is writing self-expression, the revelation of some inner truth? Or is it a social transaction, one in which language "speaks through," and thus constructs, us? We can write our lives, but our lives are—as Monette himself is acutely aware—also written. To be a gay man or woman in America is to confront (among other things) one's inscription in an often contradictory and paradoxical social text.

Can we articulate theories of literacy and of teaching that honor the complexity and urgency—and inherently contradictory and paradoxical—nature of our situations as humans? Can we also, to raise a related issue, articulate theories of literacy and of teaching that honor the rich diversity and situatedness of writing and of the processes that writers use to produce texts? In another essay in this volume, James Moffett argues that the writing process movement can be best understood as the effort to both investigate and model the practices of adult writers for students. Moffett is of course partly right. But only some writers and some practices have been included in our gaze. Why, for instance, have we generally not studied or modeled the many, many writers who dictate letters, memos, and reports? Could it be that this practice violates our field's emphasis on the recursive nature of writing and on the importance of revision? Why have we only recently begun to study and model the many, many writers who produce texts collaboratively? Could it be that this practice violates our field's emphasis on originality and on the individual nature of intellectual property rights?

There are many additional questions that seem to me worthy of our attention. Here are some of them:

Can we develop strategies that encourage us to resist our field's unavoidable tendency to reify and objectify both writers and writing?

Can we be more conscious of, and more explicit about, the models and metaphors that animate our research and the narratives that construct us as researchers and teachers?

Can we find room in our academic discourse for not only critique and opposition but also self-reflexiveness, self-critique, and self-revision? Can we develop, in other words, the sort of double vision that encourages us to acknowledge, as Kenneth Burke (1966) says, that any way of seeing is inevitably also a way of not seeing?

Can we, while recognizing the complexity and difficulty of our task as researchers and teachers, maintain the utopian and subversive desire to effect social and political change that has, at various moments, characterized our field?

There is one final question I would like to leave you with: can we revise our ambitions for our own field, our sense of our scholarly and pedagogical enterprise? In 1970 it perhaps made sense for Janice Lauer to argue that composition studies needed to strive to "reach the status of a respectable intellectual discipline" (80). Today, we may need to revise that ambition. What if, to suggest just one possibility, we conceived of our scholarly and pedagogical enterprise as nothing more—and also and emphatically nothing less—than "doing what there is to be done" (Toulmin, 485). These are in fact the words that philosopher of science Stephen Toulmin (1972) uses to describe his understanding of the contemporary scientific project. Surely we could do worse than to conceive of the field of composition studies in similar terms.

Works Cited

Berlin, James A. 1987. *Rhetoric and Reality: Writing Instruction in American Colleges, 1900–1985*. Carbondale, IL: Southern Illinois University Press.

Britton, James et al. 1975. *The Development of Writing Abilities (11–18)*. Urbana, IL: NCTE.

Brooke, Robert. 1987. "Underlife and Writing Instruction." *College Composition and Communication*. 38: 141–53.

Burke, Kenneth. 1966. "Terministic Screens." *Language as Symbolic Action: Life, Literature, and Method*. Berkeley: University of California Press.

CCCC Committee on Professional Standards for Quality Education. "CCCC Initiatives on the Wyoming Conference Resolution: A Draft Report." *College Composition and Communication* 40 (1989): 61–72.

Ede, Lisa and Andrea Lunsford. 1990. *Singular Texts/Plural Authors: Perspectives on Collaborative Writing.* Carbondale, IL: Southern Illinois University Press.

Elbow, Peter. 1981. *Writing with Power: Techniques for Mastering the Writing Process.* New York: Oxford University Press.

Emig, Janet. 1971. *The Composing Processes of Twelfth Graders.* Urbana, IL: NCTE.

Faigley, Lester. 1986. "Competing Theories of Process: A Critique and a Proposal." *College English* 48 : 527–40.

Flower, Linda. 1979. "Writer-Based Prose: A Cognitive Basis for Problems in Writing." *College English* 41: 19–37.

Flower, Linda and John R. Hayes. 1980. "The Cognition of Discovery: Defining A Rhetorical Problem." *College Composition and Communication* 31: 21–32.

Fuss, Diana. 1989. *Essentially Speaking: Feminism, Nature, and Difference.* New York: Routledge.

Graves, Donald. 1983. *Writing: Teachers and Students at Work.* Portsmouth, NH: Heinemann.

Hairston, Maxine. 1982. "Winds of Change: Thomas Kuhn and the Revolution in the Teaching of Writing." *College Composition and Communication* 33 : 76–88.

Lauer, Janice. 1970. "Heuristics and Composition." *College Composition and Communication.* 396–404. Reprinted *in Contemporary Rhetoric: A Conceptual Background with Readings.* 1975. Edited by W. Ross Winterowd. New York: Harcourt Brace Jovanovich. 79–90.

Lunsford, Andrea. 1991. "The Nature of Composition Studies." *An Introduction to Composition Studies.* Edited by Erika Lindemann and Gary Tate. New York: Oxford University Press. 3–14.

Macrorie, Ken. 1970. *Uptaught.* Rochelle Park, NJ: Hayden.

Miller, Susan. 1991. *Textual Carnivals: The Politics of Composition.* Carbondale, IL: Southern Illinois University Press.

Moffett, James. 1994. "Coming Out Right." In *Taking Stock: The Writing Process Movement in the 90s,* edited by Lad Tobin and Thomas Newkirk. Portsmouth, NH: Boynton/Cook.

———. 1968. *Teaching the Universe of Discourse.* Boston: Houghton Mifflin.

Monette, Paul. Interview by Terry Gross, 20 July 1993. *Fresh Air.* National Public Radio. WHYY, Philadelphia.

———. 1992. *Becoming a Man: Half a Life Story.* New York: Harcourt Brace Jovanovich.

———. 1988. *Borrowed Time: An AIDS Memoir.* San Diego: Harcourt Brace Jovanovich.

Murray, Donald M. 1982. *Learning by Teaching: Selected Articles on Writing and Teaching.* Portsmouth, NH: Boynton/Cook.

North, Stephen M. 1987. *The Making of Knowledge in Composition: Portrait of an Emerging Field.* Portsmouth, NH: Boynton/Cook.

Perl, Sondra. 1980. "Understanding Composing." *College Composition and Communication* 31: 363–69. Reprinted in *The Writing Teacher's Sourcebook*, 2nd. ed. 1988. Edited by Gary Tate and Edward P. J. Corbett. New York: Oxford University Press. 113–18.

Phelps, Louise Wetherbee. 1988. *Composition as a Human Science: Contributions to the Self-Understanding of a Discipline.* New York: Oxford University Press.

Reither, James A. and Douglas Vipond. 1989. "Writing as Collaboration." *College English* 51:855–67.

Shaughnessy, Mina P. 1977. *Errors and Expectations: A Guide for the Teacher of Basic Writing.* New York: Oxford University Press.

Toulmin, Stephen. 1972. *Human Understanding: The Collective Use and Evolution of Concepts.* Princeton: Princeton University Press.

Young, Richard E. 1978. "Paradigms and Problems: Needed Research in Rhetorical Invention." In *Research on Composing: Points of Departure,* edited by Charles R. Cooper and Lee Odell. Urbana, IL: NCTE.

3

"Of What Does Skill in Writing Really Consist?" *The Political Life of the Writing Process Movement*

James Marshall
The University of Iowa

My title, the first part of it anyway, comes from *Research in Written Composition*, the 1963 volume authored by Dick Braddock, Richard Lloyd-Jones, and Lowell Schoer, which is usually cited as one of the anchoring documents of our professional interest in writing and the writing process. "Of what does skill in writing really consist?" is the twenty-fourth of the twenty-four questions the authors ask in the section they name "unexplored territory," and in many ways the question, now over thirty years old, can be seen as having initiated a generation or more of inquiry into the nature of writing and writing instruction. We are at a point now, of course, where we can celebrate that tradition of inquiry, and much of our research over the last three decades can be seen as well-thought-out answers to the question put by Braddock, Lloyd-Jones, and Schoer back in the early 60's. My purpose here, though, is to come at this question from a different, from perhaps even a perverse angle. Instead of attempting to answer the question, I would like to explore our way of asking questions, or more broadly, the kinds of rhetoric and the kinds of politics we as a community have practiced over the last thirty years. This will involve something we might as well call "attitude." We've had one from the beginning—an attitude, that is—and I'd like to begin describing it by asking us to look again at the question put to us by Braddock, Lloyd-Jones, and Schoer.

"Of what does skill in writing really consist?" seems a straightforward enough question until we ask what that word "really" is doing in there. What is its rhetorical function? We might say that it is just there for emphasis, to indicate that the authors were interested in the truth, the whole truth, the "real" as opposed to the "unreal" truth. But they might have gotten that job done without the "really." The simpler "Of what does skill in writing consist?" seems cleaner, more empirical, objective, and more researcher-like in tone than it does when that "really" intrudes. Let me suggest that the "really" is there for the same reason "really" shows up in every day conversation—to call into doubt an assertion that has already been made. "I'm going to lose ten pounds over the next month," someone says. "Really?" we respond. A child tells us that the wind blew over the lamp. "Come on," we answer, "tell us what *really* happened." "Really," when used in this way, positions the speaker as a doubter, as one who knows what's what and what isn't what, as someone who isn't going to be fooled. It's the position taken by someone standing outside a field of discourse and questioning its validity, its truth, its value. "Read my lips, no new taxes." "Let's get real," we say. "What are you really going to do?"

My argument in this paper is that those of us who read and talk and write and teach about the writing process have consistently positioned ourselves in this way, that is, that we have consistently and insistently represented ourselves as outsiders who doubt the validity, the truth, the value of what has traditionally gone on in writing classrooms. I'd like to demonstrate how we've done this, and then I'd like to make some suggestions about where that attitude of doubt has taken us.

First, just what have we been doubting? Richard Young (1978) has perhaps provided the most succinct description, though we might offer our own variations. He called it the "current-traditional paradigm" and his description went like this:

> The overt features . . . are obvious enough: the emphasis on the composed product rather than the composing process; the analysis of discourse into description, narration, exposition, and argument; the strong concern with usage (syntax, spelling, punctuation) and with style (economy, clarity, emphasis); the preoccupation with the informal essay and the research paper; and so on. (31)

Here we have "the other," the thing we have doubted, in dissected form. Young begins by setting up what had already become a definitional contrast (product vs. process) and then provides a crisp and efficient list of those emphases against which the writing process movement would argue: the analysis of whole discourse into subunits; the classic modes; the hyperactive concern with correct usage.

In its youth—in the early 70's—the writing process movement was energized by an animus against this approach to writing. In fact, in some ways we might see the movement as a kind of political-pedagogical protest. This cluster of attributes or emphases was our Lyndon Johnson, our Richard Nixon. It was the power we loved to hate.

My reference to the politics of the period comes from the process theoreticians themselves, for when we read the literature on writing process from the early 70's, the rhetoric of dissent seems unmistakable. Take for instance, the following short passages from Janet Emig and Peter Elbow respectively, the first from *The Writing Processes of Twelfth Grade Students* published in 1971, the second from *Writing Without Teachers* published in 1973.

> A species of extensive writing that recurs so frequently in student accounts that it deserves special mention is the five-paragraph theme, consisting of one paragraph of introduction . . . three of expansion and example . . . and one of conclusion. This mode is so indigenously American that it might be called the Fifty-Star Theme. In fact, the reader might imagine behind this and the next three paragraphs Kate Smith singing "God Bless America" or the piccolo obligato from "The Stars and Stripes Forever." (97)

The excerpt from Emig is one of the first of many attacks on the five-paragraph theme launched by those of us interested in endorsing something entirely different. But I'm most interested here in the rhetoric of Emig's attack—in the language she appropriates to make it. It is the language we used to voice our other protests at the time—the language we used to satirize militarism and narrow forms of patriotism. We would paint that jingoism in garish versions of red, white, and blue, and then we would stand back from it. We appropriated emblems associated with an America we considered old, outgrown, and corny in order to set ourselves apart from them. It was the impulse that motivated Abbie Hoffman to wear the American flag as a shirt, that motivated Jimi Hendrix to play the "Star Spangled Banner" one early rainy morning at Woodstock, that motivated Arlo Guthrie to sing "Okie from Muskogee." Kate Smith was part of the whole domain of corny culture we were rejecting, and her inclusion here connected Emig's argument to the larger rhetorical project many of us were undertaking elsewhere.

Elbow is much more direct in positioning himself within the larger political and cultural currents of the time. He writes:

> Many people are now trying to become less helpless, both personally and politically; trying to claim more control over their own

> lives. One of the ways people most lack control over their own lives is through lacking control over words. Especially written words. (1973, vii)

By suggesting that his approach to writing—noticeably to be undertaken *without* teachers, outside of school, and thus outside of institutional control—Elbow was drawing on the power of those larger currents and doing so successfully. Thus, to the constraints of writing blocks and over-schooled prose, Elbow responds with "*free* writing"—a loaded term, considering what else was going on at the time. And as if to demonstrate just what "free" could be in writing, he chooses to use a sentence fragment—right there at the end of his first paragraph.

But my favorite example of politics from the time is not a prose passage, but an image. It is the photograph of Ken Macrorie that graces the back cover of my 1970 edition of *Uptaught*. The photo represents for me everything that Macrorie was then, when I was preparing to teach. He is sitting informally on a bench, back to a brick wall. His posture is friendly and open, his shirt and tie informal and rumpled. But it's the look on his face that's important because it's a look that says, "I can't believe you're trying to get away with this." A look that says, "I don't believe you." A look that says, finally, "No." It was, I think, what *Uptaught* was about—"No" to dishonesty, "No" to "Engfish," "No" to uptightness generally. And that "no" was somehow captured iconographically in the photograph, merging for me at last with the words of Emig and Elbow and Murray as a kind of joyful but sardonic defiance—a refusal to go along with old ways of running the country or of old ways of teaching writing.

I hope it is clear that to read these artifacts from the early days of the writing process movement in these ways is not to diminish them, but to historicize them, to reconnect them to the cultural network from which they originally emerged. In our youth as a movement we were rebels, or tried to be. We did inhale. We self-consciously set ourselves up as outsiders, and then we gloried in it.

Even in our more recent representations of ourselves, we can see traces of that original rebelliousness. Notice, for instance, the way that Nancy Atwell begins her book *In the Middle*.

> I confess. I started out as a creationist. The first days of every school year I created; for the next thirty-six weeks I maintained my creation. My curriculum. From behind my big desk I set it in motion, managed, and maintained it all year long . . . I didn't learn in my classroom. I tended and taught my creation. (1987, 3)

The reference to the deistic notion of a clock-maker god seems unmistakable here, but Atwell raises the image of divine order and authority only as a way of setting up her rejection of it. "I didn't learn in my classroom," she tells us, "I tended and taught my creation." The follow up to this, of course, is the remainder of the book—a book that argues against the teacher-centered, deistic classroom and for a far more democratic, far less authoritarian approach to teaching. "Now I have given up authority," she seems to argue, "that standing back, that teacher centeredness—now I have positioned myself as the book title implies—in the middle, not in the front, not on top."

I'm attempting to understand these texts then, for the cultural work that they have attempted—cultural work in the sense that Jane Tompkins means in *Sensational Designs* (1986) when she discusses the position of undervalued fiction in American literary history. The texts I am reading, like the texts Tompkins reads in her book, are, in her words, "attempts to redefine the social order" (p. xi). These texts, like hers, "offer powerful examples of the way a culture (or movement) thinks about itself, articulating and proposing solutions for the problems that shape a particular historical moment" (p. xi). And these texts finally, I would argue, "seek to win the belief and influence the behavior of the widest possible audience. They have designs upon their audiences, in the sense of wanting to make people think and act in a particular way" (xi).

We have done this, I would argue, by employing a range of binary oppositions, which I have outlined in Figure 3–1. Peter Elbow has argued well about the importance of not resolving these oppositions or compromising them. In fact, one of the things I have always admired about Elbow's work is his refusal to make easy choices, his efforts to stretch the boundaries of the possible. But—and it is an important proviso—though we may wish to elude the trap of binary thinking, opposition seems to be a necessary means of proceeding both discursively and politically. Thus, though John Dewey always shows the dangers of either/or thinking, his arguments seem always to proceed by means of them—setting up the either/or in order to show its bankruptcy. You've got to set them up though before you can knock them down. You've got to have structuralism before you can have deconstruction. You've got to have Lévi-Strauss before you can have Derrida.

In the case of our own discourse, I think I see implicit or explicit oppositions within these four fields—and then also in one more general or even metaphysical field. Thus, we begin with a definitional contrast—product vs. process—and from that follows several distinctions. In descriptions of the writing process, we have a privileging of the recursive over the linear, of freedom over constraint, of generating over proofreading. In evaluations of pedagogy, we have a privileging of choice over control, of student-centered styles over teacher-

Figure 3–1
Some Binary Oppositions

Process		*Product*
	Process	
Recursive	—	Linear
Freedom	—	Constraint
Generating	—	Proofreading
	Pedagogy	
Choice	—	Control
Student-centered	—	Teacher-centered
Writing to learn	—	Learning to write
	Discourse	
Informal	—	Formal
Personal	—	Public
Narrative	—	Argument
	Politics	
Reform	—	Tradition
Progressive	—	Conservative
Opposition	—	Power
	Status	
New	—	Old
Natural	—	Artificial
Real	—	False

centered styles, of writing to learn over learning to write. In discussions of discourse, we have a privileging of informal writing over formal writing, of personal writing over public writing, and of narrative over argument. And finally in politics—national, institutional, departmental—we have a privileging of reform over tradition, of progressive thinking over conservative thinking, of the spirit of opposition over the maintenance of power. Taken together these form a powerful argument *for* one particular way of seeing the world and *against* the other so that the process approach is seen as new, while the product remains old. The process approach is seen as somehow "natural" while the product approach is, quite simply, false.

Now these oppositions are familiar, maybe overly familiar, and Elbow among others has deconstructed many of them, but what I find most interesting about them is the political twist that the writing process movement has given them. I suggested that in each case we, as a community, have privileged those items on the left over those items on the right. But we have done that privileging while at the same time insisting that the items on the right were the truly privileged, the truly hegemonic, the truly dominant. Thus, to repeat my initial argument, at the same time that we were creating a community of insiders—those of us in the know about process—we were insisting that we were institutional outsiders. The *real* institutional insiders, we said loudly, were those who valorized products over processes, arguments over narratives, tradition over reform, the old over the new.

Now as a means of proceeding, as a political device, this way of representing ourselves was probably helpful—in fact, it was probably even accurate, though that's not really the point. To represent ourselves as embattled, David-like, taking the slingshot of process against the Goliath of product, not only energized our community and helped it grow, it tapped those not-so-latent political impulses that were manifested in the civil rights movement and in the protests against the Viet Nam war. The writing process movement was, if you will, a fellow traveler with other movements our generation initiated—consonant with them in motive, in rhetoric, and in direction.

But now we are in charge, and we cannot pretend otherwise. Take a look at our journals, at our textbooks, at the reports of the National Assessment or at the new forms of writing tests coming swiftly to the market. Process writing is now part and parcel of the educational establishment against which we used to raise our voices in protest. The National Writing Project is partly funded by the federal government. Chester Finn's U.S. Department of Education project of the mid-80's—the little book entitled *What Works*—actually recommends process writing and cites Donald Graves as an authority in making the case. At the University of New Hampshire—the Athens of the Writing Process—we hold conferences celebrating our longevity. Clearly, we have much to celebrate. But the price of that celebration may be the recognition that we are, as a community, as a movement, now middle-aged—and I think we need to start acting like it.

Thus, I wonder if it isn't time to undertake a middle-aged enterprise—to take stock, to examine what we've built, to ask with a critical eye, is this enough after all? Let me suggest three areas that we might usefully explore.

The first of these has to do with authority—our own hard-won professional authority. A popular film from that critical period in the early 70s when the writing process movement was first becoming visible may help us see the issues more clearly. In his 1972 role as *The Candidate*, Robert Redford portrays an earnest, idealistic, deeply liberal outsider engaged in a variety of political causes, who is persuaded to run for a U.S. Senate seat. At first he is reluctant, claiming that he has no experience with campaigning or legislative maneuvering. But the pressures to try to make a difference among political power brokers is intense, and eventually Redford agrees to the campaign. While running, he loses most of his innocence and at least some of his integrity, repeating the anemic formulas that his speechwriters have provided and losing conceptual control over the issues in an effort to stay a point or two ahead in the polls. In the end, of course, Redford wins the election. But it is the last line of the film that is telling. Looking drained and clearly older, Redford asks his campaign manager, "Now what?"

It's a question we might ask ourselves. Like Redford's character, we have employed our status as institutional outsiders to make sensible, humane, and sharply reasoned suggestions about what is wrong with the way things are done. But making suggestions from the outside, as Redford's character learned, is finally much easier than hammering out realistic and politically viable solutions from a position of authority. Being in charge means that we cannot blame our failures on a mean-spirited establishment; we must claim them as our own. It means that we cannot waste our energies beating up on those punch-drunk bogeymen: five-paragraph themes, descriptive grammars, and "traditional approaches to the teaching of writing." These are no longer realistic enemies, although our life as a movement was simpler when they were. And being in charge means finally that we must accept responsibility for demonstrating what we have for a quarter-century been claiming—that the classroom practices that we have developed actually work.

On the one hand, we have to address the fact that large-scale writing assessments, mostly notably the National Assessment of Educational Progress, have yet to show any significant improvement in students' performance on the test, even though students themselves are reporting widespread use of process instructional strategies in their classrooms. And on the other hand, we have to continue the efforts already underway to develop realistic, large-scale portfolio assessments that will persuade legislatures and tax-weary parents that our instructional practices are effective even when the most conventional or even conservative kinds of criteria are used in making a judgment. Such efforts will take years, of course, and will require the work of many hands, but they seem necessary if the ideas we have generated are to play any significant role in schools over the next twenty-five years.

The second task we might now, in our middle-age, take on as a community is a more thorough exploration of our intellectual roots.

We have been quite good about examining our history as teachers of writing—James Berlin, Bob Connors, Steve North, and others have seen to that—but we have been less aggressive in tracing our deeper, philosophical origins. We don't have to read very far in John Dewey, for example, before we realize that the student-centered, process-driven, meaning-rich pedagogy that we have been advancing since the early 70's is anything but new; in fact, Dewey's early formulations of progressive educational thought are now over a hundred years old. It was in the relatively early *The Child and the Curriculum* that Dewey offered a view of teaching I think many of us would still embrace—that the teacher's greatest obligation is to engage students in a "vital and personal experiencing" of their subject. And it was in his 1904 essay "Theory and Practice" that Dewey argued for the importance of teachers developing a fully-articulated theoretical perspective that could inform and shape their practice. What we have, as a movement, been offering as "new" is actually quite old—as old, in some cases, as the old, formalist doctrines our "new" approaches were meant to replace.

And there's the rub. By virtually ignoring Dewey and the progressive movement in developing our own theory and practice, we have not only failed to exploit a rich resource, but we also have missed an opportunity to study how a movement similar to our own, but larger and more comprehensive, fared in making the kinds of changes in schools that we hope to make. If we are, in our middle-age as a community, determined to leave a legacy, then we might ask why the legacy of the progressive movement is as problematic as it is. By the late 50's, of course, in the wake of Sputnik and the cold war, educational progressivism had been quite widely repudiated. But even before then there had been signs of trouble. Dewey himself had warned against a loosely conceived regard for student freedom in *Experience and Education*. And the press and the public were never fully convinced that progressive approaches were as rigorous or as effective as they needed to be. In a *New Yorker* cartoon published in the fifties, a young girl stands at her teacher's desk and asks plaintively, "Must we do whatever we like today?"

I am not arguing, of course, that the writing process movement, in its own venue, will necessarily follow the same troubled path as progressivism. But I am arguing that we should as a community begin to ask hard questions about why earlier efforts to reform instruction have achieved, at best, only a partial success. Such looking back is an appropriate middle-aged enterprise, and it seems necessary if we are to look ahead with any realistic sense of confidence.

Finally, in addition to exploring issues of authority and history, I think we need to examine more carefully the contexts in which we do our work. For better or worse we have tended to see those contexts as physical space—as classrooms—and we have in large measure limited our observations and our efforts to what transpires within classroom walls. Such a tight focus has yielded many useful returns: a wide range of productive classroom practices; a renewed understanding of the complexity of teachers' work; a rich and still developing conception of the relationship between talk and writing. But though we have been fairly successful at seeing what happens within our classrooms, we have often failed to acknowledge that those classrooms are nested within schools, those schools within communities, and those communities within larger networks of cultural and political life. In not addressing those larger contexts, or at least not addressing them very often, we have left out of our picture of writing instruction some of the forces that are most powerfully shaping it.

What we need in our middle-age is a picture of writing instruction within its larger educational contexts—a conceptual frame that would enable us to see how the theories and practices that we have developed over the last twenty-five years map onto other visible and sometimes successful efforts at reform. How is writing process instruction, for instance, related to the effective schools movement? To outcomes-based education? To mainstreaming? Closer to home, are writing process, whole language, and reader response teaching all part of a unified theoretical perspective? If so, what is it? How are they related to one another? I don't want to be aggressively argumentative with these questions, but I don't mean them as merely rhetorical either. I think we need to pay attention to questions like these because teachers work in environments where at least some of the questions need tending all of the time. Thus, while we can talk about writing instruction in isolation, most teachers must deal with writing in contexts where writing is only part of what students are learning. We must step back a bit and widen our lens, I think, to see more clearly how writing fits into the larger picture.

There are many more areas to explore than those I've mentioned here, of course, and most of them will be difficult. But then, mid-life is supposed to be a time of crisis, and in any case, the community that has developed around the teaching of writing over the last generation seems resilient and skillful enough to face almost any challenge. The one serious mistake we could make, I think, would be to maintain the rhetorical and political positions that we took in our youth. They worked then; I don't think they can work today. We are facing a different set of problems, and we are working now from the center and not from the margins. Perhaps we can learn something useful about our situation from that great student of middle-age, Carl Jung, who wrote:

> Thoroughly unprepared, we take the step into the afternoon of life; worse still, we take the step with the false assumption that our truths and ideals will serve us as hitherto. But we cannot live the afternoon of life according to the program of life's morning; for what was great in the morning will be little at evening, and what in the morning was true will at evening become a lie. (1978, 67)

It was Ken Macrorie, of course, who taught so well the important difference between telling the truth and telling lies when we write. I like to think of that 1970 photograph of him—the one of the doubtful eyes and the ironic expression—turned not to the old educational establishment of products and five-paragraph themes, but turned toward us. We have been successful in building classroom environments that are in many ways monuments to the vision of Macrorie, Emig, Elbow, Murray, Graves, and others. But I think that it is probably time to look carefully at those environments, and to ask the same hard questions of them—and of ourselves—that we used to ask of others.

Works Cited

Atwell, Nancie. 1987. *In The Middle: Writing, Reading, and Learning with Adolescents.* Portsmouth, NH: Boynton/Cook.

Braddock, R., R. Lloyd-Jones, and L. Schofr. 1963. *Research in Writing Composition.* Urbana, IL: National Council of Teachers of English.

Dewey, John. 1990. *The Child and the Curriculum.* Chicago: University of Chicago Press.

Dewey, John. 1938. *Experience and Education.* New York: Collier Books.

———. 1904. "The Relation of Theory to Practice in Education." In *The Relation of Theory to Practice in The Education of Teachers.* National Society for the Study of Education, Third Yearbook, Part I:9–30.

Elbow, Peter. 1973. *Writing Without Teachers.* New York: Oxford University Press.

Emig, Janet. 1971. *The Composing Processes of Twelfth Graders.* Urbana, IL: National Council of Teachers of English, 1971.

Jung, Carl. 1983. *The Essential Jung.* Princeton, NJ: Princeton University Press.

Macrorie, Ken. 1970. *Uptaught.* New York: Hayden Book Company.

Tomkins, Jane. 1985. *Sensational Designs: The Cultural Work of American Fiction.* New York: Oxford University Press.

Young, Richard. 1978. "Paradigms and Problems: Needed Research In Rhetorical Invention." In *Research on Composing: Points of Departure*, edited by C. Cooper and L. Odell. Urbana, IL: National Council of Teachers of English, 1978.

4

Knowing Not Knowing

Donald M. Murray
University of New Hampshire

> Writing is a process of dealing with not-knowing, a forcing of what and how. We have all heard novelists testify to the fact that, beginning a new book, they are utterly baffled as to how to proceed, what should be written and how it might be written, even though they've done a dozen. At best there is a slender intuition, not much greater than an itch.
> Donald Barthelme

> That is the pure pleasure of creation—the not knowing that leads you to the knowing. Bobbie Ann Mason

> You write from what you know but you write into what you don't know. Grace Paley

> The excitement is in not knowing. Alain Robbe-Grillet

> I don't write out of what I know. It's what I don't know that stimulates me. Toni Morrison

Each morning I come to my writing desk and confront a contradiction: I know how not to know.

I am both teacher and student and my curriculum remains the same: how do I learn again how not to know what I know?

I know the ritual that will bring me into the presence of mystery, the religious connotation noted. I wake at 5:30 A.M. with the awareness of what I may write on the tongue of my mind, wash while half-hearing what may be written later, listen to TV news and read the morning paper while the submerged narrative of my potential draft flows under the surface of the present, breakfast with my Bagelry cronies as the pattern of what I may write becomes conscious and is forced back to the subconscious for the moment, walk for thirty minutes while the voice of what may be written grows louder and, at last, I place my hind end in the chair and turn on the computer.

Annie Dillard says it is not discipline but love that brings writers to their desks, and I agree, but my love of writing, my compulsive need to be relieved of writing, is reinforced by schedules and resolutions and habits that sound like discipline when I describe them. I force myself to my desk and once there, I must contradict the mobilization of energy, the organization and planning and habit, the rage against interruption and trivial necessity that has brought me there, and become quiet, receptive. I must listen.

To what? I do not know. This Twentieth Century Western male, armed with watch and calendar and energy, and obsessed with productivity must encourage an Eastern Zen-like waiting.

I must plan so I can write without plan; I must practice the craft of spontaneity. The act of writing is, in a sense, my religion and I must, as the religious do, practice the rituals that allow me to confront mystery.

Oh, I have an itch, a hint of what I may say, an interesting tension within a fragment of language, a beckoning clue within an image, a shape in the mist that may turn out to be poem, story, essay. I imagine what I may write, even—at times—plan but what appears on the computer screen as I write is never as I imagine.

When I know I seek not to know. I move into new territory, perhaps following Barthelme's advice to "write about what you're most afraid of" or choosing to investigate what I least understand about the writing process.

I may take my material and confuse it by moving it into a new genre, from essay to poem, from poem to argument, from academic paper to story. I mess up the rules within the genre, changing long lines to short, writing argument in the form of narrative or vice versa, starting the story backwards, becoming woman, child, victim.

I listen to the music of my language and step up or slow down the beat, distort the melody; I turn the binoculars around and make what was large small; I connect what does not want to connect.

I write against the grain of what I have written before. I have no desire to be consistent. I was a soldier in another life and loyal but today's maxim is from Graham Greene: "Isn't disloyalty as much the writer's virtue as loyalty is the soldier's?" I am not loyal to what I have known of craft or message; I seek to do what contradicts what I have done before.

I write with velocity, forcing myself to spin out of control, experiencing those blessed accidents of insight and language that instruct, that lead me toward new meanings.

I work hard to think in writing without thought about writing, depending on instinct. Dumb instinct. How much craft it takes to allow instinct!

Craft, I have discovered in writing this chapter, is not the end of writing but the beginning. The knowing that we call craft—how to find the right word, how to rub two words together in a phrase that gives off more meaning than either word alone, the skill of allowing a sentence to find its own flowing course, the placing of emphasis within the paragraph, all the techniques I practice, all my knowing, allows me to come face to face with not knowing. I am released by the knowing of craft into the unknowing that allows me to write what I do not—and my reader does not—expect. Together we are allowed to connect, to explore, to astonish, to discover what we didn't know we knew.

This stimulating ignorance expands the longer I extend my apprenticeship. It is my comfort and my delight. Completing my sixth decade of making meaning with words, I look forward to years of increased not knowing. I will write what I do not yet know in ways I have not yet written.

Teaching not Knowing

> But what do beginners know? Too much. It is what they think they know that makes them beginners.
>
> William H. Gass

> If I know what I'm doing . . . I can't do it. Joan Didion

> I guess the most important thing I can say about my writing voice, or voices, is that they are the smartest voices I have, often teaching me things I didn't know I knew.
>
> Judith Rossner

> For me the initial delight is in the surprise of remembering something I didn't know I knew. Robert Frost

I came to teaching late, after I was an established writer, comfortable with not knowing (although I wouldn't have used that phrase to describe it then). I was told by my department head to "teach what you know about writing."

I made notes and faced the class. I told them what I knew about writing. I looked at the clock and was stunned. Ten minutes. I had thought my wisdom would fill the hour, perhaps the semester. I asked for questions. None. They were apparently stunned by the tight little nugget of wisdom I had given them. Class dismissed.

And so I discovered I had to teach what I was comfortable not knowing. I had to speak of mystery: how I could sit down and allow the words to flow, telling me what I didn't know I knew with a skill I had never tried to name.

Accepting the role of instructor, I had to instruct. I began to define, describe, deliver what I didn't know I knew about writing in class, in articles, in books. I organized my knowing—and the knowing of other members of the writing trade—in a description of the writing process, certain that academics would not take my subjective, "experiential" knowledge seriously.

And some did reject it. I was, after all, a practitioner, but many more took it seriously, often more seriously than I took them myself. I knew the unknowing would always be greater than the knowing. Braced for rejection, I had to defend myself against acceptance.

I considered process *one* way of speculating about writing, a play of possible meaning; many seemed to take it as *the* way of teaching the writing act.

I considered the writing process a way of separating the knowing from the not knowing, or, to put it differently, a way of organizing knowing so the writer could be launched into the more important world of not knowing. The process was, after all, a process of learning, exploration, speculation, discovery: the goal was always surprise, the purpose was to write to know.

This is the essential challenge of teaching composition: how do we teach not knowing?

I found my students hungry for knowledge. They wanted to know how to do it. What do you want? How do you want it?

Of course I responded to them. The less I knew, the more certain I sounded. The idea of process was a compromise if not an escape from the fundamental irony of teaching what I knew about not knowing.

I speculated about the sequence of not knowing through which experienced writers passed to get from before the first page to publication.

The process allowed me to escape, first of all, questions of content. The process would be similar for writers of left and right, of for and agin', for bucks or ideals, for popularity or craft. I did not tell students what to think but proposed ways of thinking, processes of thinking in writing.

The plural is important. From the beginning I felt no loyalty to a process. Each knowing led me to a greater unknowing. My books and articles described very different writing processes. For example, my last five books described the writing process in four different ways:

A Writer Teaches Writing [2nd ed]	*Write For Your Readers* [2nd ed]	*Read to Write* [3rd ed]		*Write to Learn* [4th ed]	*The Craft of Revision* [2nd ed]
COLLECT	FOCUS	FOCUS	<->	FOCUS	FOCUS
PLAN	EXPLORE	EXPLORE	<->	EXPLORE	COLLECT
DEVELOP	REHEARSE	PLAN	<->	PLAN	SHAPE
	DRAFT	DRAFT	<->	DRAFT	ORDER
	DEVELOP	CLARIFY	<->	CLARIFY	DEVELOP
	CLARIFY				VOICE
					EDIT

My only regret is that they are so similar they imply an excess of knowing.

I declared, whenever I wrote or talked about the writing process, that the process changed in at least three crucial ways:

- The process changes according to the cognitive style of the writer. I tend to collect or connect the specific and allow the pattern or the meaning to evolve from the specifics; others may work from theory to the specific. No matter—if the writing works. Any process is legitimate if it produces an effective text.
- The process changes according to the writing task. For example, I outline my textbooks, do not outline my novels. The genre, the audience, the purpose, the message, the tradition or expectation, may change the writing process.
- The process changes with experience. I write my 287th newspaper column differently than my third. The more experienced I am with a genre or a message or an audience, the more internal or pre-first-draft my process.

I am never quite comfortable teaching in person or in writing. I fear I always sound more certain that I am, more organized, more convincing, more authoritative. I have questions but I deal in answers.

From the beginning it was clear to me that my answers were speculations—guesses. Informed guesses but not TRUTHS. And I tried to make my idiosyncratic subjectivity clear to my students and my readers. What I had to say was based on my evolving understanding of how I wrote at that moment, how published writers I knew or studied wrote, how my current students wrote, and my personal interpretation of this information. Remember, I am comfortable with not knowing.

Researching not Knowing

> I actually try to begin writing with my mind a tabula rosa; I don't want to know, can't know what I'm going to write.
>
> John Ashberry

> I believe in not quite knowing. A writer needs to be doubtful, questioning. I write out of curiosity and bewilderment.
>
> William Trevor

> You never know what you will learn until you start writing. Then you discover truths you didn't know existed.
>
> Anita Brookner

> For me, writing poetry is a series of bewildering discoveries, a search for something that remains largely unknown even when you find it.
>
> David Wagoner

As a writer I was comfortable with not knowing but as a teacher I was less comfortable. I needed the answers to the questions my students who were not content with not knowing were asking.

At the same time that speculations such as the process approach were taking place, there was an emerging research effort in the emerging or revitalized study of composition theory and pedagogy. Janet Emig, for example, was studying the brain; others such as Don Graves were designing projects to observe and document the practices of students who wrote well; others were engaged in ethnographic studies of the conditions under which students wrote well. We seemed to be turning away from the concentration on error that had dominated so much of reading research and were looking at what children did who wrote well.

I expected an army of researchers—armed with clipboards and backed up electronic devices designed to record what happens within the mystery of writing—to supplant my speculations. Oddly enough I did not feel any fear or resentment. I felt relieved. I was too well aware of the personal nature of my speculations. Now trained observers would study what effective writers—in school and out—said and did when they wrote well. I would no longer be lonely, and if they contradicted me? Well, I contradicted myself. It is from these contradictions I found new articles and books. I was excited; I would learn.

But this is not what happened. Barbara Tomlinson is the only person I am aware of who critcially explored what writers said about writing and she had difficulty getting her work published. Robert Root is one of the few who has studied professional writers as they work. The new profession of composition theory and pedagogy turned away from practice to theory, sometimes literary, more often political.

I found much of this work important and interesting but I had expected studies that would illuminate the not knowing about writing. I hoped for illumination not elimination. I did not fear that the essential not knowing would disappear, that there would be no mystery, but hoped that we would better understand how to enter and make use of mystery.

I hungered for composition research that would increase my knowing and, I suppose at times, irritate, infuriate, but educate and stimulate me. At some level I suppose I worried that knowers would take over my territory and my dumbness would be seriously impaired, and yet I wanted to know what could be known. I even constructed a fallback position if knowing limited my not knowing. I would become an artist—I would draw, paint, perhaps even sculpt—where there would be, for me, an adequate supply of not knowing.

I did not have to worry. The new scholars entering the field of composition, largely drawn from people trained in literary studies who turned to composition because that was where the jobs were, had been uninterested in how writers made the literary works they studied. In composition they were not interested in writing practioners or classroom practice.

And so I have continued my own subjective research into what writers know that bring them to not knowing. I began when I found the "800" Dewey Decimal System section of the stacks of the Quincy Public Library when I was fourteen years old and in the ninth grade. I started copying down what Burton Rascoe, a Chicago newspaperman said about writing, and I haven't stopped copying since. This morning, fifty-five years later, I copied into my daybook what I just read Elizabeth Graver saying, "When I begin a story, I never have any idea where I'm going, but the initial image, setting, or voice (any one of these can set things in motion) needs to be rich and full of possibility, and also somewhat mysterious to me, or else the story stalls."

I have not found that knowing limits, but rather extends my not knowing as I move from superficial mysteries to more profound ones. I hoped that research into the composition process would replace my subjective speculations with more objective knowing.

If I could know how effective writers—the best writers in every class and the best of published writers—approached the mystery of writing, than I could use this knowledge to get closer to the mysteries I was compelled to explore. Research, like craft, would liberate me from small mysteries and lead me to greater ones.

I still think, however, there are hundreds of interesting dissertations, articles, and books on how writers write that need to be written. A few of the hundred topics that would interest me are:

- How do writers increase their awareness through language? Wallace Stevens said, "The tongue is an eye." How does word, phrase, line reveal?
- How does the writer's memory work? How do we remember while writing what we did not know we knew? How can we increase the range of this particular memory?
- What is the role of image in writing? I think there are close connections between the visual arts and writing. What are they? What would they teach us?
- What rituals do writers perform that place them in a state when mystery is possible?
- How do writers hear what is not yet written and follow this voice towards meaning? What is voice and how does it instruct writers?
- How do writers encourage the flow of language? How do writers "ride" on fluency towards meanings they do not expect?
- How do writers enter into their drafts, working within, not outside, their drafts?
- How do writers read drafts in process to see and hear the meanings that have just been written, are being written, are not yet written?

I hope that researchers and scholars will answer—speculate in their way—about these questions and all the others that will not eliminate not knowing but circle it, and tell how to get closer, more quickly, to the mysterious process that allows us to say what we did not know we knew in a way that allows readers to know what they did not know they knew.

> As I see it, the function of fiction is to tell someone something about himself he already knows, but doesn't know he knows.
> Walker Percy

> When you're writing, you're trying to find out something which you don't know.
> James Baldwin

> I understand it much better now than when I was writing it.
> Adrienne Rich

> If I write what you know, I bore you; if I write what I know, I bore myself, therefore I write what I don't know.
> Robert Duncan

> I am discomforted by the knowledge that I don't know how to write the books that I have not yet written. But that discomfort has an excitement about it, and it is the necessary antecedent of one of the best kinds of happiness.
> Wendell Berry

> The writer himself studies intensely how to do it while he is in the thick of doing it; then when the particular novel or story is done, he is likely to forget how; he does well to. Each work is new. Mercifully, the question of how abides less in the abstract, and less in the past, than in the specific, in the work at hand. . . .
> Eudora Welty

Works Cited

Graver, Elizabeth. 1991. Autobiographical commentary. In *The Best American Short Stories 1991,* edited by Alice Adams. Boston, MA: Houghton Mifflin.

Murray, Donald M. 1991. *The Craft of Revision.* Fort Worth, TX: Holt, Rinehart, and Winston, Inc.

———. 1993. *Write to Learn,* 4th edition. Fort Worth, TX: Harcourt Brace Jovanovich College Publishers.

———. 1993. *Read to Write.* 3rd edition. Fort Worth, TX: Harcourt Brace Jovanovich College Publishers.

———. 1992. *Writing for Your Readers: Notes on the Writer's Craft from The Boston Globe,* 2nd edition. Old Saybrook, CT: The Globe Pequot Press.

———. 1985. *A Writer Teaches Writing,* 2nd edition. Boston, MA: Houghton Mifflin Company.

Root, Robert L. Jr. 1991. *Working at Writing: Columnists and Critics Composing.* Carbondale and Edwardsville, IL: Southern Illinois University Press.

Tomlinson, Barbara. Unpublished manuscript.

Section Two

Teaching the Writing Process

5

Process, Product, and Quality

Ken Macrorie
Santa Fe, New Mexico

As I look back on my experience as a teacher of writing. . . . Stop right there! What I've just said is misleading. I should have said, "When I look back on the experience of my students as writers . . . " because it wasn't until their experience began to appear in stories that their writing counted for them, their peers, me, and outsiders. For seventeen years I had tried maybe a dozen different methods in an attempt to get my students writing powerfully. When they made a breakthrough, it wasn't because I had found the right process but because I had put them into a position from which they could bring themselves into the university as persons.

In books and speeches for many years I've been saying those words: "their writing counted for them, their peers, me, and outsiders," and few readers or listeners have understood their significance. By "counted," I mean "to have meaning for." I didn't say for the writers, peers, me, *or* outsiders," but *and*. It's not enough to talk about *process* without bringing the *product*, or evidence, to the courtroom.

Some teachers have made a career, and gotten tenure out of talking about *writing process* without showing a significant number of student writings that corroborate the process they espouse. In doing that, some of them have left out students. That's a common happening in bureaucracies. I did that for seventeen years, all the while thinking I was concentrating on my students. But who were they? How did I know?

Institutions grow old and eventually exist principally to perpetuate themselves. Not intentionally. When I say "institutions" here, I'm referring to the people in charge, the administrators and teachers, not the "lower classes," the people who are supposed to be learning and performing. The older, the better-read, the more experienced people become lost in their hierarchies and create lowerarchies to look down on. I've heard teachers say, "Students can't write. They haven't had enough experience to write about."

I believe that
writing teachers
enter into
an unspoken contract
with students
to help them
become better writers
by the end of a course.

What do I mean by "better writers"? If the writing is better than before, it must be on its way toward "good" or "powerful" writing. But what's good or powerful writing?

If we teachers of writing and literature have no answer to that question, shouldn't we be resigning and looking for another line of work?

In 1982 at the Bread Loaf (Graduate) School of English in Vermont, when I was asked to teach two sections of the course in Writing Prose Non-Fiction, I put my students through a writing process and acted as editor and publisher of a magazine of student work issued five times in the six-and-a-half-week term. In that enterprise I alone decided which were the best writings. Almost all of my students were experienced high-school teachers.

This process continued for the next five years. Not until the summer of 1988 did I stumble into setting up a comprehensive experiment that finally made me comfortable when asked that wicked question, "What is good writing?" The change I made was to ask the fifteen teacher-students in the Non-Fiction writing course to form teams of three editors for the five issues. Each team had to receive the writings and choose which should be published. At lunch on Wednesdays, the magazine, named *Yeast*, appeared on the tables in the dining room.

To help the editors, I established routines. The class met for two-and-a-half hours on Tuesday and Thursday afternoons. In groups of five, one editor per group, the teacher-students exchanged papers and read them to themselves silently, or mumblingly, so that when their turn came to read another student's paper aloud to the others in the group, they would understand what it was saying. When they knew that, they could read its lines with the normal emphases, pauses, changes of pitch, etc. which they all give to ordinary spoken sentences that communicate their intended meanings. If they couldn't make out what a word was, or didn't understand something, they asked the author to clear up their confusion. That meant that when the three editors later met to determine the writings for *Yeast*, they each were already acquainted with five out of the fifteen submissions for that day, and they had noted the response to them by members of their small group. Each editor's own writing had to face the same test in the small group. Editors scheduled conferences with the authors of writings they thought they might publish. Sometimes a writer would meet outside class with a single editor or all three editors to discuss as many as three drafts of a story.

As the project developed over the years, we added refinements, most of which were designed to protect the feelings of writers, editors, and readers. A full elaboration of all the changes we made in the process will have to wait until I can discuss them at book length.

With all our concern about not destroying the confidence of writers, these teacher-students still fought and suffered. Several cried over the way editors had treated them. Editors expressed to me outrage or disbelief about the way writers had taken their suggestions for improvement of their work.

In the summers I was directing this class, I was also a member of a group of professional writers in Santa Fe, New Mexico. I noticed that constantly we professionals were encountering the same problems in our writing as the *Yeast* editors and writers were encountering in theirs. For example, in both groups, the opening paragraph in most first drafts didn't get a piece going; it tried to say too much at the beginning. Again and again, editors would react strongly to a passage in a work for the same reasons. We were all unconsciously building a set of criteria for what we thought was good, or powerful, writing. Later in the term, I asked these teacher-students to begin making notes about what criteria seemed to lie behind this or that comment of theirs.

Sometimes in these sessions, which were often heated, both writers and editors were exposed to sharply differing responses to pieces of writing that tested their own responses. What seemed to me at once most unsettling and educational was the move for everyone from writer to editor, and back to writer again. This wasn't an exercise in imagining what it might be like to be an editor. This was a real magazine, published to a real audience of student peers. Also in the audience were English and Drama professors and Equity actors. Each week, a teacher-student submitted two pieces of writing for consideration. If, as happened at times, both works during a week were turned down for publication, the writer was usually frustrated or hurt. All the editors were aware of what was involved in rejecting a work under these circumstances, and yet they felt obliged to hold to high standards. Their names would appear on the masthead of the issue of *Yeast* they had edited.

Again and again, these teacher-students found a clear *voice* in writings. It seemed to come when the writer was relating events and relationships as truthfully as possible—not just interesting ones, but deeply felt, unforgettable experiences. Then the writing was carrried out with such intensity that the drama of those events and relationships often came out in rhythms: slow, fast, mounting, suddenly abrupt, smoothly floating, or whatever, as the sentences embodied the actions and physical reality rather than weakly characterized them with adjectives. Consider this story, written in 1992, by Karen Field.

To the Woman on the Bus

> I was struck by how different I must have looked to you that day you sat next to me on the bus in Suva. Before it arrived, I watched as you poured coconut oil from an old Coke bottle onto your arm and smoothed the cloudy liquid into your black skin. The oil took away the ash and made you glow.
>
> You sat by me because the bus was crowded. You looked like other Fijian women with your long Afro and broad white smile, but you were more beautiful. I remember thinking you must be twenty-one, but now that I have watched shades of skin age, I'm sure you were older. Tall and lean, you appeared cramped in the seat and held your cloth bag filled with bananas, cabbage, and potatoes on your lap.
>
> I caught a glimpse as you stared at my skin, my hair, my clothes. With the inquisitive look of a child in a petting zoo, you reached out and stroked my arm just once, cautiously. My eyes followed the slow movement of your hand down my white freckled forearm and then up to my blonde hair. I did not flinch. We briefly smiled at each other. You gazed out the window.
>
> —From the Woman Who Shared Your Seat

Karen made this event happen, movement after movement. Her writing possessed the consistency of diction and manner that we imply when we say that writing has a *voice*. Instead of discussing multiculturism, she had put us in a certain place at a certain time when two very different persons surprised each other but evinced no outward signs of shock. We call that act *telling a story.*

Five years after arriving at Western Michigan University, I asked my students to try harder than ever before to put down some kind of truth, not *the* truth (whatever that is) but their truth. I remember being surprised to find that within the space of three class meetings they were all writing stories. I asked a student why, and he replied that he had noticed that when read aloud to the class, the writings in story form held people's attention more than those in the form of essays, "themes," or reports. And he said, "When you asked us for truths, I realized that I had better write about my own experiences, because I could be surer about being truthful than when I was writing about other people's ideas and experience." I felt uncomfortable about this because as an English teacher who frequently required students to analyze canonized stories, I had written few stories myself, and published only one, which I felt was awkward and lacked a convincing voice.

In 1968 John Bennett, a high school teacher, and I began publishing a broadsheet of our students' writing. I called it *Unduressed.* I watched those students, and later, graduate students take to writing stories as if they had been telling them throughout their lives. Then I realized that indeed they had been telling stories throughout their lives. But they had been speaking them, not writing them. When we are children we all tell stories constantly to our peers, or to our mother or some other adult in the kitchen. As adults we exchange stories with hundreds of different people.

Once in the early 70s when I was talking about *story* with graduate students in English at the University of Virginia, a young man said to me, "Do you know Crites?" I liked those students of Professor Hal Kolb. They talked to me as if they and I were colleagues. I looked up Stephen Crites's article in *The Journal of the American Academy of Religion* and found that he worked in philosophy of religion at Wesleyan University. His article was titled "The Narrative Quality of Experience." He, and later, Scott Momaday, Joan Didion, and Leslie Marmon Silko all spoke of telling stories as the principal human way of communicating. Through my friends Jimmy Britton of the University of London, and Bob Boynton, a founder of Boynton/Cook Publishers, I learned that Barbara Hardy of the University of London in 1968 had anticipated what all of the above people and I had later come to observe about storytelling:

> We dream in narrative, daydream in narrative, remember, anticipate, hope, despair, believe, doubt, plan, revise, criticize, construct, gossip, learn, hate, and love by narrative. In order really to live, we make up stories about ourselves and others, about the personal as well as the social past and future. (13)

So there were many others besides me who had finally understood that story is the first form for human beings wanting to communicate with each other. Most of us English teachers are so in love with stories that we have arranged to be paid for "teaching" them. Yet few of us ask our students to write stories of their own experience.

In the *Unduressed* and *Yeast* classes on the first day, I showed students past issues of the broadsheet or magazine they were going to write for. Besides asking them to try hard for their truths, I said to forget about spelling, punctuation, grammar, and trying to write what they thought would impress me. Almost all of them did, and soon in our classroom we were listening to surprise after surprise. When people tell stories that count for them they usually choose events that had once surprised them, and maybe still do. I think of this story that Marti Buckingham wrote at Bread Loaf in 1988. She was from Wyoming and had worked with sheep during a good part of her youth.

Country Kids

> Dear Mr. Moore:
> I understand you got out of the penitentiary early on account of good behavior. You were teaching illiterate inmates how to read.
>
> When I found out, I felt a lot like I did the time I walked to the outhouse and then looked back at a rattle-snake coiled next to the path. An eerie feeling of what might have happened haunted me for days. There were only five to seven of us in that little K-8 rural school. If you had molested one of us, would we have known any better? Would our parents have suspected anything? I don't know. We were just country kids with a lot of common sense but not much street smarts, and our parents thought things like that happened only in the cities out there somewhere else. It came out in court that you were a victim of incest yourself. I can't buy that as an excuse, regardless of the television commercial that says something about abused children becoming child abusers. I'm damn sure that those two little girls and their parents can't buy it either—even after all these years. Would you, if it had been your daughter?
>
> You made us feel very grown up and important when you bought us each our own clipboard. Each morning we would come in and find it hanging next to the door with that day's "task menu" on it. You listed everything we needed to accomplish that day, including instructional periods with you, but the time we took to get the work done and the order in which we did it was up to us. If we finished early, you let us select our own pastime.

Then in this story Marti tells what she did with the classroom freedom Mr. Moore gave students. I must leave out several paragraphs here to save space. I pick up the story again:

> Sometimes you would come outside during recess and play kickball with us or push the merry-go-round so fast that the world continued to spin for several minutes after we stopped. We loved those recesses. They made us realize that growing up didn't mean you had to give up the great things about being a kid.
>
> When that rural school closed, I was terrified of fifth grade in town, but you had more than prepared me. Academically, I was ahead of my classmates, and socially, well adjusted.

No one will ever trust you with a group of kids again. You were one of the best teachers I ever had.

Thanks.

Marti Buckingham

Once in a *Yeast* class, the teacher-student whom most other students right away looked to as the best writer, said in a class discussion of somebody's story, "This is good, but I think it would be much more powerful if it *showed* more and *told* less." Everyone except me nodded in obeisance to the wise one. I was remembering Marti's letter to Mr. Moore, which told more than it showed. I found it moving. In her piece, she summed up points and made moral judgments. She maintained a cool voice that seemed to me to carry a strong undercurrent of passion.

In those writing classes that was the way the students and I slowly built up our criteria for good or powerful writing. We examined our own reactions to the writings we read or heard. We kept changing or modifying those criteria. We watched and listened to other people responding to writing. One criterion that we all agreed on is that good writing contains surprises.

Maybe the events and relationships surprise, maybe the language. Clichés and other forms of trite language don't surprise, so we figured that good writing doesn't contain them. But surprise for whom? Or trite for whom? Since we were working in that neat little white box that contained people we knew and had at hand—both writers and editors—we could get answers to those questions. Often we didn't have to ask a question. After hearing a story read in the *Yeast* class, listeners might say something like this: "I found it sort of boring," and the writer would begin to consider the question of surprise.

A listener to a story read aloud might say, "I got lost here in the beginning. There were too many people introduced all at once." Or, "when you say 'problems,' whose problems are you talking about?" and the writer faces another requirement for good writing: it must be clear. This is such a fundamental expectation that both professional and amateur writers and editors often don't put it on their list of criteria for good writing. It's a tricky matter, because many highly sophisticated writers, literary critics, and professors are so enamored of meaningfully ambiguous writing that they forget that unintended ambiguity may confuse and irritate readers until it destroys a piece of writing.

And so as we worked to produce five issues of a magazine in a short summer term at Bread Loaf, individuals kept responding to the stories, and bringing up other possible criteria for good or powerful writing. When Brian McEleney, one of the Equity actors in the Bread Loaf Theater Ensemble, visited our class he was asked how actors manage to learn a long part in a play. He said that for a good actor, remembering the words in a script isn't as crucial as understanding the events and relationships in the play. "What's going on here in this scene? Who's talking to whom, and for what purposes?" Brian said that if actors knew who they were as characters and understood the events and relationships in the play, forgetting a word in a line wasn't a catastrophe because they knew what might be said at that point and could furnish words that would put them back into the script quickly. Once he said that in our class; I have repeated it in every subsequent class. If *Yeast* writers focused on rendering the events clearly, no one said, "Be more specific," a teacher's injunction that has seldom helped writers. In this class, we found that lists of suggestions had no place in our discussions, but side-coaching did. "I don't get it. Did you fall down because you were so nervous about meeting this girl, or simply because your cousin had laid a trap for you?"

We learned that whenever writers focus on the events of their stories, they quit being self-conscious about their relationship to their readers. Nothing is worse than a writer who is forever wanting to sound like a Writer. Carol Elliott McVey, the teacher of acting at Bread Loaf, sometimes shouts at a student on the practice stage, "Don't act! Be somebody. Who are you? What's the event you're in? Now try it again." Being unselfconscious is a key to good acting and good writing. Time after time we found in the *Yeast* class that a writer who concentrated on events found that her language took on certain rhythms (I'm not referring to metric pattern) that forcefully ended a story. Without any mention of this strategy, frequently writers would compose their last lines principally in words of one syllable. Marti Buckingham ended her letter to Mr. Moore by saying:

> No one will ever trust you with a group of kids again.
> You were one of the best teachers I ever had.
> Thanks.

Out of these twenty-three words, twenty are of one syllable. Such an unselfconscious strategy comes from years of participating in spoken conversations. We have a feel for finality. We know in our brain's emotion center the power of using the simplest, most ordinary kitchen language at moments of greatest stress. Shakespeare knew that. In his tragedies, at the realization of death or some other major understanding, many of his characters lower their elevated language in that way. When I first started reading Shakespeare's plays with students, I gave him credit for planning every word he wrote. Now when I see students aged fifty or fifteen using that strategy, I believe that Shakespeare and those students were both usually unaware of their shift in language. If you look at TV news shows, and study samples of the speech of real people who have just survived a catastrophe, you'll find that many of them eloquently pronounce judgment on the experience and reveal their feelings in kitchen language heavy with one-syllable words.

That's why some writing teachers ask their writers to center upon telling their truths and focusing on events and relationships. I think any practicing writer will tell you that when he tries to think up a metaphor, he seldom finds a brilliant one. Good alliteration, metaphors, and rhythms *come to* people writing. I think you can see why. If we look to our words to produce power, we usually begin by thinking of old phrases and patterns, rather than allowing the events in a story to call up appropriate words for us. This is not to say that in revising we can't sometimes spot a weak passage and consciously make it stronger, but it has a better chance of being brilliant if it comes to us in context rather than if it is consciously devised as a remedy.

You might wonder why most of us English teachers cripple our students by giving them formulas like five-paragraph themes and topic sentences. We don't know any better. Through all our professional lives we've lived with rotten writing by students and it's hard for us to believe that those people have in them unselfconscious language powers. That's because we see them as members of a lowerarchy—for many reasons, which I haven't space to go into here.

I think of a story that received enthusiastic responses from everyone in the *Yeast* class and all but one person in our Santa Fe professional writers' group.Why would one person receive this story differently from the way all the others did? I know her. She's a formidable professional writer and one of the quickest at learning to improve her work whom I've ever met. I'm sure that her differing response is due to some strong experience in her past. This story probably gave her an expectation different from that which other students in her class experienced. Some word, manner, or attitude in the text may have put her off. Our past experiences, as well as what we're looking at right now, build our expectations, and hence our perceptions. To an extent each of us is going to perceive any single thing or event slightly differently from the way others do, because we all have had different experiences—not totally different, but different enough that we will see something as good that other people see as bad, or vice versa. Here's the story. It was published in *Yeast*, Number 5, 1991.

> Dear Times-Square Mugger,
> You never sent me a copy of your poetry. It's been ten years and I've long since moved. I suppose I'll never see you again, yet I still remember the night we spent together.
>
> I'll never carry my wallet in my front pocket again. When you flashed that serrated kitchen knife at me in Times Square, I realized

that my upbringing had not prepared me for the possibility of you. Thanks for letting me buy a coffee and you a Coke before we negotiated about the money. I hope the thirty dollars you eventually got from me was enough to take your son to Coney Island. I had enough left to drive to my new job in Florida.

I'll never forget when we came out of the coffee shop, you standing behind me with that knife inches from my back. I'm glad that I had some good pot with me. When you told me that you weren't going to kill me as my shaking hands tried to roll a joint on that bench, I realized that you didn't like to do the mugging thing. I still count our conversation that early morning to be one of the most wonderful I have ever had. When you told me what you wanted the money for, and what getting out of prison was like, how could I resist? When we stopped and looked at each other, you, black dressed in black, and me, white dressed in white, I realized that was not how the script was supposed to go. You brought me into another world. The mugger and the muggee shouldn't have enjoyed each other, shouldn't have had common ground to talk about. But we did. The pride in your voice when you told me about your son helped me to better understand you, to understand that you too were a victim. He must be a teenager now. I hope he's still in school.

Maybe *you* learned something that night, too. When you told me that the only reason that you stabbed your targets was because they resisted and because you hated yourself for what you were doing, I could feel your desperation. I know I resisted that night. Thanks for not stabbing me. When you told me about your experience in school, I understood completely what started your problems. I hope you believed me when I said you were smarter than you thought. I don't blame you for being pissed when your teachers thought your poetry was dumb. It was probably wonderful. They just had to get through their curriculum. They were trapped too.

I thought it was funny when we both took some of my money out of our pockets and changed it into quarters to play pinball. I've never played pinball since that night. I told you that sucked. I still can't believe that I beat you by 25,000 points.

The image of our walking through Times Square as the rising sun turned the buildings gray will stay with me always. Watching you call out to the hookers and point out those guys who were looking for marks to roll has helped me to be more careful in cities at night. Thanks for walking me to the subway. I felt safe with you.

My friends thought I was crazy when I told them I gave you my address. Somehow I couldn't imagine you would stray very far from your territory. I did hope that you would send along your poetry, though.

I'm spending the summer in the Southwest. I don't know if you know where New Mexico is, but the sky is big here. From the ground you can see farther than from the top of the Empire State Building.

Ned Bradford

That story, like the other two stories I've presented so far, is in the form of an imaginary letter. Over the years that has been one of the most successful assignments I've given in white box classes. I think that's because the letter isn't going to be sent. In one way this is one of the most difficult forms to write in because the author has to keep two audiences in mind at once: the person he's addressing in the letter and readers of the publication the letter appears in. Yet all three of the writers of the imaginary letters I've presented seem to have had no difficulty in writing their letters. I think that's because this form allows a writer to put down truths that arise in the story without risking injury or a libel suit by the recipient of the letter, unless the writer is foolish enough to use real names in his letter.

In all these writing classes for *Unduressed* and *Yeast*, I gave a suggestion for each writing: "Tell us about an event in your childhood you can't forget." "Write a story of someone (could be you) who made a large unexpected change." Then I always say, "If something else is asking you to be written, write that."

For me, "Times Square Mugger" by Ned Bradford is not an essay, a report, or a critical paper. It's very personal and very objective at the same time. Its meanings rise above and beyond its moment. Like that other reader I mentioned earlier, you may not feel the same way.

What is good or powerful writing? From my experience with some thirty writing groups, I would say it has meaning for several different audiences at the same time; the writer, the writer's peers, editors, and larger audiences the writer had in mind. It surprises, in what it says or how it says it, or perhaps in both. Its dramatic rhythms come from the events the writer has chosen to reveal, and from her relationships with those events. Few, if any, of the characters are one-dimensional. The more the author tries to show herself off as a writer, the more likely the events and relationships at the heart of her work will be weakened or lost. Good writing doesn't waste words. It's not sentimental. It dramatizes its crucial moments. If it's powerful writing, at the same time it rises above those moments and tells us what it's like to be alive on this earth.

Tomorrow, listening to writers I work with, I may be adding to or subtracting some of the above criteria, because like language, we human beings are always immersed in new events that change our perceptions of the world. That may sound foolish to you, my saying that language perceives events, but it does. It's like a huge animal swimming along as the host to hundreds of little growths that keep changing as they multiply or diminish, as new ones attach themselves to the beast. It still swims and dives to the depths and comes squirming up to leap out of the water. We are in it and of it. How splendid it is!

You could take these remarks of mine and move in many directions with them. For example, at the moment they make me think of the idea of writing across the curriculum. Some composition teachers ask their students to choose a field they're interested in, say, law, mechanical engineering, medicine, history, or business management. And then they ask them to look into a question in that field and report it in the language and form of the field. This is an overwhelming and foolish request of most students, who probably don't yet know the field well enough to be comfortable in such a task. So they pontificate, writing awkwardly in what to them is a jargon of a foreign language. And they're required to write with it in an unfamiliar form. Within these fields each company or group of professionals has worked out forms and terms particular to them alone. This language and these forms can't possibly be imagined by a student without experience in the field.

We need to feel confident with the language we write and speak. All of us were born into a world of story. We have to tell stories to live with other people. If in school we're encouraged to tell stories in our mother tongue and we see those stories registering on listeners and readers, we can keep going and learn and grow. With the confidence we gain from writing in our own mother tongue powerfully, we can relax and absorb other languages more quickly.

Finally, you may be saying to yourself, "I just don't believe all people have these latent powers—to speak and write in their mother tongues. Only the talented." I can understand that response. The three stories I've presented so far were written by high-school English teachers in graduate school, who are in love with written language. When they arrived at Bread Loaf, they already ached to be powerful writers. But in my files I have dozens of strong stories by younger, less-schooled people.

From 1968 to 1974, I was publishing the broadsheet *Unduressed* with John Bennett, who was then a teacher at Central High School in Kalamazoo, Michigan. Recently he sent me a copy of the current publication of his students' writings in a class in British Literature, at Loy Norrix High School in Kalamazoo. I was taken by this story:

Don't Do This To Me, Ron

I remember when I just told my mother I was talking to a white girl. When I first told her she thought I was playin' and she had a little smile on her face and said, "Yeah." When she finally realized I was serious, she had that evil woman stare in her eyes and said,

"Don't do this to me, Ron."

I asked her, "Do what?"

"You know I have problems of my own."

> After she said that, I kept quiet for a little bit and sat down and watched T.V. After I watched T.V., I started thinking about what she said. Finally I got up and asked her, "How is this a problem to you? I'm the one talking to her, not you."
>
> "I just don't want you goin' with a white girl. One day she might get mad and call you 'nigger this, you black whatever,' and then what you goin' to do? And if you have kids . . ."
>
> "Kids? Mama, it's not like we're getting' married. And I'm not going to have any kids with any girl I don't know."
>
> "Well I got to go, so I see ya when I get back."
>
> *Ron Hemingway*

I asked John Bennett why students in a British Literature class were writing stories like this. Were they supposed to be parallels or contrasts to stories the students had been reading?

"No," he said.

"Then why are you having them write them?"

"Well, these kids have been reading Shakespeare for a while. And then Milton. They want a change, so I let them write these stories. People think that kids are dumb. They're not dumb. They know they've been reading stories. Then *they* write stories. They see the connection."

You may say that "Don't Do This to Me, Ron" is no more than a piece of a story. That could be said. But if this is just an episode, it's an episode with completeness. It really ends. The last line, spoken by Mom, sounds out a finality, as the ending of Marti Buckingham's story did. "Well I got to go, so I see ya when I get back." Every word in that sentence has only one syllable. We find that students attempting to write more truthfully than ever before often write endings like that *unconsciously*. They staccato a feeling just as Ron's mother did when she spoke. I would like to read more episodes of Mom and Ron talking to each other, but what's here reveals to me a relationship. They're at ease with each other. They can talk about tough things. I was eager to hear each next sentence.

To encourage and support truthtelling in his students' writing, John Bennett requires all of them to use pen-names when their work is published.

Why is Ron's story so short? How long has it been since you visited a high-school classroom? The students are gyrating with energy. They like to try something, and move on. In his story Ron has let us see something of himself as a person. He's aware of its ironies. He talks to an adult as an equal. I'll take this story. It requires great leaps of understanding from me. The class is reading British Literature. Not much time for writing stories. I chose this writing for use here partly because it is short, and neverthess, I think, powerful.

Ron wrote me from an army post where he was training. He accepted a small payment and gave me permission to reproduce his story. It was a gracious note that contained a statement that stunned me: "I don't consider myself a writer. As a matter of fact, I don't like to write."

If I sat down on the first day of this class as teacher or student with Ron, I would be wondering, who is this person? I would expect to be working alongside him for three or four months. Knowing something of his life would help me judge what he says or writes in this course. I don't care if the class is math or history or psychology. A good part of the time I want a large part of him there. Not in a scorecard or analysis from the Student Records Division, but in a few stories he has written himself. Then I can judge the degree of objectivity he's mastered in such tellings.

The people who think stories about one's own experience are bound to be soft and squishy don't know the stories I've heard by high-school and college students. Because they're not familiar with this body of writing, understandably they don't realize that students who have learned to write of events and relationships as truthfully as they can often achieve a high degree of objectivity. Sometimes these doubters don't realize that the hardest thing to be objective about is oneself.

We might start every course with our students writing truthtelling stories. First we need to give them powerful models written by students who have gone before them. If you can't find any around, you might use the four stories that I've presented here. It won't be long before others begin to appear before you.

Works Cited

Crites, Stephen. 1971 "The Narrative Quality of Experience." *Journal of the American Academy of Religion* 39: 291–311.

Didion, Joan. 1979. *The White Album.* New York: Simon & Schuster.

Hardy, Barbara. [1968] 1978. "Toward a Poetics of Fiction: An Approach through Narrative." In *The Cool Web,* edited by Margaret Meek, Aidan Warlow, and Griselda Barton. New York: Atheneum.

Momaday, N. Scott. July 9, 1991. Address to the Bread Loaf Santa Fe Community.

Silko, Leslie Marmon. 1981. *Storyteller.* New York: Arcade Publishing.

6

The Process of Poetry
Rethinking Literature in the Composition Course

Daniel Reagan
Saint Anselm College

> In the rhetorical tradition it is not uncommon to start by having students create discourse—speeches or essays—start by having students figure out what *they* have to say about the topic. These discourses often become the text for reading and listening and further speaking and listening. In the poetic tradition, students seldom write except in response to hallowed texts.
>
> Peter Elbow

This comment from Peter Elbow's account of the 1987 English Coalition Conference, *What Is English?*, challenges us to apply what we have learned from the writing process movement when we design LITCOMP courses (to adopt Wayne Booth's [1983] term).[1] The sort of course I am identifying here is listed in our catalogues under the heading Freshman Composition, but has a title—"American Literary Realism" or "The American Short Story," for example—which suggests that the matter to be studied is a series of literary texts rather than the process by which meaning is made through reading and writing. This species of course appears frequently in writing across the curriculum programs, in composition courses which are governed by the view that students must be provided with a subject to write about, in "special topics" composition courses, and in courses that are meant to serve the dual curricular purposes of providing both writing instruction and an introduction to literature. The dual purposes and competing subject matters inherent in LITCOMP courses make them difficult to design and teach, and the most frequent design I have seen and adopted myself is to drop COMP and turn the courses into LIT with some writing. In this Chapter, I will suggest some ways to reinsert COMP into LITCOMP courses.

Most scholars who have written about the relationship between reading and writing during the past ten years agree with Elbow that initiatory writing most frequently drives the structure and logic of composition teaching while responsive writing drives the organization and tasks of literature courses. David Bleich articulates that difference most bluntly when he observes:

> It is widely held in the language and literature profession that, while literature and composition are both central subjects in the domain of "English," they are essentially separate. There has been a "standard" way of relating them to one another—by having students write "compositions" about "literature"—but this rarely leads anyone to believe that the two subjects are intrinsically or conceptually related. (1983, 81)

My LITCOMP courses in the past have reflected this standard relation by privileging responsive rather than initiatory writing—students read works, we discussed them, students wrote about them, I held conferences with students about their essays, they revised the pieces, and I graded them. My training in the teaching of writing perhaps helped me respond to these writers, but what I was teaching was unabashedly a literature course with a strong writing component, not a composition course.

Elbow's insistence on "the importance of writing to initiate —writing to start a conversation" (1990, 180) even in literature courses, however, suggests a way of reasserting the primacy of COMP within the LITCOMP classroom because it reverses the traditional hierarchical relation between literature and writing that Bleich describes. Certainly Elbow is right that to "start our classes with speaking and writing" is standard practice in composition courses which emphasize a process approach, and he is also right that this same practice appears much more radical when applied to literature and LITCOMP courses. In this chapter, I will discuss the results of just such a radical structuring of a LITCOMP course around Elbow's advice that initiatory rather than responsive writing be primary. The classroom activities I will describe center on what Elbow calls "output." They are designed to help students experience certain difficult but essential aspects of the writing process, such as how writing provokes its own thought and logic, how generic models can shape and limit thought, and how conscious choice works in revision. Ultimately, however, I have found that these same initiatory writing activities serve as an ideal mechanism for developing students' understanding of literary works themselves and of the kinds of responsive writing activities they will be called upon to produce in other contexts.

The title of my LITCOMP course, which is the second in a two-course freshman composition sequence, is "What Is Poetry?"; in it we work with short lyric poems.[2] My primary goal in the course is to help students reconceive their processes of both writing and reading as acts of making meaning. I urge students to apply discoveries made while working with poetry to other types of writing, primarily the expository essay, which is the primary genre taught in the course. I chose lyric poetry as the material for study because of its practicality; it provides short, compressed, self-contained uses of language, which can be dealt with easily as whole texts. But I had another motive for choosing lyric poetry—to confront the negative, often blatantly hostile attitude toward poetry emanating from most of my students—and not just first-year students. Because the primary activities I designed for the course all attempt either to make familiar language seem alien, or alien language familiar, I chose a genre that I assumed would be farthest from the reading my students would choose themselves. The idea of initiatory writing exercises, however, carries with it an initial and necessary caution about making assumptions. Elbow's idea implies that we need to test our assumptions; we need to learn what our students actually think and know before we move into the reading material of any course. I began the course therefore with three writing activities designed to reveal student attitudes about poetry. First, I asked them to attempt an answer to the question that heads the course, "What is Poetry?"; second, I asked them to write a poem; third, I asked them to explain why what they wrote was a poem. The answers surprised me.

I assumed the source of their hostility rested in the observation frequently made by students that poetry is willfully obscure, difficult to read, and filled with "hidden meanings"—hidden by the poet from inexperienced readers, but for which the teacher has some answer key, some grand *Cliff's Notes* that contains *the* meaning of every poem.[3] The responses to the three exercises, however, revealed that the students' hostility was not directed at poetry, but rather at what English teachers do to poetry.

Virtually every student in this class articulated, in some form, that poetry is radically expressive. Two responses to the question "what is poetry?" will reveal what I mean. Jeanne wrote "Poetry is the pouring out of emotions and feelings onto paper." Kristine agreed: "Poetry for me is a type of writing that allows you to express some of your innermost feelings into words. Poetry is a lot of times just a way for some to escape everything and just be in their own world and write whatever they want to say at that particular time." Note here that, when responding to the question, these students and most others in the class described writing, rather than reading, poetry.

The same expressionism emerged in the explanations of why each student's writing should be considered a poem. Indeed, most students gave the expected nod toward formal features in response to this task. Lisa, for example, wrote, "I suppose the form makes it a poem—it is divided into stanzas, the form LOOKS like a poem—blah-blah-blah-blah." She added, however, "but I don't really think that is what is important." Dennis summed up what most in the class felt was important: "It's a poem because it is an expression of me. It is what I think about and what I feel."

A number of important implications about writing and reading poetry emerge from this view. These students consider the act of writing poetry to be radically private, akin to journal or diary writing. Because they view it as a pouring of emotions onto the page, they trust immediate inspiration rather than revision as an effective method of composing poetry. Such a view, according to John Crowe Ransom, makes of poetry "less a form of knowledge than a form of 'expression'" (1941, 130). If poetry is not a form of knowledge, then any rhetorical imperatives to communicate are secondary to the therapeutic value of composing itself.

This last point also explains much about student attitudes toward reading and discussing poetry in classes. Students assume that the poet's words are private; therefore, to probe too deeply into those words is an egregious invasion of privacy. The language of poetry is alien and should remain so, because the words belong to the writer, not the reader. This assumption suggests two radically different theories about reading poetry. First, reading a poem involves reconstituting its words within our own emotional experiences and then writing our own poem, which would be inspired by, but not accurately represent the words we have read. According to this theory, poetry can mean anything we want. No reading is better than another, since each is merely a personal expression of the reading experience. Second, if poetry is private language that has no intentional rhetorical feature, then we have no authority to make any statement about it. It can be enjoyed, but it cannot be interpreted or evaluated. In either case, class discussions that attempt to develop either a normative reading or a series of readings authorized by the text directly challenge students' understanding of the nature of poetry.

It is no surprise then that when we analyze poetry or other arts many students respond as one sophomore did (in a humanities class I also taught) during a discussion of the Sistine Chapel Ceiling. When I asked students to consider the problem Michelangelo faced in choosing an appropriate subject matter for the ceiling, one student who had not participated in the discussion could restrain herself no longer. She burst out, "How do we know he thought about all this so much? It's like poetry. English teachers always read all this stuff into poetry and I think they make it up. Writers don't think about all the stuff English teachers say they do. I know. I write poetry, and I just put down what comes into my head."

Obviously I disagree with the description of poetry posited by my class. There would be no reason to teach literature and writing if I did agree with it. But their view suggests how important it is to challenge the notion that poetry is an inspired private language not meant to be read as other texts are. This view makes of poetry a sacred text: "hallowed" is Elbow's word. Heaven forbid that our students project this view onto other texts they encounter—the words of political candidates, of advertisements, of their teachers. My first activity is designed to break down that notion by presenting writing and reading of poetry and other texts as a series of choices in which differing imperatives compete for prominence.

I give students this text:

> My heart leaps up when I behold a rainbow in the sky so was it when my life began so is it now I am a man so be it when I shall grow old or let me die the Child is father of the Man and I could wish my days to be bound each to each by natural piety

You will recognize Wordsworth's poem, "My Heart Leaps Up," stripped of all punctuation and line breaks. I break the class into groups and ask each group to reconstitute the shape of the poem and punctuate it. An examination of the choices students make in shaping what Wordsworth wrote as the first two lines will indicate the issues this exercise raises. The groups shaped and punctuated the lines this way:

1. My heart leaps up.
When I behold a rainbow in the sky,
2. My heart leaps up when I,
Behold a rainbow in the sky.
3. My heart leaps up
When I behold
a rainbow in the sky.
4. My heart leaps up when I behold a rainbow in the sky;

The point of this activity is not to guess what Wordsworth did; the point is to examine the advantages, disadvantages, and reasons behind their choices. The first group wanted to isolate what they considered to be the central action in the poem, so they separated the subject and verb not only into a first line, but into a first sentence. The second heard a rhyming couplet and leapt on it as an organizing feature throughout most of the rest of the poem. They were able to find couplets with *I/sky, began/man, I/die*, then a problem line ending with "Man," and finally a couplet formed with the rhyme of *be/piety*. The third group heard three lines rather than two because the rhythm seemed more "natural" to them. The fourth saw the words as one syntactic unit and were reluctant to break up its coherence by separating it into lines. Some of these reasons are stronger than others, some principles of choice are sustained better than others throughout the shaping of subsequent lines. But the point is that each group decided on a different solution, and each had a cogent explanation for that decision.

After discussing the groups' shapings of the poem, we can compare them to Wordsworth's:

> My heart leaps up when I behold
>   A rainbow in the sky:
> So was it when my life began;
> So is it now I am a man;
> So be it when I shall grow old,
>   Or let me die!
> The Child is father of the man;
> And I could wish my days to be
> Bound each to each by natural piety.

The first thing students notice is the complex rhyme scheme—ABCCABCDD—and are surprised to discover rhymes they did not initially hear. (Group Two wanted to know why Wordsworth's choice was better than theirs.) They also note the irregularity of line length and discuss why the setting off of "Or let me die!", which three of the groups also set apart, is appropriate. The point here is not to observe the profundity of the discussion, but to observe its subjects. The class immediately begins to ask why Wordsworth made the choices he did, and why those choices were different than theirs. They even focus on the differences between his punctuation and theirs, and note how punctuation can further meaning. This activity does not recover Wordsworth's composing process or his intentions in the poem, but it does present the poem as a matter of choices made among competing imperatives rather than as a matter of unguided inspiration. And though their readings emphasize different imperatives, students discuss both Wordsworth's and their choices with impressive insight. The exercise helps students experience an active form of reading because they are authorized to take possession of and manipulate

Wordsworth's words to see what they will yield. Each group can compare its choices with the others', not to determine what is right and wrong, but to explore what we can learn about the text from each response. Reading itself becomes a collaborative activity.

The second exercise moves in an opposite direction from the first. Instead of asking students to take possession of others' words, this activity, which involves writing three collaborative poems, forces students into a defamiliarized relationship with their own words. The point here is to help students experience what Don Murray identifies as "the process of evolving meaning—a constant revolt against intent—[which] motivates writers" (1982, 18). This process of discovery through surprise, through the unexpected revelations of language, is something experienced writers feel and know how to cultivate, but is difficult to engender in inexperienced writers. Many first-year college writers do not know how to read their own prose from a distance, as a third party, to see if it yields what they do not expect. I find that they simply miss surprise in their own language because they do not read it carefully enough. This activity forces their words to return as surprise.

For this activity, the class is divided into three groups. The class produces three collaborative poems of twelve lines; each group is responsible for four of the lines in each poem. First, each group begins a poem by writing two lines. They also write and keep a description of how they think the poem should develop both in form and content. The first two lines establish parameters for the poem, but the next group must decide the direction of the poem given those parameters. The second group has one week to compose the third and fourth lines of the poem; the third group has a week to compose lines five and six. By the time the first six lines have been written, the half-finished poem returns to the writers of the first lines. The poem goes through another round of writing in the same manner, and when the twelve lines are composed, the poem returns to the first group to be named.

One group began the poem they eventually named "Blind Hunter" this way:

> Thunderheads engulf the sky, and his woolly hound
> Stands watching, Zephyr gently bends the acreage of heather.

These lines pose interesting problems of form and tone. The beginning does not establish a rhyme scheme (the other two groups began with a rhymed couplet), nor does it establish a consistent line length or rhythm. The next group must choose either to impose a particular rhyme scheme and metrical pattern, or allow the poem to develop in some organic, non-regular way. The group who in fact received these lines also found the diction to be a problem because they considered the word choice—engulf, Zephyr, acreage of heather—to be sophisticated and unfamiliar.

The lines also pose problems of content. No one in the group who received these lines knew the meaning of Zephyr. After finding out, they had to decide if they would continue a pattern of allusion to Greek references, if they would continue a pattern of personification, or if they would ignore these features. At a more basic level, they had to decide what the subject and action of the poem would be. Would the subject be the hound (it turns out this was the first group's intention) or would it be the person who owns the hound? And what would happen? Would the poem carry forth some narrative action, be meditative, be descriptive? The second group's continuation:

> The distant laughter of the loon beckons him
> Forward, summoning the mighty hunter to his destiny.

The group here takes the poem in a direction other than the initiators planned by identifying the person as a hunter and by identifying the hunter as the subject of the poem. The third group decides to establish scene and leave the defining action to the first:

> Approaching the swampy water edge he spots his game
> As drops of rain fall and his woolly partner awaits his call;

These six lines offer a narrative direction, a subject, an action, and a formal pattern that make the initial lines a radically different act of language than the first group meant it to be.

These six lines illustrate how students are forced to reread their own words as an unfamiliar text that offers surprises in direction, so I need not analyze the development of the rest of the poem. It is worth, however, glancing at the first group's response to these six lines, because it suggests how liberating such impositions of language on their plans could be. The group decided to turn the poem into a farcical tragi-comedy by doing away with the woolly hound altogether since it could not be the subject of the poem:

> Almighty hunter's thunderstick, poised butt-end on his shoulder,
> The woolly beast lies motionless, the barrel still asmoulder.

Each group was outraged by the narrative direction the sets of lines took because they had envisioned very different poems when they wrote the first two lines. Even so, they were compelled to resee the poems, to reread their own lines as they now were constituted, and to come to terms with the changes in meaning and form that the first six lines directed.

In addition to these exercises, students worked on individual drafts of two poems throughout the semester. One was the poem they wrote at the beginning of the course, the other was written in response to the final activity I wish to describe. I gave the class four sonnets (it isn't important which ones) and asked them to list all the features the poems had in common. I did not identify the poems as sonnets, and I did not ask for interpretations of them. My point here was to generate a catalogue of features that would begin to identify a genre. The list we generated was highly predictable—each poem had fourteen lines; the great majority of the lines were ten syllables long; the poems had essentially the same rhyme schemes, which broke the poem into three quatrains with an ending couplet (but with minor variations in the last six lines). You will recognize here the formal features of a Shakespearean sonnet. I then assigned each student the task of composing a poem that met these restrictions. I assured the class in this, as in all the exercises in which they were writing rather than reading poetry, that the quality of the product was not a primary concern. Rather, I asked them to attend to how they wrote the poems.

Very few students were able to fulfill all of the features in the first draft. Some abandoned any concern for line length, some did not get fourteen lines, a few wrote in rhyming couplets rather than in the more complex rhyme scheme we had described. My questions for class discussion were first: "how did you write the poem," and second: "what difficulties did you encounter?" Most privileged the rhyme scheme first, and thought of all the words that would end their lines, then wrote to connect those words in some sensible way. This proved a wonderful strategy for helping students experience the ways in which language can create its own meaning, because they found the imperative of making meaning in constant tension with the imperatives imposed by the formal restrictions. Most students agreed that the necessity to rhyme kept forcing them to take the poem in different directions than they intended, although the directions they found themselves taking often interested and surprised them. Those who honored the restriction of line length found the problem exacerbated.

By comparing the experiences of writing this sonnet and their first poems (which had no preestablished generic restrictions), students were able to explore how generic conventions shape thinking. When we then turned our attention to their essays, we were in a position to consider further how both conventions of genre and the imperatives established by their own drafts function to shape and limit their patterns of thought.

The experience of writing these sonnets also allowed us to ask why anyone would choose to write under these severe, formal, generic restrictions. The class suggested a variety of interesting answers: because the constraints of form help create unexpected meaning; because writing with these restrictions is challenging, so to do it successfully is an impressive display of skill; because the successful results are beautiful; because it forces one to think hard about all aspects of writing—not only what one means, but how one sounds. All of these answers are very far from the expressive theory of poetry that many students brought to the course, and when I read some of their initial definitions back to them, they agreed that those statements were in need of revision.

It was only after the class had an opportunity to discover the processes by which poetry is created that we turned our attention to reading poems written by people outside the class. Each student was responsible for teaching one poem of his or her choice to the class, and those teachings were marked by an effort to identify points of difficulty in the poems and the proposal of solutions to the difficulties, not only from the presenter, but from the class as a whole. Poems became texts to read, to work with, to learn from.

Elbow's initiatory writing therefore provides a model that could be valuable not only in composition, but also in literature courses. In LITCOMP courses, and indeed in any course which aims to help students learn to read literature, initiatory writing makes "learning" rather than "literature" the central noun of the course. Reading "imaginative literature" involves understanding the choices writers make about genre, character, setting, modes of representation, tropes, and all the other features of literature; the initiatory writing activities I describe here lead students to experience choice itself as a central activity of both writing and reading. If students try their own hands at genres—not only a sonnet, or lyric poetry more generally, but fiction (the short-short story), or drama (a scene from a play)—with the goal of identifying the process of conscious and at times subconscious choice that acts of writing evoke, they are better able to read critically the literature of the genre.

Of course, this sequence of initiatory writing activities affects the kind of responsive writing we should require in LITCOMP and literature courses. As we all realize, the primary genre in these courses is the critical analysis essay, which has very restrictive conventions. The critical analysis must have a clear, arguable thesis that is proven by evidence marshaled from the text. It should be organized to present an argument rather than a sequential accounting of the text (summary) or a narrative history of the student's thoughts.

The essays many students in my class wrote in response to the poetry, however, challenged the conventions of the traditional critical analysis by focusing explicitly on their processes of reading. I asked students to choose from our anthology (*The Oxford Book of Short Poems*) three poems that shared some feature in common. Each student wrote an essay on one, two, or three of the poems. Because I did not define a genre for this essay—I did not explain what a "critical analysis" was nor did I require that the students write one—the students developed their own strategies for responding to the essay. A few wrote about the forms and genres of the poems, and some wrote about the subject the poems suggested, but virtually all of them incorporated into their texts the process by which they came to understand the poem or poems. Three quick examples will demonstrate the way in which process became topic for these students.

The most overt and simplest strategy students used was to describe their own process of reading. One student's introduction can stand for many others:

> To assist you in understanding the significance of the poem, I will first interpret it line by line. Then I will proceed with laying out some type of impression of how I pictured the poem in my mind, and then explain how the poem's idea of turning to someone for help and hope is evident.

Such a description of process often replaces a thesis in student writing, and it rarely produces effective essays. But this strategy does allow students the room to discuss their own puzzlement and confusion about certain aspects of their poems. This sort of discussion—marked by the haziness of "laying out some type of impression of how I pictured the poem in my mind"— may not be particularly valuable in a critical analysis essay, but it does keep the student's process of reading open, active, and honest.

The essay that most closely resembled a critical analysis was titled "Epigrams." The student who wrote this essay thought he was taking the easy road by choosing three two-line poems, but he quickly discovered that, if he was going to have sufficient information to write an essay, he would have to look past the poems. He wondered what these poems were, so I sent him to a dictionary of poetic forms, and he discovered that the three poems he had chosen were epigrams. His essay defined "epigram," offered a reading of each poem in light of the definition, and discussed how each poem differed. This student was led naturally to explore the nature of genre, and his process of discovery provided both evidence and a topic for his essay.

The most spectacular example of how process can become topic is an essay on Vachel Lindsay's "Factory Windows Are Always Broken." The writer of this essay was initially stumped by a line from the poem: "Something is rotten—I think, in Denmark." She could make no sense of this because the poem did not seem to be set in Denmark. I sent her to a dictionary of quotations, where she discovered the source of the allusion. She then read *Hamlet* to understand the significance of the allusion. When she wrote her essay, its subject was not Lindsay's allusion to *Hamlet*; rather, it was the importance of understanding allusions in poetry. Her experience of coming to meaning with this poem became the example she used to explain how one can track down allusions, and to discuss the rewards of such a pursuit.

The conventions of the critical analysis essay would not allow for the sorts of essays my students produced. The conventions demand that we erase all marks of the process by which we reach understanding; such essays speak to their readers as if understanding were shared and always present. I am certainly not advocating the elimination of the critical analysis essay from literature and LIT-COMP courses. I believe it is a valuable genre to learn. But as a step in the progress toward learning the genre, I think it may be more profitable for our students, particularly our freshmen, to focus first on the surprises, discoveries and misunderstandings that words can produce. They should write about this process of discovery repeatedly before they are asked to erase any traces of it from their critical essays. The convention of erasing the narrative of reading from criticism is partly responsible, I think, for students' anger and frustration about what English teachers do to poetry.[4] If we present poems as already understood, students are left with nothing to consider but their own inadequacy, revealed by the gap between their accounts of the poem and ours. Our students deserve better. They deserve the empowerment that emerges from their deeper understanding of the processes of reading and writing. As long as students continue to view poems as what Elbow calls "hallowed texts," and we position ourselves as privileged interpreters of the sacred, we will leave "the making of meaning" shrouded in mystery.

Notes

1. Booth observes that to "argue against separating 'comp' from 'lit' is easier than to develop and teach courses that counteract our increasingly sharp divisions" (57). This problem is restated in almost every essay contained in *Composition and Literature,* a collection of essays which itself grew out of a discussion about "the increasing separation between composition and literature" (Horner, 1) at an executive committee meeting of the Teaching of Writing Division at the 1980 Modern Language Association Convention. One can trace a direct line from *Composition and Literature,* through Robert Scholes' *Textual Power* and Stephen Mailloux's *Rhetorical Power,* to Elbow's statement. In fact, Elbow points to Scholes' book as an important item on the suggested reading list for the Coalition Conference. The project this lineage traces is an effort to revise the structures of English departments, the logic of the English curriculum, and teaching strategies within the classroom. My chapter is intended as a contribution to the last aim, and I wish to acknowledge how deeply the works of Scholes, Mailloux, and Elbow permeated my thinking here.

2. My initial impulse for choosing poetry was to test Nancy Comley's and Scholes' assertion that the "short, accessible modern poem is often a reservoir of compositional techniques" (102). They urge an exploration of a different aspect of writing—voice—than I am focusing on in this essay, but my results led me to agree with their claim that a "writing approach to literary texts, in which students write in the forms they are reading or use such texts as intertexts for writing in other forms, not only improve their ability to write in all forms of discourse, but will also improve ability to read and interpret texts" (108). Other genres, it seems to me, could be used effectively in the course I am describing, as long as the examples are not too long. Nonetheless, I believe that short lyric poetry holds a special advantage over other genres in this type of course because it tends to demand a confrontation with language through its attention to both the accuracy and surprise of its words.

3. Tom Newkirk observes the same reaction: "Students frequently speak of the 'hidden meanings' of poetry, and by that expression they usually mean hidden for them but open to another class of readers—professional readers, teachers" (209).

4. I agree with Newkirk's observation that we also erase the narrative of reading from our teaching: "Traditional practices of teaching literature in introductory courses promote the view of 'inspired reading' because they obscure the process of forming an interpretation. In the traditional classroom the instructor rarely reveals what happens in his or her initial contact with a poem" (210).

Works Cited

Bleich, David. 1983. "Discerning Motives in Language Use." *Composition and Literature: Bridging the Gap,* edited by Winifred Bryan Horner. 81–95. Chicago, IL: University of Chicago Press.

Booth, Wayne C. 1983. "'LITCOMP': Some Rhetoric Addressed to Cryptorhetoricians about a Rhetorical Solution to a Rhetorical Problem." *Composition and Literature: Bridging the Gap,* edited by Winifred Bryan Horner. 57–80. Chicago, IL: University of Chicago Press.

Comley, Nancy R. and Robert Scholes. 1983. "Literature, Composition, and the Structure of English." *Composition and Literature: Bridging the Gap,* edited by Winifred Bryan Horner. 96–109. Chicago, IL: University of Chicago Press.

Elbow, Peter. 1990. *What Is English?* New York: Modern Language Association.

Horner, Winifred Bryan. 1983. "Historical Introduction." *Composition and Literature: Bridging the Gap,* edited by Winifred Bryan Horner. 1–13. Chicago, IL: University of Chicago Press.

Lindsey, Vachel. 1985. "Factory Windows Are Always Broken." *The Oxford Book of Short Poems,* edited by P. J. Kavangh and James Michie. 190–91. New York: Oxford University Press.

Mailloux, Steven. 1989. *Rhetorical Power.* Ithaca, NY: Cornell University Press.

Murray, Donald. 1980. "Writing as Process: How Writing Finds Its Own Meaning." *Eight Approaches to Teaching Composition,* edited by Timothy R. Donovan and Ben W. McClelland. Reprinted in *Learning by Teaching: Selected Articles on Writing and Teaching.* 17–31. Portsmouth, NH: Boynton/Cook.

Newkirk, Thomas. 1990. "Looking for Trouble: A Way to Unmask Our Readings." *To Compose: Teaching Writing in High School and College, 2nd. ed.,* edited by Thomas Newkirk. 209–21. Portsmouth, NH: Heinemann.

Ransom, John Crowe. 1941. "Criticism As Pure Speculation." *The Intent of the Critic,* edited by Donald A. Stauffer. Princeton: Princeton University Press. Reprinted in *Selected Essays of John Crowe Ransom.* 1984. Edited by Thomas Daniel Young and John Hindle. 128–46. Baton Rouge: Louisiana State University Press.

Scholes, Robert. 1985. *Textual Power: Literary Theory and the Teaching of English.* New Haven, CT: Yale University Press.

Wordsworth, William. 1985. "My heart leaps up." *The Oxford Book of Short Poems,* edited by P. J. Kavangh and James Michie. 113. New York: Oxford University Press.

7

Rend(er)ing Women's Authority in the Writing Classroom

Michelle Payne
University of New Hampshire

"Michelle, is it okay if I don't come to conference tonight?"

The rest of Kyle's peers were making their way out of the classroom, talking about the fate of our team-taught writing course. As a class, we had just tried to "democratically" plan the rest of the course by negotiating four different proposals the students had spent the last few weeks creating in small groups. The process of negotiation this period had been quite chaotic, as most democratic processes are, especially when they are experiments. Amid this chaos, Kyle, an eighteen-year-old journalism student who had begun the course by asking whether other sections were taught more "traditionally" than it seemed mine would be, had spent his time in class this day trying to read a novel despite my presence next to him. When I suggested he put the book away, he grunted and remained silent the rest of the period, hanging his head. As he had made clear to me before, he had no interest in planning a writing course he didn't believe he could

I want to thank two people who have been significant to the development of this article: Tom Newkirk, who urged me to get this out of my computer and into the hands of other readers; and my husband and colleague, Steve Barrett, whose support, ideas, and many conversations helped me to see my way through the web of conflicting feelings and ideas that had begun to undermine my teaching and my sense of self. He encouraged me to write my way through a difficult situation, and I did. Thank you.

learn from anyway. Now he was asking my permission to skip a conference, a group conference, no less.

"Why do you want to skip conference?" I asked. My back was to the blackboard. Only a few inches taller than mine, Kyle's stocky, broad frame was poised to go out the door.

"I have too much other stuff to do."

"I think you need to decide whether you want to stay in this class or not."

Motionless, he stared at me.

"What?"

"It seems to me you don't agree with what we're doing and don't believe you can learn from this situation, and there are plenty of other courses to choose from. I think it would be in your own best interest to take another section. I created this course to be designed by students so that everyone could find a space to get what they wanted out of it. You don't have to be here if it isn't meeting your needs." I took a deep breath, noticing from the corner of my eye the three male students who were waiting for our conference. I knew, based on my previous conferences with Kyle, what was coming next—he would challenge me, try to intimidate me, get defensive, and try to deflect from my point.

"When did I say I didn't want to be in this class? I don't remember saying that. I don't understand what you're talking about." He faced me squarely now, fixing his unblinking, dark brown eyes as firmly on me as he had positioned his feet firmly on the ground.

"It's the sixth week of classes and you haven't done the dialogue journal, you haven't even begun your learning log, and your last paper, which didn't even fulfill the assignment, makes it loud and clear you don't intend to learn anything in this class. Your body language in class announces your apathy and resistance. Technically, I could fail you not only for failing to do the work but for being mentally absent in class a number of times and then not coming to conference tonight." Remember, I said to myself, stay focused on the point.

"What do you call being mentally absent? If you just mean not talking, then half the people in this course should fail. I worked in my group—just ask them. I put time in and they'll tell you I contributed a lot. How can you say I was mentally absent?"

"I'd say reading a book in class is being mentally absent."

"I thought what we were doing in class today was stupid."

Was it stupid? Did anyone else feel that way? Had we accomplished anything? Should I have said something when Karen said she didn't see why we should read in a writing course? When Amy said we should only write for ourselves?

"Why was it stupid?" I asked.

"Because it was like high school." In the writing he *had* turned in he had repeatedly criticized his "liberal" high school, particularly his English teachers who made students write about their "feelings."

"Well, there are twenty-seven other students in this class who think this is college. If you don't think so, then you need to find another section. You don't have to be here. And I don't have to teach apathetic students. I'm tired of teaching students who don't want to be here. The whole premise of this course is that students need to participate in their own learning. If that isn't what you want, then you need to find another section." After several weeks of Kyle's passive-aggressive behavior, I was beyond frustration.

"I was going to ask you if I could audit it."

"You need to talk to the director about that. But I suggest you change sections."

"I can't drop this class. I need it. And about that last assignment—I thought you told us that if we didn't like an assignment, we could write about whatever we wanted . . ."

"I find that hard to believe. Why would I create a specific assignment and then say that?" Had I said that?

"I don't understand why you think I'm apathetic. I never said that. Plenty of other students seem apathetic to me. Why are you focusing on me?"

"Not turning your work in and reading a book in class seems like convincing evidence to me. And you just said you thought the class today was stupid." Was I only focusing on him? Was this only one incident that I was blowing out of proportion?

"But I haven't been like that all semester . . ."

"Kyle, what do you think you need to do to pass this class?"

"Turn in my portfolio. Show up for class."

"No, Kyle, you need to learn something. You need to put some effort into learning something about your writing, and you need to not only do all the work, but participate in class."

"You can't fail me if I turn a portfolio in. If I show up for class and do all the work, you can't fail me. What about all those other people who are apathetic and not doing their work?" He folded his arms across his chest and stood with his feet wide apart.

I wanted to say, "Watch me." I hesitated. He was asking important questions, even if they were deflecting from our discussion of his own behavior. Did he know of other resistant students trying to deceive me? Could I really fail him for all these reasons? Would the director support me? Would he think I was out of line?

"The portfolio is only part of your grade. You haven't done all your work, and your attitude in class has given you two absences. If you have a problem with this, you can talk to the Director of Freshman English. For the moment, you have to decide whether you're going to stay for this conference."

"I guess I don't have any choice."

I recreate this incident in such detail because it represents for me not only one of the most difficult situations in being a writing teacher, but one of the most significant issues of being a female academic. Despite James Berlin's criticism of the belief that "[my] privately determined truths will correspond to the privately determined truths of all others" (1988, 486), I want to argue that what I have experienced as a female graduate teaching assistant in a Composition and Literature doctoral program may speak to more female academics and writing teachers than I (we) realize. But, maybe not. It may be, as I once heard a professor say of Richard Rodriguez, that I'm speaking out of my own neuroses. Or, as Kyle once said of Rodriguez and Nancy Sommers, I may be writing one of those "confessional narratives" that seems to have no particular audience except the self. Regardless, what I hope to do here is explore the ways in which my personal history, my gender, and my education in Composition and critical theory have created for me a rather interesting, sometimes frustrating, always conflicting internal dialogue about my own authority (and authority in the abstract) that often renders me hesitant and distrustful, vulnerable and decentered. In doing so, I will harken back to those "prior texts" in Composition and post-structuralist theory that seem most useful to my task, and I will also share a good deal of my personal history.

And that makes me nervous.

As much as I value the marriage of public and private discourse, academic and personal writing, I find it increasingly difficult to "allow" myself to "indulge" in such a marriage in my own writing. It's hard enough to write a piece where my voice "appropriates" the discourse of others and uses that discourse to further my own argument. To invite my own experience into the dialogue seems particularly . . . threatening. I've always feared that one of these days, someone would come along like Toto and inadvertently slide the curtain away to reveal that the Wizard of Oz wasn't quite who he made himself out to be. By sharing my personal experience, and certainly my feelings, I may be inviting someone to come along and determine I am unfit, unstable, too emotional to be in a position of power—that my presentation of efficiency and capability is exactly that, a presentation. A pretty common feeling for many of us, I know, but one that has become increasingly difficult for me to shake. The more frequently I'm in positions where I need to "authorize" myself, the more threatened I feel. I think this is what Peter Elbow means when he says "there is what I would call a certain rubber-gloved quality to the voice and register typical of most academic discourses—not just author-evacuated but showing a kind of reluctance to touch one's meanings with one's naked fingers" (145). Well, I'm about to touch my meanings with my naked fingers.

I rarely read about students like Kyle who reject process teaching, or about teachers like me who feel riddled with self-doubt. In our continuing re-evaluation of the teaching of writing, we have created a pedagogy (at least one) that we believe, on some level, will reach every student and bring out his or her latent powers of language. In blaming current-traditional writing instruction for the hatred students felt toward writing and for their poor writing skills, we have almost defined ourselves as the "saviors" of students—and of learning in general. In bringing students to the center of our classrooms, we have taken them more seriously, granted them more respect and intelligence than had been acknowledged before, and this is good, this is important. But in my experience it has left little room for the growing anger I feel at apathetic students (anger that is created, in part, I think, by the belief that my success as a teacher depends on reaching everyone). It has left little room for exploring my experience as a writing teacher, specifically those moments when I'm not quite sure I'm making the best choices. In romanticizing our students, we may have inadvertently silenced a very important part of the teaching of writing—our experiences as complex individuals who don't always have everything figured out and who interact with, affect, and are affected by complex students. This is not to say we haven't written about "not having things figured out" or that all the various pedagogical theories in our field have an evangelistic tenor to them. It is to say we need to pay closer attention to our beliefs about our students and about ourselves as teachers. And we need to write about them. Although the situation with Kyle is not the worst case I've dealt with, it strikes me as painfully emblematic of the "heteroglossic" (in all its connotations) nature of my teaching experience.

I was angry, had been angry for a number of days, that Kyle could sit so calmly in class and make comments pointing out the absurdity in what I was saying or trying to get the class to do, and that he could sit in conference with me, late at night with no one else around, and refuse to answer questions like "What are you trying to do in this paper? What ideas do you have for revision?", only to get defensive when I would, at his request for more directive comments, share my various responses and ideas for his paper. I was simply tired of having at least one male student—but usually more—who had no problem telling me, often in writing, that I didn't know what I was doing, that he didn't like the course or what I was asking him to do, and that he didn't feel like he was learning anything. "I'm paying for this course. I came here to learn from *your* knowledge—how can I possibly create a course to teach me something I don't know yet?"

Although his behavior was unacceptable to me and the philosophy of the course, I could see his point. I had sat in on the various groups of students as they talked about the goals of a college writing course, their past experiences, what they thought the roles of teachers and students should be in creating an "exceptional" learning experience. Prior to this group work, they had individually been writing in response to a sequence of assignments, reading (Paulo Friere and Richard Rodriguez), and researching about learning and education under my own guidance. I had developed the questions I thought they needed to consider—I wanted their plans to be informed decisions to the extent they could be. I had anticipated an outbreak of creativity and excitement. What I saw was excitement that gradually gave way under the pressure of time, the struggles of negotiating and accommodating so many personalities and ideas, and what I sensed was an increasing fear that they wouldn't really learn much in this course. What I realized as I sat in on their planning sessions was that I had a lot more to offer these students than I realized—ways of creating the experiences they wanted and helping them to learn something about writing from those experiences. I also realized that in planning this course, they were coming in with so many beliefs about writing that I didn't agree with (but that didn't surprise me), that I didn't think were productive, that I didn't want them to walk away with. This grand experiment was beginning to look too risky. I was experiencing the same self-doubts I always do when I teach: Was this the right thing to do? Am I wasting their time? Have I created a too-difficult task? A too-easy one? Will they give up, decide they can't learn from this class and turn into passive, "good students" who humor the teacher just to get through the course? Should I, as Bartholomae, Bizzell, Delpit, and others say, be teaching them what they would need to know about writing in the university instead of asking them to participate in determining what they might need or want to know and do?

I would call this an identity crisis. In asking my students to design their own course, I was opening myself up as a teacher for criticism and doubt, inviting them into a relationship with me that was more co-equal than many of them had experienced with teachers before, and also inviting them into my own personal and professional struggle with who I am as a writing teacher. Together, we were asking: What is a teacher? What does she or he do? Why? What is her or his relationship to students and their relationship to her or him? From the perspective of many "libertarian pedagogies" as well as many process, student-centered pedagogies, this situation is ideal—students and teachers are learning from each other, both learning within a community of people reflecting on their world and their place in that world. I have certainly embraced these values or I wouldn't have created such a class. But from the perspective of a woman who was socialized to have what post-structuralists call a "split subjectivity," who already commands from most students less authority and power than a man, yet who has embraced pedagogies and post-structuralist theories that decenter authority, and who also sees the value of "apprenticing" students into the academy, asking students to question my authority was overwhelming at best, debilitating at worst.

In exploring this "identity crisis" and how I see my conversation with Kyle as emblematic of it, it would be nice if I could create a palimpsest, a multi-voiced text whose columns speak back and forth to each other as they seem to in my head. Unfortunately, that would be too difficult to read and to produce on paper, so I'll have to settle for a linear text that tries as best it can to weave these multiple voices in and out in a productive tension.

Personal History as Text

As many social constructionist and post-structuralist theorists have argued, an individual is more than a unitary, coherent self—she or he is "constructed" of all the prior texts and prior discourses she or he has engaged with. I have very little difficulty agreeing with this; my sense of self has always seemed fragmented, fluid, and dialogic. Because of my personal history, I have been "constructed" around a certain view of myself that many post-structuralists might find . . . inviting. In many ways I am a series of texts that all seem to "deconstruct" themselves regularly. In spite of all my efforts to the contrary, my attempts at authorship—in all the connotations of that word—usually end up dismantling themselves. In other words, post-structuralist theory has merely given me language with which to discuss processes I have been experiencing for years now. Ironically, this makes critical theory both comforting—I have a language for my experience—and threatening. It just intensifies the internal conflict and self-doubt that seem crippling in situations with students like Kyle.

One of the most powerful discourses that has influenced my identity as a writing teacher—and that is often ignored in theoretical and pedagogical discussions—has been my experience as a woman from an emotionally abusive childhood home. In sharing this I am quite conscious of the myriad reactions I might receive. Not only am I making myself vulnerable, but I'm "telling on" my family and breaking the cardinal rule of most academic work—keep your distance, be objective and theoretical. Many, though not all, of us seem to value students writing about their family life and care about our students not just as writers but as people, yet we seem reluctant to share publicly the various ways our own private lives have influenced us as scholars and teachers. We are quite willing to turn a psychoanalytic eye on "literature" and use psychotherapeutic methods in the writing classroom, but do we ever think about ourselves in these terms? Do we ever consider the impact our theoretical and pedagogical ideas might have on those of us who didn't have "normative" childhoods? We are only beginning to understand how our students' family experiences may influence their learning and behavior in our classes, and it seems equally important that we begin to understand what may be influencing us. Maybe these are issues that can only be worked out in a therapist's office. Then again, maybe these are issues that can't wait for the therapist's office.

We have certainly learned a great deal about what it means to be female in this culture, particularly when it comes to women's social and intellectual experiences. My own experiences might sound familiar to many. Very early in life I was convinced that I was as gullible, naive, irrational, and emotional as my father and younger brother said. Whenever I had an opinion about something, they would argue with me, sometimes through intimidation, always to the point of me getting "emotional." In their bastardized version of logic, my personal experience was always skewed and my responses were emotional over-reactions to their simple, clear, rational points of view. Even as an undergraduate, when I came home one weekend and shared with my father, a dentist, what I had learned male doctors had done to marginalize and criminalize midwives and to radically change the experience and function of childbirth for women, he became increasingly angry. He couldn't believe, he said, that I could be so gullible and uncritical, believing everything I read or heard from a teacher. How could I expect to function in this world believing everything I read? I tried to explain what I had read, recapitulating the argument as best I could given that I was quickly losing confidence in my ability to remember anything. My father pointed out everything I didn't know about this issue, including the incredible benefits of modern medicine, reinforcing my belief that I was, as he had always said, merely a bookworm who knew nothing more than what I read and couldn't function outside the limits of the university.

My father once told me that my brother, on the other hand, had natural talent and "understood" things, even though his grades didn't reflect it. I had gotten through school and done well, from my father's perspective, by the sheer force of my desire to please, not by any intellectual prowess on my part. This reinforced my already pervasive belief that I was "faking it" and would one day be discovered as a fraud. This inability to trust myself was reinforced by my father's reaction to our sibling fights. My brother would try to humiliate me verbally and, no matter what we were arguing about, I was always stupid and wrong, and certainly too emotional. Even though I felt my brother was being a jerk, my father often told me it was my fault, and this compounded my sense that I was easily deluded. Although my father and brother now realize the debilitating impact all this had on me, it has seemed from the time I was in second grade, when my father attributed the sexual abuse I had suffered from his cousin to my over-active imagination, that my sense of self has been constructed around a belief that I am usually and easily deluded.

At least three of the arguments that have historically been used to dismiss women's experiences are (1) she's deluded, irrational, "mad"; (2) she's just angry and emotional—it will pass; and (3) she created the situation herself. Interestingly, Kyle, the student I began this piece with, used all of these arguments, besides physical intimidation, to undermine my authority at various points in the semester. The conversation with Kyle I have recreated evoked memories of my father and brother, and I struggled not to fall back into my role of "victim" and allow him to convince me that I was at fault, that I was simply angry and picking on him, or that I was under an "illusion" about his behavior and feelings and couldn't see what was going on around me with the other students. A week after our first conversation, Kyle brought the subject up again after class, saying he didn't understand why I was so "down" on him. "You're just upset that I don't agree with your teaching philosophy, that's all," he said. Through a series of verbal attacks, reminiscent of my brother's, he essentially told me I was making this all up; I was creating a double-standard because I didn't like him; my anger was not justified; I didn't know how to teach; I had no power over him. Later, when Kyle and I were discussing this with the director, I said, "Kyle, one of the central issues here is that you don't respect me. You don't believe that I have anything to offer you." He nodded his head.

Composition Theory as Text

When a female teacher walks into a first-year writing class, she inevitably evokes responses from students a male teacher most likely does not. Students come in with so many assumptions about teachers, authority figures, and women as teachers and authority figures that how a teacher interacts with students becomes incredibly important. Most process, student-centered pedagogies define the teacher's primary role as facilitator, the one who creates an "enabling environment" where students can experience the process of discovery, the "motivating force of revision." The teacher is a questioner who sits back and lets the student tell her where the draft is leading him, modeling for him the questions he needs to ask himself in order for the teacher to be needed no longer. A writer herself, the teacher is patient and listening, responding to where each student is coming from.

In this model, the teacher is nurturing, non-directive, non-content oriented. Her authority derives from her experience as a writer, but more importantly from her partnership with the students. In order for the best learning to take place, the hierarchy of power must be broken down so teachers and students learn from each other and share authority (though sometimes we speak of "transferring" the authority and power to students). For theorists like Paulo Friere, the classroom becomes democratic and communal; for someone like Donald Murray, the institutionally-endowed power of the teacher is evident primarily in the pressure to write daily, participate in workshops, and come to conferences. For many teachers—particularly, I imagine, for women—decentering the teacher's authority feels comfortable, manageable. If, as Carol Gilligan (1982) says, women are attuned to relationships and try to avoid threats to those relationships, a co-equal, non-authoritarian, non-confrontational writing classroom seems ideal.

That was certainly my response when I began studying composition my senior year in college. I was preparing to teach the following year as a Master's student and I was terrified I wouldn't know what I was doing. "What right do I have to be in front of the classroom?" I asked my professor, Mary Fuller. "I'm only four years older than my students. I know so little about writing. . . ." Mary assured me, as did the writings of Murray, Elbow, Emig, and Knoblauch and Brannon, that my experience as a writer was all I needed to qualify me as a writing teacher. I didn't have to lecture, I didn't have to demonstrate my knowledge to my students in careful commenting on their texts. I was comforted. After all, I did the non-directive thing well. Having been my brothers' caretaker from the time I was ten, I was nurturing, responsible, and adept at creating non-threatening environments. I had been responsible for everyone's feelings and fearful of their anger and displeasure, so I became a chameleon, trying to prevent "unpleasant" situations by understanding everyone's point of view and reading everyone's mind. The last thing I wanted to do was put myself into a position of responsibility that carried overt power and authority—power and authority meant humiliation and silencing for me. I felt I would either stand before my students to be revealed as a fraud, or I would silence them and create hostility.

It soon became evident, however, that decentering my authority was not creating the situations I read about in the journals. My students were not motivated by their writing—they took advantage of my openness and unwillingness to create friction by doing as little work as possible. I had been following my interpretation of the Murray-method of response, and when a student said, "Nowhere—I like this draft just fine," to my question, "Where is this draft leading you?", I didn't know what to say. I knew the draft wasn't "good enough," but then again, the students were the ones determining what was good, what felt right, not me. I was there primarily to facilitate their natural impulse to write and give them the freedom to write about whatever they wanted so they could shake off the shackles of high school writing teachers. (In effect, it seems, I was exchanging my power and authority for their comfort and affection). They were supposed to be learning to enjoy writing and learning again. My class was supposed to be the one they would never forget. Instead, they seemed to sit back and write with the same attitude they did in high school—I'm not learning anything, but I have to do this, anyway.

Gradually, I changed my style. I was starting to read people like David Bartholomae and Joseph Harris, and their arguments about empowering students with academic discourse made sense. As a graduate student I was certainly aware that I had to learn academic conventions and personas—I was an apprentice who knew that personal experience papers wouldn't get past the professor's desk. Plus, I was discovering through a rhetoric class that if I had known anything about logic and argumentation, I would have known how to defend myself against my brother and father's mal-adaptations of it. I'd always known language was empowering, and now I was learning *how* it was empowering. Why not share that with students?

I worked my way into creating sequences of assignments around a single topic that asked students to "theorize" from their experiences what it meant to, say, conform in our society, or to play roles, or to be a female. I structured the class with assignments that still asked them to write personal experience papers and that eventually led to open topics, and I maintained the same nurturing, flexible, non-authoritarian stance I had assumed in my less-structured classes. I still talked about the writing process and writing to discover. The only thing different was that I was handing out general assignments. The students by and large, after the first four weeks, reacted with open frustration. Instead of male students trying to flirt with me and get out of doing any work, some of them began to respond hostilely in their writing. ("This is bullshit." "I can't believe you picked this story. It's stupid." "I don't care about this."). They began to act out in class—falling asleep, not working in their groups, and goofing off. Whether their behavior can be attributed to the way I asserted my "control" over their writing or to what I now see as a general trend in this kind of behavior, I'm not sure. Whatever the case, their behavior complicated my already conflicted internal dialogue about my role in the writing classroom and the extent and nature of my "control" and "authority."

After a series of unusually passive and quiet students (with noticeable exceptions) who I feared had not learned much from my course, I was about ready to give up on teaching. I realize now that how my classes responded to my teaching—their resistance and apathy—translated for me into failure. The students could see that I had no real power, just as my brothers had seen it. Plus, no matter what I taught, I seemed condemned to fail: the dialogue in the field about what and how we should be teaching corresponded well with my personal conflicts and experiences with the emotional and the "rational," what had been marginalized for me and that which marginalized it.

In other words, I knew first-hand that Western male (academic) discourse was empowering; I had come to believe such discourse was what I needed. But I also knew it was threatening, used to disempower, and I wanted to value my feelings and personal experiences, not continue to marginalize them as my father and brother (and education) had done. So what should I teach? Should I ask the women to learn a new discourse that for many is threatening? Should I encourage them to write from their strengths in personal, self-reflective pieces? Should I encourage the men to learn new ways of thinking about themselves and relationships, or reinforce the discourse that seems based on a devaluation of such personal discourse?

The way academic discourse has been structured seems to demand that this is an either/or choice. Bartholomae's metaphors of mastery and appropriation for acquiring academic discourse seem anathema to what has traditionally been associated with women's values and experiences. At the same time, as Lisa Delpit (1988) has argued, we can't empower disempowered students by refusing to teach them the power language. Ironically, this "public" discussion of these issues is incredibly personal for me. I cannot separate them, especially now that I have language to talk about their differences. In this sense, such a dialectic is productive, stimulating. But as I said before, when I walk into the writing classroom so well-versed in this debate, knowing that some students value non-directive teaching and others value explicit teaching, I feel like double-exposed film.

I want to add one more element to this discussion before I move on to the post-structuralist critique of these dichotomies. I would argue that the choices set up by the process-model/academic discourse debate create a no-win situation for a female teacher. If she chooses the non-directive approach and works to share authority, it might reinforce the men's devaluation of her as an authority figure (and invite them to turn that power differential in their favor, as Kyle tried to) and it might send the women a signal that power and authority are inappropriate for women (even though the women might feel comfortable with a co-equal teaching situation). If the teacher decides to teach academic discourse (which seems to demand more direction), she might create resistance in the men at a "woman" holding power over them, and resentment in the women for disturbing the relationships with them and with the men (especially in a period like now when women reject anything that will label them—or any other woman—"feminist" or "bitch").[1]

A female teacher's authority, though endowed by a degree and the university, is tenuous no matter which pedagogy she embraces. And if teaching is a matter of persuasion in the classical rhetorical sense, then women may have a more difficult time being taken seriously by their students when the very fact of their gender undermines their ethos. As much as I wish this weren't the case, my power and authority—my effectiveness as a teacher—is dependent on how much power and authority my students grant me (in addition to the support the administration grants me). When they can't even agree on what constitutes "legitimate" authority, and I'm still torn myself, what do I do on Monday morning?

Post-structuralist Theory as Text

Deconstructive critics, as I understand their method, would consider the previous paragraphs a deconstructive moment. I tried to demonstrate that our traditional definitions of "authority"—a teacher's authority—can be "decentered" when we begin to take into consideration what happens when the marginalized term (women have not traditionally been considered authority figures) is brought into the system. Authority is not transcendent or transmissible. It is arbitrary and contingent, definable only in relation to its opposite.

For a number of people, post-structuralist theory seems jargony, elitist, unnecessarily abstract, and sometimes nihilistic. I have certainly experienced it as all these things. But as I said earlier, I have also experienced post-structuralism as something that describes my experience of myself and my world. Very few things have remained stable for me, and structure and power have always seemed arbitrary and conflictual. What people said was not necessarily what they meant, so signifiers and signifieds only rarely seemed to line up. To this day, with the help of post-structuralist theory, I can still argue myself into and out of any situation or feeling, as well as into utter hopelessness. I have welcomed difference and criticized power relations, arguing for multiplicity and tolerance.

But when I am in charge of a classroom of students, when I carry with me the "power of the state" and participate in what is always some form of indoctrination, how does multiplicity and tolerance work? I have relatively specific goals (which are constantly in flux) and I try to direct the classroom so that students can learn something, but what if my goals are in conflict with a student's (like Kyle's)? What happens when I ask students to critically consider the role of teacher and student and redesign their course to meet what they determine their needs are? Where do my needs and what I think is important fit in? Does the class have to be either the students' or the teacher's? Do I have to "give up" power for them to become empowered? What if they decide I don't know what I'm doing as a result of the questioning I have asked them to do?

If we are arguing in literary theory that we need to redefine the canon to reflect multiple views, and that this means we must consider the literary piece within its own culture and its culture's values, does this also mean we must consider each student (and his or her paper) within his or her own culture, regardless of how it conflicts with our own? I'm not arguing here for a return to a universal standard or the dominance of one discourse community over another. I'm primarily wondering how I can possibly *not* marginalize someone in the classroom, especially in a situation where we are required to evaluate students' work. Should I, for example, sit down with Kyle and try to "talk this through" by sharing what I sense is going on, as one of my colleagues suggested? When it seems that Kyle operates within a community where authority figures are direct about their requests and their information, would that work for me, trying to do what Delpit says is a white, middle-class method of making my power inexplicit through a series of questions that imply commands (289)? As a feminist, should I be disturbed or enraged (which I am at times) that I have to put up with more from male students like Kyle than my male colleagues do? In my efforts to be tolerant and egalitarian, do I have to value male values that I see as ultimately hurtful?

I realize that critical theorists don't see their value system leading inevitably to relativism and "anything goes"—they value the dialectic, the discussion that occurs when conflicting paradigms engage each other. Ideas and people are ultimately changed in the bargain. But for someone like me, whose sense of personal power was eroded from childhood on, and who knows that power does exist and is held by certain people, being a deconstructive text is becoming more and more debilitating. Theoretically, we are not unitary individuals with one "self" we need to find in order to be whole. We are multiple selves that have been constructed over time from the various "texts" we have encountered. I have organized this chapter based on that premise. But right now, I would really like to have a unitary self, a set of values that I can live by, even though I know they are not absolute and probably not common. I would like to be comfortable walking into class with a plan I will stick by no matter how many students grumble. I'd like to know my students *are* learning something from my class. I would like to be able to comfortably tell someone like Kyle that he cannot stay in my class and to know that I won't get sued by his parents for discrimination or fired for not being able to "handle" discipline problems—and that I won't get tossed out of the profession for having the "wrong" attitude toward students.

Note

1. See especially Susan Jarrett's "Feminism and Composition: A Case for Conflict" in Harkin and Schlib's *Contending with Words*, pages 105–123.

Works Cited

Bartholomae, David. Spring 1988. "Inventing the University." *Journal of Basic Writing*. 5:109–28.

Berlin, James. September 1988. "Rhetoric and Ideology in the Writing Class." *College English* 50:477–94.

Delpit, Lisa D. August 1988. "The Silenced Dialogue: Power and Pedagogy in Educating Other People's Children." *Harvard Educational Review* 58:280–98.

Donahue, Patricia, and Ellen Quandahl. 1989. *Reclaiming Pedagogy: The Rhetoric of the Classroom*. Carbondale: Southern Illinois University Press.

Elbow, Peter. February 1991. "Reflections on Academic Discourse: How It Relates to Freshmen and Colleagues." *College English* 53:135–55.

Friere, Paulo. 1970. *The Pedagogy of the Oppressed*. New York: Herder and Herder.

Gilligan, Carol. 1982. *In a Different Voice: Psychological Theory and Women's Development*. Cambridge: Harvard University Press.

Harkin, Patricia, and John Schilb. 1991. *Contending With Words: Composition and Rhetoric in a Postmodern Age*. New York: MLA.

Murray, Donald. 1992. *Learning by Teaching*. Portsmouth, NH: Boynton/Cook.

Rodriguez, Richard. 1982. "The Achievement of Desire." *Hunger of Memory*. New York: Bantam.

Sommers, Nancy. December 1980. "Revision Strategies of Student Writers and Experienced Adult Writers." *College Compostion and Communication* 31:378–88.

Section Three

Institutionalizing the Writing Process

8

The Politics of Intimacy
The Defeat of Barrett Wendell at Harvard

Thomas Newkirk
University of New Hampshire

In *Lives on the Boundary* Mike Rose tells the story of a young faculty member who pleaded not to be nominated for a teaching excellence award for fear it would hurt her tenure chances. She worried that it would make her appear insufficiently committed to scholarship. In my own department there is often concern that young faculty members will spend too much time with students, be too available, thus limiting the efforts they can put into research. Student contact is viewed as a form of seduction, the tempting gingerbread house that lures young teachers from their stern duty. After all, student contact puts a premium on personality, on empathy, on the capacity to listen (the "softer" virtues), rather than on more purely intellectual skills. And no teachers, historically, have suffered more from this devaluation of student contact than composition teachers.

In this chapter I will argue that the fundamental conflicts that confront our field are not between the cognitivists, expressivists, social constructionists, and other "ists", interesting as these debates (sometimes) are. A more fundamental conflict concerns what I call here "the politics of intimacy," the systematic devaluation of individual contact that marginalizes the work of all committed composi-

Excerpts from the Barrett Wendell papers are quoted by permission of the Houghton Library and the Harvard University Archives. I am grateful to both libraries and their staffs for assistance on this project.

tion teachers, no matter what their epistemological stripes. I will focus on Barrett Wendell and his career in composition at Harvard in the 1880s and argue that his defeat at the hands of the Harvard administration prefigures the history of composition in the twentieth century, as composition teachers became an underclass in colleges and universities, even though they often provided the most individualized attention to students. But to view Wendell in this way requires a revision—almost an inversion—of the generally accepted historical narrative.[1]

Most historians of composition—whatever their differences—have agreed on two points. The first is that Harvard exerted a strong, even dominating, influence on the direction of composition teaching in the United States at the end of the nineteenth century. And second, that this influence was negative and regressive. The narrative, in oversimplified terms, runs like this. Beginning in the 1870s, universities responded to the call for "more English" by instituting writing courses in the newly-forming departments of English. Composition became an established subject. But rather than drawing on a rich rhetorical tradition, teachers at Harvard (particularly Adams Sherman Hill and his protege, Barrett Wendell) seemed content to teach a watered-down version of Bain's modes combined with a ferocious attention to mechanical correctness and contempt for the public schools that forced this obligation on colleges. According to James Berlin, the harshest critic of Hill and Wendell, writing instruction at Harvard was essentially positivistic, stressing "the kind of writing most valued by a technologically oriented business community"—a depersonalized form of exposition (1984, 63).

Thus an opportunity was missed. Composition teaching rigidified into the "current traditional paradigm" and slipped into the stagnant Dark Ages of the early twentieth century, emerging only slowly in the 1960s as scholars began a rediscovery of classical rhetoric and researchers began to examine the writing processes and, more recently, the social and political contexts of the writing act. In this narrative, Fred Newton Scott is portrayed as the voice that failed, a man who could envision the possibilities of composition teaching and scholarship, but was unable to slow the descent into darkness.

But recently, as scholars (Adams, Jolliffe, Simmons) have begun to explore the extensive material—student papers, class notes, letters, journals—that Wendell placed in the Harvard Archives, a more complex and sympathetic interpretation is coming to light. Wendell appears as a failed reformer, a major innovator in composition pedagogy who never gained the needed support from the Harvard administration and particularly from its president, Charles Eliot. By the end of his career Wendell felt his attempts to make composition a humane and intimate discipline were a total failure. According to Oscar Campbell, who knew him during his last years at Harvard, he was revolted at the "huge machine inexpertly devised for teaching Freshmen" and felt that mechanically minded men perverted his methods, setting "this Frankenstein in motion" (177-8). The story that emerges is one of profound professional defeat, one that would be reenacted so often in college composition programs.

Overcoming Resistances

Wendell's innovations in teaching should be seen against a background of student resistance or passivity. While instruction in the late nineteenth century is often perceived as more autocratic than that of contemporary classrooms, the students at Harvard actually held a number of high cards. The gentleman's C would not, after all, keep them from entering law school or taking over the family business or entering the ministry (a large number of Wendell's students became small town lawyers). Although Eliot's elective system had improved the classroom climate, students could still easily, and without penalty, withdraw from any engagement with their teachers. In 1877 Henry Adams gave up teaching at Harvard, in part because it was impossible to get students to talk to him. The *Harvard Crimson* advised students in 1876 to avoid asking questions or making observations in class. "Your questions will bore the students, and your observations will bore the tutors. And don't talk to tutors out of hours" (quoted in McCullough 1981, 201).

Significantly, W. R. Castle, one of Wendell's assistants, claimed that Wendell's main task was to overcome this lack of engagement. According to Castle (1924), Wendell gave "unreservedly of his strength to break down the barriers of indifference, or inertia, or obsti nacy, which bound or choked back the intelligence of the young men who made up his classes" (10). This indifference took a number of forms. It was, for example, common to have fewer than half the students present on the first day of class in October. Students regularly complained in their daily themes about having to attend class, or of the difficulty of writing the 150-word "dailies":

> I think the work in English 12 is a pretty heavy drain upon a fellow's mental energy. The daily theme requires an immense amount of work. A fellow feels uncomfortable all day until he has his theme written . . . But the worst thing of all is that a fellow must attend lectures three hours a week. These lectures consist chiefly of reading themes. Now the fellow who is stupid enough to listen to another fellow's themes is a little bit more stupid than anybody in Harvard. (McAfee 1876, "Themes")

In another daily theme, a student wrote about the reluctance of a peer to write about the topic Wendell assigned, social life at Harvard:

> Shortly after the first lecture in English 12 I heard between two students the following conversation which is a stinging comment on "Life at Harvard":
>
> "Well, George, what do you think of the subject for our first theme?"
>
> "Oh, it will do. We can make something up. Of course, we can't tell how we spend our time; it would be a confounded disgrace." (Woodman 1886, "Themes")

Wendell addressed this issue in an essay he wrote on social life at Harvard (completing his own assignment) and read to the class, inviting response. It begins with the admission that "at the moment the relations between the students and officers [i.e. teachers] of the college are by no means as intimate as could be wished" ("Social Life").

The central teaching issue, then, was how to engage a group of privileged students who saw their primary education as occurring in the dormitories and club life of the university. Without the sanction of grading, with graduate schools that would admit virtually any Harvard graduate, with jobs largely dependent on family and personal connections, with Eliot's elective system allowing almost free choice of courses, what hold could teachers have on students? Clearly, one major hold was the energetic projection of personality, the harnessing of eccentricities. The published lectures of William James suggest an irreverance barely under control. We have Samuel Scudder's classic account of Louis Aggasiz's anatomy class where students "looked at the fish" for three days. Wendell was a bundle of eccentricities: his dandyism, his twirling his watchchain as he lectured rapid-fire in a high-pitched voice, his cutting criticism, and his habit of stopping class when someone was snoring until the culprit suddenly sprang back to life. But to view these as only personality quirks is to trivialize one of the few sources of authority that teachers possessed.

Though loyal to his mentor, A. S. Hill, Wendell recognized that Hill's approach to teaching failed to break the gridlock in teacher-student relationships. Often pictured as one of Hill's disciples, Wendell explicitly rejected the negativity and overly conscientious attention to error that he saw in Hill's approach. If Hill was a model for Wendell, he was a model of what to avoid:

> His tendency as a teacher was to grimly eradicate faults rather than sympathetically to stimulate promise. Partly his infirmity of health, partly his extreme near righteousness, partly his dry and biting manner, partly the thin rigidity of his red-bearded countenance, and most of all a temperamental shyness, made him seem aloof. ("Recollections," 71)

Although Wendell could be bitingly critical of students (his ultimate term of rebuke being "Germanic"), his primary approach was far more positive and self-revelatory. One of his students recollected the contrast between Wendell and his previous English teacher, "a sanctimonious old fellow" who "trained us to use long involved sentences. If I had used fire instead of conflagration I should have been thrown out of class. Imagine, then, my horror at sitting in front of a man who was human, and who frankly admitted some human weaknesses" ("Booklet").

We get some sense of Wendell's personal invitation to students in his opening remarks to the 1888-9 English 12 class:

> So far as I can stimulate you and you one another to feel what life is; to feel the inevitable inadequacy of all expression thereof; to feel, more and more, the beauty for all its inadequacy, of the great expressions that have been made for us—the ugliness and vileness of the mean ones;—we shall do well. We shall help one another to gain from this work training that will make us if not better writers at least better men. (Notes on Lectures, October 3, 1888)

Wendell also was extraordinarily generous with his office hours; he was available on Monday and Friday afternoons and on Saturday mornings, a generous ten hours in a week filled with class meetings and theme reading.

Wendell elaborated on his pedagogical creed in a *Boston Advertiser* column published in 1896 criticizing normal schools and the "methods" courses required in them. Wendell saw two requirements for teaching: sound scholarship and "the power of stimulating and holding attention," a power that derives from "vigorous individuality." To teach well required the primarily personal attributes that enable the teacher to maintain a stimulating relationship with individual students. Teaching "methods" had little to do with it. Yet, paradoxically, Wendell's great invention, his English 12 writing course, was such a pivotal pedagogical experiment, such a methodological innovation, that it anticipated many of the reforms that we have come to see as more recent—writing conferences, the use of student writing as the primary texts of the course, peer critiquing, analytic evaluation tools.

The Course

Students in English 12, a year-long junior course, were required to write twelve fortnightly themes, each of which would be revised to deal with criticisms of the teacher and, in some cases, the student critic. The order of assignments followed a modified version of the modal approach: description, narration, summary and criticism, exposition, and argumentation. Though Berlin claims that Wendell was a strong adherent of the modes approach, this was probably not the case. In fact, in the late 1890s he would write a critique of the modes that anticipates the position of James Kinneavy (see Newkirk, "Barrett Wendell's Theory"). And even in the 1880s he probably used the modes only as a loose guide to the types of writing he wanted students to try.

A much more central concept in the course was "point of departure," a method of helping students find topics to write on. Wendell modified the practice, very likely as old as writing instruction at Harvard, of using quotations to stimulate composing. Traditionally, this building on quotations prepared students to preach sermons. Just as the minister might look through the Bible for a particular verse, a point of departure to elaborate on, Wendell asked students to peruse Palgrave's *Golden Treasury*. One student, for example, settled on two lines in Thomas Moore's poem, "The Journey Outward," to begin his fortnightly theme:

> As slow our ship her foamy track
> Against the wind was clearing.

The lines reminded the student of a time he sailed from Provincetown to Vineyard Haven. The poem served as a prod to memory. In effect, Wendell took an approach that typically had led to moralizing (another term of rebuke), one which caused twenty-year-olds to sound like Polonius, and *secularized* it.

In class, Wendell spent considerable time reading student themes—strong and weak—to illustrate the principles of good writing. And of all these criteria, he seemed to stress "force," that mark of "vigorous individuality" above the others. On December 1, 1886 he read a student theme on smoking opium, suggested by DeQuincey's *Confessions*, which he had assigned, perhaps for shock value. For one student, though, this theme clarified what Wendell meant by "force":

> Never until today have I had a clear idea of the difference between force and elegance in a piece of writing. Hitherto I have always had the idea that the two were synonymous, but the theme that we read today on opium smoking showed very clearly the difference. The theme had, to me at least, more force than any that has been read. I could see the opium joint plainly as the writer described its minute details. (Howard 1886, "Themes")

Like other overwhelmed composition teachers, Wendell also devised shorthand notations for indicating mechanical problems, though some students complained about the inadequacy of the system. One wrote:

> Here [on your theme] you find an expression which you thought particularly happy marked with an "x" which being translated is "error too obvious to need particularizing"; there you see a metaphor, which required half an hour's thought to straighten out into what you thought something quite poetical, marked "m"—mixed metaphor. Under the circumstances is it any wonder that the copy [i.e. revision] you made is just as abominable as the former. (Peale 1886, "Themes")

Complaints like this one appeared on the daily themes, Wendell's most obvious addition to the composition course.

The guidelines for the daily themes were relatively simple: students would write one page, about 150, words every day except Sunday, focusing on what made that day in some way particular. In his opening talk to the 1886–7 English 12 class, Wendell listed four objectives for the dailies:

1. Regularity of practice.
2. Ease of writing—an art that I believe is essentially a habit. Force—the power of holding attention, and the fundamental quality of efficient style, comes like ease of manner, from practice.
3. Cultivation of the powers of observation, wherefore I advise that daily themes be written on topics that transpire day by day.
4. Correction of habitual errors. (Notes on Lectures, October, 1886)

Students were given almost absolute choice in their topics for the dailies, although during the course Wendell "blacklisted" some that were being overworked, the trolley strike and the weather, causing one student to protest that "the weather has always been my short anchor" (Howard 1886, "Themes"). Another student, who was working his way through the life of Martin Luther, wrote, probably at Wendell's insistence, "I shall not afflict you with anything more about Martin Luther" (McAfee 1886, "Themes").

In addition to the cultivation of the habit of observing and writing, the daily themes bridged the gap between social and academic life. They were a way of achieving intimacy, of participating in the primary learning that occurred in the dormitories and the streets. The range of topics was vast: watching an amputation at the medical school, the joys of the ukelele, the novelty of typewriting and electric lights (they were installed in the gym before they were installed in the library), roommate problems, football (or "foot ball") games, watching a drunk being carried off in a wheelbarrow, attending the performances of Sarah Bernhardt and Edwin Booth, the mistreatment of horses on the Cambridge-Boston line—and again and again, the difficulty of coming up with topics.

On the back of each theme Wendell wrote the title and a one-word evaluative comment, and once he had accumulated a month's worth of themes, he would comment on the set and return them. A listing of the one word comments suggests the qualities Wendell was looking for:

> *Terms of Praise*—sensible, vivid, simple, sympathetic, easy, colloquial, to the point, empathic, sincere, spirited, clear, conversational, some vivacity, forcible, delightfully direct.
>
> *Terms of Criticism*—diffuse, heavy, padded, rambling, not very interesting, windy, not much substance, prolix, vapid, vague, slight, hasty, a little formal, trivial, confused, labored, moralizing, bad ink.

Compare this list to the one Kenneth Macrorie (1970) offered students in *Telling Writing*: "Most good writing is clear, vigorous, honest, alive, sensous, unsentimental, rhythmic, without pretension, fresh, metophorical, evocative in sound, economical, authoritative, surprising, memorable, and light" (21).

Wendell saw as his goal the eradication of the sententious moral discourse that was characteristic of Harvard in earlier times. Take, for example, this opening paragraph written for Edward Channing in 1838 to the assignment, "State some of the reasons why criticism of recent works is to be mistrusted." Bear in mind that a twenty-year-old is writing this:

> That an author has enemies who gladly seek opportunity for gratifying private spleen by condemning his work is, obviously a reason we should be cautious what credit we pay to criticisms upon recent works. Instances have occurred, where, based on prejudice, men have poured forth a torrent of invectives on work no ways deserving censure. (White, "Themes")

White's essay proceeds on this level of generality, never once mentioning a *specific* work that had been censured. Often the writer simply stitches together ready-made moral commonplaces. A few years before Wendell began his teaching career, Mark Twain parodied this style in *The Adventures of Tom Sawyer* where he quotes an examination theme written to the topic "Is this, then, Life?" which begins:

> In the common walks of life, what delightful emotions does the youthful mind look forward to some anticipated scene of festivity. Imagination is busy sketching rose-tinted pictures of joy. (198)

It was against this sententious style that both Twain and Wendell waged war.

The daily themes also served as a means for students to comment on the course; in fact Wendell invited them to be critical. To the contemporary reader, some of the student comments seem extraordinarily blunt, even rude. One student commented on Wendell's notorious high speed speaking style by suggesting—in a daily theme—that he "should take a few lessons in elementary elocution" (McAfee 1886, "Themes"). Another began, "I am disgusted with your criticism of my fortnightly themes" (Richards 1886, "Themes"). While contemporary response approaches tend to emphasize support, the writer's ownership, and criticism often couched in oblique language, Wendell prized candor and directness. The final theme in his 1888–9 English 12 class was an evaluation of the course, and he urged his students to "make [their] criticism as specific, as true, as frank as possible" (Notes on Lectures, May 17, 1889). For teachers, just as for students, the real enemy was complacency; without "manly opposition" from students, faculty tend to "develop that arbitrary self-confidence and impatience of contradiction" that Wendell saw as characteristic of the ministry (Howe, 89).

The dailies, then, provided a regular channel for students to criticize English 12, often at Wendell's encouragement. Though grade complaints were fairly rare, they did appear. A typical grade distribution for English 12 was 0 A's, 6 B's, 15 C's, 9 D's, 0 F's (Notes on Fortnightly Themes, 1889). More typical were complaints about the sharpness of Wendell's criticism when he discussed papers in class. One student wrote, "it is a question whether it is best to make a man believe that he is a blockhead; for although it was not distinctly said that either of the men criticized were blockheads, the remarks might easily have been interpreted to mean that" ("Peale 1886, Themes"). The same student objected to Wendell's comment on the first half-year's writing, "Your work is exceptionally uneven, whence I infer that you do not always take pains." The student wrote back, making an interesting comment on the composing process:

> I think the cause of the unevenness in the work is not so much lack of pains as lack of interest in the subject. You may say that this amounts to what you said. Partly it does. For a great deal of work is done unconsciously on a subject you are interested in. But this ought not to be called "pains" for the very reason that it is unconscious work. The amount of conscious effort on every theme but one has been about the same. (1886, "Themes")

Students also expressed disagreement, probably at Wendell's invitation, at the peer critiques of their papers. Each student, identified only by number, wrote evaluative comments on another student's paper (Wendell then added his comments to those of the peer critic). One common criticism of student work was the recycling of encyclopedia information without citation, leading in one case to this angry defense:

> If the "crank" will show me the encyclopedia from which, he thinks, "I culled these facts" I shall be much obliged. . . . I think it is a very unjust remark to make about a classmate's theme unless the critic is sure it is true. The theme was a pretty poor one, and some of the remarks are very just. The critic ought to have his head pushed in a snowbank and kept there all night. (Atwood 1886, "Themes")

It is necessary to read such criticism as Wendell probably read them, not as the breakdown of community, but as a form of engagement, a dialogue. Students clearly were drawn by Wendell's commitment to writing. As one of them recollected years later, "No one could write themes for Mr. Wendell, could visit the austere work room in Grays 18, without feeling the seriousness with which the work in English Composition was carried on" (Herrick, Booklet).

Just how many students Wendell taught in the early years of English 12 is not clear because he was not responsible for reading all of the themes (though he seems to have been the main reader for the dailies). Judging from the numbers assigned to student critics, a figure of 160–200 seems likely for the course in 1886–7. Since the undergraduate enrollment at that time was about 1,000, it appears that *almost the entire junior class chose to take the course*. The demands on Wendell were so extreme that he would describe himself at the end of an academic year as "tired out," "deprived of health and strength," "limp as a wet rag" (Notes on Lectures, 1885–86). One student sympathized in a daily theme, "How pitiful it must be for a man to peruse about 200 odd sermons [i.e. daily themes] every day, week after week, and worst of all, like the shades in Hades, not be permitted to die" (Hesseltine 1886, "Themes").

Defeat

While Wendell supported (with some reservations) Eliot's elective system, he was almost crushed by it, defeated by his own popularity. Though students had almost complete choice in their courses, resources did not necessarily go with them. This became a source of contention, particularly when Wendell took on role of English Department chair in the 1890s. Even late in his life Wendell remembered bitterly his dealings with Eliot:

> When I was chairman of the department of English, I had to submit to him a budget of annual salaries, which he found inconveniently

> large. I ventured to suggest that, under the free conditions of his elective system, so many courses in English had been chosen by students that the proportion of tuition-fees thus earned by the department was about four times as much as our total list of salaries....His answer took my breath away; he rather sternly said that my argument seemed to him vulgarly commercial. . . . In this instance he forgot, or neglected, the fact that for some generations his ancestors and mine had been engaged in self-respecting mercantile pursuits. (Recollections, 46–7)

This was just one of many battles focusing directly on money, but indirectly on the possibilities for personal contact, intimacy, in writing instruction.

As department chair, Wendell made a sweeping proposal for the overhaul of both English A and B, the freshman and sophomore courses. His long memo to Eliot, describing the rationale for the changes, provides an illuminating look at the problems Wendell saw with the course structure. The major one was the lack of support it gave to the rewriting process:

> As the course is conducted at present, each instructor after spending *20* hours in correcting themes spends *10* in the examination of written work and then *4* in consultation with the students who choose to come to consult him in regard to written work. Attendance at consultation is voluntary. No more than a third of the class (this is a liberal estimate) avail themselves of the opportunity for consultation; a good many never come to consultation. Thus a large part of the time spent in examining written work is, so far as the student is concerned, practically wasted: for the matter of change of marks by quality of rewritten work is of little real value. (Proposed Plan for English A)

Wendell proposed to cut time spent attending lectures in half, so that there would be only thirty during the entire year, thereby reducing the number of lecture summaries students would write. The time gained would be used in helping students revise their work. The entire freshman class (about 600 in 1894) would be divided into sixteen to twenty-four sections for the rewriting of themes, to be done in class with the instructor there. This smaller setting (about thirty students) would allow for the type of in-class consultation that would be popularized by Roger Garrison eighty years later. In addition, Wendell's plan called for scheduled conferences (called "consultation") between the teacher and each student, about six per year. According to Wendell, "the value of this consultation, both to student and instructor, cannot be overestimated."

Wendell goes to great numerical pains to prove that this conference-based system could be initiated with no increase to the staff of five instructors . Yet the strain it would place on these men is difficult to imagine. We don't have Eliot's response, but later correspondence shows he clearly was unwilling to provide additional staff to move in this direction. The opposite seems to be true. He wanted the departmental budget cut, a demand which led to this *cri de coeur* from Wendell to Eliot:

> One and all of us have labored not to shirk work, but to make our teaching effective. To my mind, and I think myself at one with my colleagues, the reduction of work proposed will mean that our teaching will suffer almost beyond words. [I]f this reduction must be made we must . . . limit that personal contact which we have found mutually stimulating. The utter lack of heart with which we are forced to what we all deem professional inefficiency is the one thing I hope you fully realize. What we now propose—as the only means we can profess of meeting the conditions you have stated—is literally the abandonment of all the methods which have made us hope that study at Harvard might mean more to students than study elsewhere. (Letter to Charles Eliot, November 20, 1896)

Even thirteen years later, as Eliot was leaving the presidency, the wound was still fresh. In a curious poem, entitled "De Praeside Magnifico," which appears at the end of his essay collection *The Mystery of Education*, Wendell commemorated Eliot's retirement and embedded in the poem several criticisms:

> He seemed—one never knew—so full of change
> That if you let your imagination range
> In untried regions of experiment
> You had his ear; but if you paused content
> To better, if you could, your daily task
> He gave you little—so you ceased to ask. (259)

This is an unmistakable reference to Eliot's unwillingness to support composition teaching. Eliot responded stiffly, "In your description of me there are some things I do not understand, or recognize as correct" (Letter, January 10, 1910).

History and Hagiography

As researchers begin to explore archival material and to place major figures in composition *within* their institutional settings, some of the widely accepted historical generalizations will inevitably be challenged. It is, for example, implausible to argue that writing instruction at Harvard, in the 1880s and 1890s, focused on depersonalized exposition. Wendell's teaching, his writing, and the writing he asked of students was viewed as an energetic projection of personality. One of Wendell's main goals was to overcome the emotional flatness, the gridlock, in teacher-student relationships.

It is also misleading to speak of Harvard as some unity in the evolution of composition teaching. It was a site of almost perpetual conflict. The Overseers were constantly monitoring the writing program, often fixating on student errors. Eliot, under financial pressure, was unwilling to go along with Wendell's proposal for conference-based writing courses. Wendell and Hill, though often viewed as very much alike in their approach to teaching (though not in temperament), had vastly different ideas about writing instruction. Wendell worked to strip from the writing course many of the elements Hill had introduced—lectures, a prescriptive focus on style, a central textbook for the course. Katherine Adams has claimed that English 12 was Wendell's "revenge on Harvard," his own assault on the way writing had been taught.

Wendell's harsh treatment by historians also raises the questions about standards of hagiography: how do we claim significance for figures in composition history? Is the standard "influence," and, if so, how is influence determined? Or do we seek out figures that most resemble contemporary composition specialists? Do we look for likenesses? If so, then someone like Fred Newton Scott is clearly closer to the ideal of the academic composition scholar. He published extensively in academic journals, he was interested in the conceptual and rhetorical issues involved in writing, and he developed a graduate program in which his students explored these issues. He was one of us.

Wendell didn't fit this mold. Though he wrote extensively, he usually wrote for a popular audience, and on a wide variety of topics (his biography of Cotton Mather is still in print). He had little to do with the development of graduate programs, feeling that they focused too much on narrow specializations and drew resources away from undergraduates, particularly freshmen. And he distrusted the elaborate conceptual apparatus that was being imported into composition teaching (e.g. from logic). The key words for Wendell, are "intimate," "stimulating," "habit," and "simplify." Taken together they outline a pedagogy that rested on the personal and mutually stimulating (though not always gentle) relationship between teacher and student. He saw writing itself as primarily a habitual form of behavior, and the successful writer becomes automatic in certain skills from regular practice. He also saw that by keeping the conceptual principles rigorously "simple" (always a positive term in Wendell's lexicon), they are better able to be internalized and transformed into unconscious behavior. He demonstrated this small set of terms through regular discussion of student writing, which became the major text in the class.

Given the politics of specialization and academic reward, Wendell's position was doomed. It was too craft-oriented, too student-oriented, too much the work of a generalist. The tensions within the Harvard English Department were evident early in Wendell's career there, and they came out in the open over issues such as advanced studies in literature. Here is Wendell's account of a departmental discussion in 1889 concerning a course called "Special Advanced Study and Research":

> Yesterday, without having a quarrel, we managed to declare two views of what it ought to be, which portend trouble. One is Child's, which appears to be that no course of study which does not involve actually professional minuteness of investigation is of the slightest value. He does not insist on philology, but holds that a single author, for example, is more than enough for a year's work. In short, he treats the matter, to my way of thinking, as if we were a technological school, engaged solely in turning out men equipped for lecturing and editing. (Journal 6)

Wendell stated the opposing position that diverse reading might be the best thing "for many students, who care more for the effect of education on themselves than for the tangible acquirement that may come of it." But even then the tide was moving toward those like Child's protege, Lyman Kittredge, who, Wendell feared, viewed his work in composition as "amateurish and trivial."

By the early 1900s he admitted defeat and withdrew from composition teaching, calling his efforts a "waste." To the extent that his career was a tragedy, it is one that would be enacted time and again in the twentieth century as writing teachers would find their time-consuming work with individual students unrewarded, while priority went to specialists who no longer bothered with the younger and less-prepared students.

In a cruel historical irony, those few composition specialists who began to earn academic status in the 1970s and 80s did so by following Child's prescription for professionalization. To preserve time for this work, they (and I include myself in this generalization) often had to protect themselves from the kind of intimate, one-on-one writing instruction that Wendell saw as the *center* of his work. As this process of institutionalization continues, it seems to me, composition studies increasingly aligns itself with the traditional biases of English departments: a lack of interest in literacy learning at the elementary and high school levels (and among those in the workplace); a preference for theoretical or historical studies over empirical investigations of writers; a belief that the most gratifying work comes from teaching the best prepared students; a suspicion concerning the scholarly status of pedagogical work; and, most maddeningly, the condescending dismissal of earlier work in writing as theoretically naive, or "amateurish."

For twenty years, bearing a teaching load that only the most overworked community college teacher can imagine, Wendell fought the trend of professionalization, often with a bouyancy and energy that a century later still has the capacity to inspire. It is this earlier Wendell that we need to remember:

> A dull business this seems to many, yet after ten years' study I do not find it dull at all. I find it constantly more stimulating; and this because I grow more and more aware how in its essence this matter of composition is as far from a dull and lifeless business as earthly matter can be. . . . For he who scrawls ribaldry, just as truly as he who writes for all time, does that most wonderful of things,—gives a material body to some reality which till that moment was immaterial, executes, all unconscious of the power for which divine is none too grand a word, a lasting act of creative imagination. (1891, 40)

Notes

1. The basic lines of this narrative come from Albert Kitzhaber's groundbreaking history of rhetoric instruction in American colleges. Contemporary historians, particularly Donald Stewart, have drawn from Kitzhaber, presenting an almost binary view of historical development with Scott at Michigan the hero and various teachers at Harvard the villains. The most extensive published treatment of Wendell was done by Wallace Douglas, whose portrait is entirely negative. James Berlin makes the untenable argument that Wendell and Hill favored a depersonalized form of exposition that could serve the rising merchantile class that Harvard sought to attract, a claim that entirely misses the mark so far as Wendell is concerned.

Wallace Douglas is, however, undeniably correct when he argues that Wendell was an elitist who endorsed some of the most extreme views of the Brahmin class to which he belonged. Even Charles Eliot criticized the emphasis on class, breeding, and family origins in Wendell's *Literary History of America* (James, 1930). For example, here is Wendell on abolitionist Theodore Parker:

> For this [i.e., his tendency toward vituperation] might be pleaded the excuse that Theodore Parker, like Garrison, sprang from that lower class of New England which never intimately understood its social superiors. A self-made man, however admirable, can rarely quite outgrow all the limitations of his origin. (348)

He is continually praising men "of the better sort" and saw his task at Harvard as that of educating such men. For this reason, it is easy to dismiss him as a reactionary, which in many ways he was, particularly in his later years. But what I argue in this chapter is that, whatever his political view, he responded to the institutional challenges that Harvard presented in the 1880s and created a bold experiment in writing instruction, his English 12 course. His insights into issues like fluency are not ultimately limited to any class.

Works Cited

Adams, Katherine. 1991. "English 12 and Professional Writing." Paper delivered at the Meeting of the International Society for the Study of Rhetoric.

Berlin, James. 1984. *Writing Instruction in Nineteenth-Century American Colleges*. Carbondale, IL: Southern Illinois University Press.

Booklet of Quotations by Former Students. Barrett Wendell Collection. Harvard University Archives.

Campbell, Oscar. 1939. "The Failure of Freshman English." *English Journal* (College Edition) 28:177–85.

Castle, W. R. 1924. "Barrett Wendell—Teacher." *Essays in Memory of Barrett Wendell*, edited by W.R. Castle. Cambridge, MA: Harvard University Press, 3–10.

Douglas, Wallace. 1983. "Barrett Wendell." *Traditions of Inquiry*, edited by John Brereton. New York: Oxford University Press.

Eliot, Charles. January 10, 1910. "Letter to Barrett Wendell." Wendell Family Papers. Houghton Library, Harvard University.

Garrison, Roger. 1974. "One to One Tutorial Instruction in Freshman Composition." *New Directions for Community Colleges* 5:55–83.

Howe, M. A. DeWolfe. 1924. *Barrett Wendell and His Letters*. Boston, MA: Atlantic Monthly Press.

James, Henry. 1932. *Charles W. Eliot, President of Harvard University 1869–1909*. Boston, MA: Houghton Mifflin.

Jolliffe, David. 1989. "The Moral Subject in College Composition: A Conceptual Framework and the Case of Harvard, 1875–1900." *College English* 51:163–73.

Kinneavy, James. 1971. *Theory of Discourse*. Englewood Cliffs, NJ: Prentice Hall.

Kitzhaber, Albert. 1953. "Rhetoric in American Colleges 1850–1900." Ph.D. Diss., University of Washington.

Macrorie, Kenneth. 1985. *Telling Writing*, 4th ed. Portsmouth, NH: Boynton/Cook.

McCullough, David. 1981. *Mornings on Horseback*. New York: Simon and Schuster.

Newkirk, Thomas. 1991. "Barrett Wendell's Theory of Discourse." *Rhetoric Review* 10:20–30.

Palgrave, Francis. 1883. *Golden Treasury of the Best Songs and Lyrical Poems in the English Language*. New York: Crowell.

Rose, Mike. 1989. *Lives on the Boundary: The Struggles amd Achievements of America's Underprepared*. New York: Free Press.

Simmons, Sue. 1991. *A Critique of the Stereotype of Current-Traditional Rhetoric: Invention in Writing Instruction at Harvard, 1875–1900*. Dissertation Abstracts International 52:04a.

Stewart, Donald. 1985. "Some Historical Lessons for Composition Teachers." *Rhetoric Review* 3:134–144.

"Themes on Daily Life." 1886. Ms. Curriculum Materials. Harvard University Archives.

Twain, Mark (Samuel Clemens). [1873] 1946. *The Adventures of Tom Sawyer*. New York: Grosset and Dunlap.

Wendell, Barrett. 1891. *English Composition*. New York: Charles Scribners and Sons.

———. Journal. Ms. Wendell Family Papers. Houghton Library. Harvard University.

———. November 20, 1986. "Letter to Charles Eliot." Charles Eliot Collection. Harvard University Archives.

———. [1900] 1927. *Literary History of America*. New York: Charles Scribners.

———. [1909] 1971. *The Mystery of Education*. Freeport, New York: Books for Library Press, 1909.

———. "Notes on Fortnightly Themes, 1888–89." Ms. Barrett Wendell Collection. Harvard University Archives.

———. "Notes on Lectures in English 12, 1885–6." Ms. Barrett Wendell Collection. Harvard University Archives.

———. "Notes on Lectures in English 12, 1888–9." Ms. Barrett Wendell Collection. Harvard University Archives.

———. "Proposed Plan for English A 1894–5." Charles Eliot Collection. Harvard University Archives.

———. 1917. "Recollections of Harvard." Ms. Barrett Wendell Collection. Harvard University Archives.

———. 1885. "Social Life at Harvard." Ms. Barrett Wendell Collection. Harvard University Archives.

———. n.d. "The Study of English Composition." Ms. Curriculum Materials. Harvard University Archives.

White, W.O. "Themes, 1845." Ms. Curriculum Materials. Harvard University.

9

How the Writing Process Came to UMass/Amherst
Roger Garrison, Donald Murray, and Institutional Change

Charles Moran
University of Massachusetts

In 1981 the University of Massachusetts had what Richard Young and Maxine Hairston then would have termed a "current traditional" freshman writing program: some subject-matter (literature, film), interspersed with writing assignments that were completed, then graded, then returned. In 1982, one year later, the university had a radically different writing program, one based on the work of Janet Emig, Peter Elbow, Roger Garrison, Donald Murray, and the other pioneers of what was then known as a "process" approach to writing. This new writing program received some national attention: it was one of twenty-eight programs described in the 1986 MLA book, *New Methods in College Writing Programs*. How did such a radical change come to pass?

I thank Tom Carnicelli and Lester Fisher, of the English Department at the University of New Hampshire, for the help they have given me in tracing the career and influence of Roger Garrison. I thank Marcia Curtis, Jim Leheny, and Sara Stelzner of the University of Massachusetts for their thoughtful comments on this chapter as it was being written. I thank, too, Roger Garrison, a man I never met, and Don Murray, a man I count as a friend, for the help and guidance both gave me at a crucial time in my life. And I thank Kay J. Moran, journalist, wife, and best friend, for the insights she has given me into her profession.

What follows is a narrative, one that begins in 1973 with a meeting between my colleague Jim Leheny and the dean of a local community college. The narrative includes people, texts, and political/economic forces, each a contributor to the change that would take place in the university's writing program in 1981–2. The narrative will illuminate the complex processes of institutional change in higher education, and specifically in English departments in four-year, research universities. The story is extraordinary in at least these respects: an English Department at a Ph.D.-granting research university was instrumental in undergraduate curricular change; an English Department served as the locus for curricular change in a field it apparently did not value, the teaching of writing; and an English Department at a Ph.D.-granting research university was influenced by texts from two communities it did not often encounter, the community of professional writers and the community of two-year college teachers.

First among the cast of characters is Walker Gibson. Our story may be said to begin in 1967 with Gibson's arrival at the university—a senior professor, widely published, a man who believed that writing could be taught and whose principal field of scholarly endeavor was rhetoric. Gibson believed, and often asserted, that the field of rhetoric was more ancient, prestigious and useful than the field of literary study as it was then defined. Gibson did what he had been hired to do: he combined the existing speech and freshman English requirements into a required two-semester rhetoric sequence. When the English Department wanted nothing to do with this course, Gibson asked the department if it would mind if he established a separate unit, the Rhetoric Program. The department was delighted; now it could teach what it wanted to teach: British and American Literature. So in 1970 Freshman English left the English Department.

Next in the cast of characters are two young English professors, myself and Jim Leheny—both scholars trained as specialists in eighteenth century British literature, both in 1973 tenured or about-to-be tenured, and both at least open to new directions in their careers. I had always thought of myself as a teacher, not a scholar, and my CV at this time bore this out: a few reviews, a few articles on the teaching of literature, but nothing that suggested (tenure-memo prose notwithstanding) that I'd contribute to the world of scholarship in literary studies. Jim had published a fine book, the Oxford edition of Addison's *Freeholder* papers, but heavy-duty scholarship, though he had shown he could do it, was not where he would make his mark. Jim was to go on to a career as a high-level academic administrator; I was to be the first director of a new Writing Program and was to accumulate in my CV not articles on Laurence Sterne, my dissertation subject, but on the teaching of writing. In 1973 neither Jim nor I knew much about the teaching of writing. We had done it, but we'd not read in the field. We were not committed to a particular pedagogy and were more-than-open to suggestion.

Additional players in the scene were political and economic forces that operated on our nation and upon our home institution. In the activism of the late 60's and its effect on required courses, our English Department had lost its enrollment-generator, a required two-semester sequence called "Masterpieces of English Literature." Coupled with the loss of the two-semester rhetoric sequence, also a university requirement, the loss of the "Masterpieces" requirement did dreadful things to the department's faculty/student ratio. We became, in 1971, a department of 107 tenure-track souls with shamefully few students to teach. The dean therefore began a campaign of retrenchment that was to reduce the Department by 40 percent. The dean also began to weaken the Rhetoric Program, using its budget to absorb the mid-70's budget cuts that came his way. The dean deeply believed that English should be responsible for the teaching of writing and was willing to use his power to make this happen. If English would take over rhetoric, then it would lose fewer faculty. The English Department resisted for more than a decade, some of us believing that the Rhetoric Program was in good hands, others fearful that English would become a writing, and not a literature, department.

To counter the appearance of departmental inactivity, and to give the more adventurous among us something socially useful to do, our department head, Joe Frank, began in 1971 to encourage outreach activities of all kinds. He drew on Walker Gibson's energy, enthusiasm, and contacts, which produced initiatives that sent us to teach English to inmates of local jails, to teach paraprofessionals in Bedford-Stuyvesant as part of a grant won by our School of Education, and to teach undergraduates in the CCNY Writing Center under the direction of Mina Shaughnessy. One of the supported outreach activities was a cooperative internship program for our graduate students at Springfield Technical Community College, an effort led by Jim Leheny. Another was our connection with the Springfield Public Schools, just a thirty-minute drive from the campus. These outreach activities, begun in 1971–2, continued into the early 1980s, driven by the department's enrollment needs and, after the 1975 *Newsweek* article "Why Johnny Can't Write," by a national sense that the teaching of literacy skills was of crucial importance. This outreach effort brought Leheny and me, members of an English Department at a four-year, research institution, into professionally-extraordinary contact with English teachers at other types of institutions: two-year colleges and secondary/elementary schools. We were traveling "down" the vertical metaphor that defines American education. This outreach effort also brought us, Ph.D.'s and literary scholars, into contact with MFA graduate students, people who identified not with the community of literary critics but with the community of professional writers. For these people, in contrast to our Ph.D. students, teaching in two-year colleges was a job, not a fall from grace.

Into this mix of individual, institutional, and national imperatives came, in 1973, two texts: a mimeographed thirty-page monograph titled *Teaching Writing: An Approach to Tutorial Instruction in Freshman Composition*, by Roger Garrison; and *A Writer Teaches Writing: A Practical Method of Teaching Composition*, by Donald Murray. Both authors were ex-journalists. Both authors extrapolated from their professional writing experience to the freshman writing classroom and described a classroom in which writers wrote, under the supervision of an editor-in-chief who circulated among the working writers and advised them as they wrote. Garrison described in detail a classroom-management system that would permit one teacher to edit the work of twenty-five student writers. Murray gave to the teacher-editor a sense of how writers wrote and of how a teacher-editor might best "coach" young writers.

Though Garrison and Murray promulgated remarkably similar pedagogies, though both were New Englanders, and though Garrison taught at Murray's home institution during the summers of 1973–77, the two men hardly knew one another. Yet they often appear together in the literature of our field, as they appeared to us in 1973. Both Garrison and Murray contributed chapters to the 1985 Coles and Vopat collection of student writing and teacher response. Garrison's own work is not often cited, but when it is, a citation from Murray's work is never far from it. The two appear together in the literature of one-to-one classroom teaching strategies (Carnicelli "The Writing Conference;" Collins & Moran; Foster, Laque & Sherwood); in the literature of writing centers (Almasy; Flynn; Harris *Teaching*; Olson, Reigstad & McAndrew); and in the pre-network literature of computers and writing (Collins & Sommers; LeBlanc & Moran; Rodrigues & Rodrigues). Eight years after our encounter with Garrison and his work in an instructor's manual that accompanied *How a Writer Works* (1981), Garrison would include Murray's book in a "Select Bibliography" for writing teachers, with this generous note: "Perhaps the best writing text available. Suitable for grades ten through college freshman level. Murray is a Pulitzer Prize winner (journalism), and the book is crammed with valuable advice. Beautifully written"(16). Murray does not cite Garrison in the suggested reading list he includes in his 1985 revision of *A Writer*

Teaches Writing. Nor does Garrison's work appear in other places one might expect it to be: the reading list at the end of the Judys' 1981 *Introduction to the Teaching of Writing*; the "Annotated Bibliography on Revision" appended to Ronald Sudol's 1982 NCTE anthology, *Revising: New Essays for Teachers of Writing*; or in the indexes of James Berlin's and Stephen North's 1987 histories of the field. Don Murray's works are listed in each of these places.

The reasons for the difference have to do with character and situation. Garrison was a self-styled outsider and iconoclast, a person who deliberately remained outside the growing community of scholars in the field; Murray was, and is, a generous and sociable man who moves comfortably in the world of professional conferences. Perhaps linked to the difference in character was a difference in situation: Garrison and Murray were working in different cultures. Two-year college English teachers have easy access to the published work of their colleagues who teach in four-year research institutions; their own knowledge, not often cast in the form of the published research article, circulates, most often oral and embodied, within their two-year college community—except in the extraordinary circumstances that brought Garrison's work to our attention in 1973. The cultures of the two-year college and the four-year college/university are still separate today.

It follows, therefore, that we learned of Roger Garrison and his work through Jim Leheny's visit to a two-year college, Springfield Technical Community College—one of our department's "outreach" efforts enumerated above. Jim tells the story thus:

> The academic dean of the community college—John Dunn—was a former graduate student in Political Science at the University; a mutual friend had introduced us. One day, while Dunn was in Amherst on other business, he rang my office and we arranged to meet for a drink at the end of the day. We had already had some conversations about the internship program, and this meeting was, as I recall, intended to move that program along. Because it involved joint funding from the two institutions, we were each struggling with budget issues. After discussing what seemed the most important topic at the time—money—we started discussing what seemed like more peripheral issues: how community college faculty felt about having our graduate students invade their turf, how our department would select and supervise the graduate students, and so forth.
>
> Casually, and almost as an afterthought, Dunn mentioned that some of the English faculty at his college were interested in the work of Roger Garrison—"he teaches somewhere in Maine," Dunn said. Garrison was a name I did not recognize, but Dunn went on to say that he had funded a Saturday workshop at the college. Garrison would be there to discuss his work. He invited me to join the group.

Jim continues to describe the effect of the workshop on him:

> My day with Garrison changed how I thought about teaching writing. We sat around a large conference table, about eight or ten community college teachers and I, and Garrison began in his no-nonsense, Maine woodsman kind of way to describe how and why so many traditional writing classes don't work. . . . He then proceeded to describe the methods he used at Westbrook College: the steps involved in leading beginning writers into the writing process.

Garrison's workshops and summer seminars, we now know, were tremendously influential—but in the world of two-year colleges, not four-year colleges. Garrison himself taught at what were then termed "junior" colleges: Briarcliff and Westbrook. With Tom Carnicelli and Lester Fisher, both professors in the English Department at the University of New Hampshire, he ran the "UNH-Westbrook College Summer Institute for Two-Year College Writing Teachers" for a period of four years, 1973–77, and then moved it to Westbrook and ran it himself for two more years, 1978–9. Each summer he taught with forty to eighty teachers who took his program back to their colleges and passed it along to their colleagues. Garrison's work never appeared in *College Composition and Communication* or *College English*; it was the center of the occasional conference presentation at CCCC, not of scholarly papers, but of special interest groups (1981) and post-convention workshops (1982); but chiefly it circulated among two-year college teachers, in mimeographed and even blue dittoed form, never reaching the growing community of scholars in composition studies who were based chiefly in four-year research institutions. Garrison's text was distributed in seminars like the one Jim Leheny attended, teacher to teacher, as what Louise Phelps has termed "practical knowledge" and what Steven North has termed "lore." Garrison's program was transmitted most powerfully, as Jim Leheny's words above suggest, face-to-face, in the physical presence of its author. Well after his work had been widely "published" through workshops and lectures, it was put into print in 1974—appropriately, in a series titled *New Directions for Community Colleges*.

Shortly after Garrison's text entered our world, Donald Murray's *A Writer Teaches Writing* presented itself to us through an MFA graduate student, Wayne Ude. For us, Murray's book reinforced what Garrison had begun to help us see: that students were writers, people working through a complex activity, one that teacher/editors could help them with as they wrote. Murray's book came to us, as had Garrison's monograph, through channels outside those normally open to professors of English Literature at research universities. Indeed, as Tom Newkirk has recently suggested, Murray's approach "was defined as *in opposition to* writing practices of the university"(6). As its title suggests, Murray's work drew on a non-academic, "writerly" tradition—he himself a Pulitzer Prize-winning journalist, a novelist, and essayist. In his "Writing Teacher's Library," appended to *A Writer Teaches Writing* (1968), Murray includes such section headings as "Writers on Writing" (e.g. Robert Frost, George Orwell), "Manuscript Studies," "Master Writers" (e.g. Rachel Carson, John McPhee), "Biographies of Writers," "Letters of Writers," and "Writers' Journals." This "writerly" tradition made his book acceptable to our MFA program in English, one that consisted of poets and novelists-in-training. As did Garrison, Murray presented his work as rooted in practice. The subtitle of his book was *A Practical Method for Teaching Composition.*

In 1973 these two texts, and their model of the classroom in which writers wrote, with guidance and feedback from the teacher, rescued us from a difficult situation. As part of our department's outreach efforts, Jim Leheny and I had been co-teaching a practicum seminar for MAT candidates with Jim Collins, a teacher at Springfield Technical High School. Jim Collins had opened his tenth-grade English class to us as a teaching laboratory for the seminar. As we first structured this seminar, each MAT candidate prepared and taught a lesson to the 'lab class' in Springfield. This format turned out to be a dismal failure: our MAT candidates would teach as best they could and then would endure a soul-killing critique from their peers. Garrison and Murray gave us a way out. If we set up the "lab class" as a Garrison/Murray writing room, the teacher would be less the center of activity, the student-as-writer would be foregrounded, and the situation would be substantially detoxified. The new structure achieved our ends—a much more positively-oriented MAT seminar—and it achieved the school's and students' ends as well. Jim Collins, the teacher at 'Tech,' saw the potential for his students in this classroom format and asked me to join a team of Springfield teachers who, in the summer of 1974, redesigned the school's tenth-grade English curriculum as a year-long alternation of activity-centered writing and reading workshops.

This collaborative work led Jim Collins and me to co-author an article that would describe the Garrison/Murray writing laboratory class, an article that would be quoted in the instructor's manual that accompanied Garrison's *How a Writer Writes* and that would later appear as a chapter in Muriel Harris' 1982 anthology, *Tutoring Writing*. As we taught and wrote, and as we presented our work to other teachers, the Garrison/Murray texts became ours, fully integrated into our own teaching. When, therefore, Walker Gibson encouraged us to apply to the National Endowment for the Humanities for a

"Extended Teacher Institute," Garrison and Murray were our primary texts. To the 1978 and 1980 Institutes came two sets of sixty Massachusetts secondary English teachers, all of whom spent time teaching with Jim Collins in our Garrison/Murray writing classes at Springfield Technical High School. All these teachers read Garrison's monograph and Murray's book. And we, in preparing for these institutes, read in the rapidly-emerging literature of composition studies, educating ourselves. We brought to the NEH summer programs the work of such scholars in the field as Nancy Martin, Lee Odell, Peter Elbow, and Anne Herrington, and we assigned, as reading, books written and edited by such theorists in the field as Janet Emig, Charles Cooper, James Moffett, Mina Shaughnessy, and Lee Odell. Given our prior experience, however, we saw these new experiences through the "terministic screen" of Murray's and Garrison's work. That the Moffett of *Teaching the Universe of Discourse* was a rhetorician somehow passed us by; his chapter "Learning to Write by Writing," we read as confirmation of the "common sense" we had first read in Garrison and Murray. That Shaughnessy was a linguist who advocated, finally, the teaching of grammar, seemed to us much less important than did her redefinition of "error" and her belief in the intelligence and dignity of all her students—a belief that we perhaps had had all along, but which was certainly echoed and intensified by Murray's frequent assertions that student writers were able and interesting beings who could, if offered guidance, find their own way and become fine and powerful writers.

So in 1981, when the Rhetoric Program finally collapsed after a decade of underfunding and the resultant bad publicity, our experience had prepared us to design a writing program of a certain kind. We had what seemed sufficient knowledge, and we felt grounded in the field. We designed for the University a new writing program that drew for its first-year writing course on what we had learned from Garrison and Murray. The program also included a junior-year, writing-across-the-curriculum program that drew on other sources: the University of Michigan Composition Board and the work of such four-year college teachers as Elaine Maimon, Toby Fulwiler, Art Young, and Anne Herrington. To the teachers of the new freshman program, we distributed copies of Garrison's monograph, of the Collins/Moran article that derived from that monograph, and of Donald Murray's *A Writer Teaches Writing*. These were first in the canon of the new program's sacred texts. Most present in our minds were also, in alphabetical order, Peter Elbow, Janet Emig, James Moffett, and Mina Shaughnessy.

In the books and articles we gave to the teachers in our new program, we can trace the Garrison and Murray influence, sometimes as two parallel lines, and sometimes as a fabric. In the new program's first year, each teacher received a copy of Dawe and Dornan's *One to One: Resources for Conference Centered Writing*, a book that was part of Garrison's two-year college world. Dawe and Dornan taught at a two-year college, Orange Coast College, in Costa Mesa, CA.; both had collaborated with Garrison in a post-convention workshop at the 1982 CCCC; and the book was introduced by a "Foreword" written by Garrison. Each of our teachers received as well a copy of Lester Fisher and Don Murray's 1973 *College English* article titled "Perhaps the Professor Should Cut Class," which described their move at the University of New Hampshire toward an entirely conference-based writing course. Fisher had co-directed Garrison's UNH summer programs, and so was part of Garrison's world as well as of Murray's. In addition, we had available in our program's library multiple copies of Donovan and McClelland's 1980 anthology, *Eight Approaches to Teaching Composition*, which began with Don Murray's chapter, "Writing as Process: How Writing Finds Meaning," and included Tom Carnicelli's chapter, "The Writing Conference: A One-to-One Conversation," in which Carnicelli often refers to Garrison's work. Carnicelli, too, with Fisher, co-directed the Garrison UNH summer institutes and, by his own account, had been deeply influenced by the man and his teaching.

So, although the new freshman writing program announced itself to the university community as one which "incorporated the best contemporary theory and practice in the field of composition," it was founded on assumptions we had first encountered in Garrison's and Murray's work, and here I quote from Program documents: "that writing is primarily an activity, and not a subject; that one learns to write by writing and receiving feedback; that writers need to become aware of their own writing process; and that the primary text of the writing course should be the students' own writing." English 111, called "Basic Writing" in honor of Mina Shaughnessy, was a "conference-centered writing course designed to meet the needs of students who have difficulty writing rapidly, fully, and accurately. Students write in class under an instructor's supervision, working at their own pace through a structured sequence of assignments with defined audience and purpose."

The Newsroom

Both what now seem to us the good and the bad in Garrison's and Murray's work inhere in the analogy they drew between the freshman writing classroom and a journalist's newsroom. Garrison called his classroom model a "workshop," but, with its partitions and editor's office, it looks much more like the workspace in which newspapers are written. The "newsroom" analogy is no accident; both men had been journalists before they were teachers—Murray an editor at the

Boston Globe, and Garrison a journalist and the author of three books on writing and on education.

An aside: Freshman English is a soft structure, living as it does outside the protection of disciplines and departments. It is subject to definition from without: cultural literacy, literary criticism, the research paper. Given its ancestry, the freshman course is pressured to teach "grammar"; given its location in English departments, it is pressured to teach literature. Freshman English draws eagerly, therefore, on anything that may seem to permit it to define itself. This definition may be an academic purpose, as in David Bartholomae's argument that the course is an "introduction" to academic discourse; it may be a non- or even anti-academic purpose, as Peter Elbow sometimes gives it, an island in which a writer can find and employ a non-academic, authentic voice. The definition may be an assumed connection to the non-academic world, in which case the course will draw on work-based genres such as the *curriculum vitae*, the business letter, the report, the memorandum—an assumption most powerfully present in "technical" or "professional" writing courses. Garrison and Murray bring the newsroom—a writer's workplace—into the regular freshman writing classroom, and it is accepted, despite what might seem to be a bit of a problem—there's no newspaper. The analogy catches on because it permits Freshman English to define itself as distinct from English, and from the teaching of Latin grammar. It catches on, too, because of our need for definition, and perhaps, too, because both newsroom and classroom have similar power structures and loosely-comparable writer/editor ratios.

For both Garrison and Murray the teacher is an editor, the students are cub reporters, and there are facts to be collected, column inches to be written, deadlines to be met. Within the "newsroom" metaphor there is nested a medical metaphor: the teacher is a diagnostician whose diagnoses lead to prescriptions. Here is the ex-journalist Garrison using both metaphors: "The writing teacher is a good listener, a fast reader, a good diagnostician: in short, an editor-on-the-spot." And Don Murray, when he describes the ideal writing classroom, sees the ideal (for him) newsroom: private workspaces for the reporters, and a soundproofed, separate, glass-windowed office for the editor to work in—watching the newsroom, conferring in private with reporters and writers. In Murray's 1968 newsroom/classroom, as in Garrison's, writers work alone, and deal not with one another but with the editor-in-chief.

Beyond the Newsroom

Since its inception in 1982, the University Writing Program has evolved, with the field of composition studies, away from the models we first found in 1973 in Garrison's and in Murray's work. So, too, has Don Murray. While Garrison remained outside the culture of composition studies to the end of his life (he died in 1984), Murray has evolved with the field and has lived long, holding fast to his base but acknowledging and incorporating the theory and practice of his colleagues in the profession. James Berlin notes a post-1975 "tendency of certain rhetorics within the subjective and transactional categories to move in the direction of the epistemic" (183); Murray, and we, have participated in this move. Indeed, Murray's entirely-rewritten second edition of *A Writer Teaches Writing* (1985) is one of the three books that our Writing Program gives today, in 1994, to each of its new teachers.

We can't say that we have improved, though we may think we have, but we can say with assurance that we have evolved. It is my belief that the model that Garrison and Murray provided in 1973—the one-to-one editorial conference—has made this evolution possible. In individual conferences, we could, if we wanted to, focus closely on individual student-writers at work and begin to attune our pedagogy to their needs and situations—a feedback loop that would permit, and even cause, change. The first publication that arose from our work (Collins & Moran) was a Janet Emig-inspired case study of one writer, "Theresa," at work at Springfield Technical High School. Jim Collins would later leave the Springfield schools to teach at SUNY-Buffalo, where one of *his* graduate students, Elizabeth Sommers, would construct a similar study of a single writer, "Michael," composing on a computer. In 1986, when our writing program began to teach in computer-equipped classrooms, we brought Garrison and Murray into this new environment and Paul LeBlanc, one of our graduate students, closely observed six students composing on-line and discovered what was then news: that writers used computers in diverse and individual ways. This student-centered perspective, a close and "thick" view of the writer at work, was not available to us in the current-traditional classroom with its proscenium format and stacks of finished papers to be graded. In the current-traditional classroom, students are almost inevitably seen as an ill-defined, collective problem to be solved, their definition most often a projection of the teacher's or the institution's needs, less often the result of actual knowledge of the students' situation. The Garrison/Murray writing classroom format made it possible—not inevitable, but possible—that we would see and understand our student writers, modifying our pedagogy to suit particular students and particular times.

Perhaps for this reason, conferencing is still, in 1994, an important part of our teaching today. For two weeks during the semester we suspend classes and confer with students one-to-one. Our classes are still centers of activity today: writing takes place in class as well as outside of class. While students write, teachers often circulate and read their work—particularly in the computer classrooms. Students publish their work in-class four times per semester, following Murray's 1968 dictum that "The act of writing is not complete until a piece of writing is published and read, and the teacher should seek whatever ways he can in his own school to achieve a variety of publications for his students" (162). We're also more aware today of issues of dependency, difficult to solve when the editor/writer relationship is your model. Garrison's words here still sound wise: "Students need to learn how to diagnose their own writing difficulties and how to resolve them with less and less dependence upon the instructor" (1974, 56). And, with Murray and Garrison, we still look upon the carefully-worked-out assignment that the student should follow as not terribly useful; we prefer to see the assignment as a "prompt" that gets the writer going in *some* direction, one that may not be the final direction but is movement, movement that will make discovery possible. We tend, too, not to grade individual papers, but to proceed very much as Garrison announced in his syllabus: no grades for the first six or seven weeks; after that, "your work will be graded occasionally, and only if you request it" (1973, 18). And we still believe, with Garrison, that "the content of a writing course is what a student is writing, has written"(1973, 6; 1974, 62). It is not too much, we think, to see in Garrison's grading policy and his sense of the course's "content," and in Murray's preferred grading practice (1968, 138) a forecast of evaluation by portfolio.

We have also left behind a great deal of what we learned in 1973. I have distanced myself from the role that Garrison assumed: the iconoclast, the practical man in a crowd of pedants. In his monograph, Garrison presents himself as the ingenious Yankee, the outsider, the tinkerer, the home handyman, the popular mechanic—all in the American nativist tradition. "There's a problem; we'll fix it," he seems to say, and with plain, old common sense. To Jim and to me in 1973, then newcomers to the field of composition studies and sometime dwellers in the world of eighteenth century British literature, this "common sense" was an attractive fiction. Things were, really, quite simple, if one looked at them clearly. Now, in 1994, I am much less the rogue English Department person taking a flyer at a new field. I am more aware now of the complexities of these activities we call "learning" and "teaching." I have new colleagues—Marcia Curtis, Anne Herrington, Peter Elbow, Sarah Stelzner, Jean Nienkamp—and graduate-student colleagues in our graduate program in Rhetoric and Composition. Through them, I am part of the community of writing teachers.

What I hope I never borrowed from Garrison was his sometimes-dismissive attitude toward his students, perhaps a necessary precipitate of his highly personal, charismatic teaching style (Carnicelli, Fisher). Both in his unpublished monograph and the revision that was published in 1974, Garrison refers to his students as "perfectly ordinary, pleasant, unmotivated students" who are hopelessly driven before a "slob culture" (1973, 1; 1974, 55). I don't think that Jim Leheny and I shared this attitude. One of the teachers who worked with us in the Springfield classrooms tells me that what she most remembers from this experience was the sound of Jim's voice, reading student writing aloud in a way that said that this writing was valuable—that it was literature. I can't say anything about Garrison's actual teaching, because all I have is his writing—but that writing often betrays an assumption that students aren't really very smart or able. Here's how Garrison opens his monograph: "This manual is the result of twenty-five years of frustration with the usual methods of teaching freshman composition. It represents three years of intensive tinkering with methods of instruction that might reduce this frustration—both for me and for my students. I was fed up, as most English teachers are, with endless stacks of mediocre papers" (1973, 1).

Woven into the texture of this narrative is the assumption that student writing is really "endless stacks of mediocre papers." Garrison discovers the cause of this mediocrity in existing teaching methods, of course, but he does not anywhere define the particular mediocrity of which he speaks, nor does he suggest that these papers might not really be mediocre, if read with a sympathetic eye. Murray, too, despite his evident faith in the latent skill and competence of student writers, occasionally engaged in some genial student-bashing. "No teacher," Murray wrote, "will convert all the hard-core anti-writers" (1968, 160). Shirley Brice Heath, and the London Schools Project, and ethnographers such as Anne Herrington, Marcia Curtis, and Linda Cleary, have given us ways of seeing beyond our own teacher-fictions into students' worlds and cultures. From this perspective, students are not infidels, in need of conversion. If they seem to be "hard-core anti-writers," we need to find out, from them, how they see the teaching-learning situation that we're all part of.

We've left behind, too, Garrison and Murray's early-1970's belief that there is a single style, a single "good." Both men were essentialists and positivists. Beneath all that fat there was bone. "Good writing," Garrison told us, "is explicit. It deals with facts, comparisons, sights, sounds, and evidence. . . . It is usually *show* rather than *tell*. Good writing is as forthright as a punch in the nose" (1974, 63). "Take that," he seemed to say. Less the pugilist and more the man of letters, Don Murray quoted Frost—in support of his dictum, "be specific; don't generalize;" "Intellectuals deal in abstraction. It's much safer that way" (1968, 5). In "The Writing Teacher's Library" appended to *A Writer Teaches Writing*, in the category of "Desk Books and Texts" Murray listed Strunk and White's *Elements of Style* and noted that it "deserves its reputation as the best book of its kind" (1968, 247). According to Murray, this single, "good" style will work for all people, in all situations. In writing about audience, Murray wrote of the writer, "If he finds himself he will find an audience, because all of us have the same common core" (1968, 4). These assumptions—that there is a single good style, that this "good style" (Hirsch, in 1977, would call it "readability") is a superior communicative instrument, one with special access to our "common core"—sit nicely with New Criticism, still in the 1970s the dominant school in literary studies, and with our colonial past, but not so well with post-structuralist criticism and a post-colonial, emerging cultural democracy. Moreover, our move since 1980 into "Writing Across the Curriculum" is founded upon the belief that the *differences* among worlds of discourse are an appropriate focus for our pedagogy.

In addition, we've left behind the early-70's assumption, found in both the Garrison and Murray texts that came our way in 1973, that writing is at its most important level a-social, a transaction between writer and text and, occasionally, a transaction between writer, teacher/editor/diagnostician, and text. We guess that Garrison's and Murray's a-rhetorical view of writing was the result of three factors: the a-rhetorical stance of most English departments, then and now (rhetoric went, with speech, to departments of communication); our continuing reluctance to look at the rhetorical situation of the student in what we call "academic writing" (it's really an extraordinarily murky context—writing-to-be-evaluated-by-someone-you-don't-know); and the fact that both Garrison and Murray were journalists. I'll expand only on the third of these. For the journalist, the audience is a given. It is also, from the editor's perspective, a mass audience, easy to conflate. Its heterogeneity can be discovered through market research, but the focus of this market research is commonality, areas of agreement—inevitable, because the same editorial has to be written to the entire, diverse readership. Further, the journalist's audience is an audience that one "learns" on the job and which, once learned, disappears from the writer's consciousness. A newspaper has many styles, really—an editorial style, a sports-page style, an obit-style, a "feature" style—a range of styles that the neophyte learns as "true." After a time, these lessons learned, the writing proceeds without a powerful conscious sense of audience "out there."

So it is that Murray could write about "audience," but in a way that suggested, finally, that this audience was not an important consideration for the writer. At one moment, Murray could be very much the rhetorician: "The writer does not exist without a reader. The purpose of writing is not to arrange ink on paper, to provide a mirror for the author's thoughts, but to carry ideas and information from the mind of one person into the mind of another" (1968, 3). Sure, there's an audience out there. But Murray could also write, in his next paragraph, "Many of the world's most popular writers have never been aware of their audience; they have merely written in terms they themselves understand. . . . This does not mean that they do not know an audience; it means that they know it subconsciously; and, if we are to discover what the writer does, we must develop this conscious sense of audience if we do not have an unconscious sense of audience. The writer may be his own audience, but only after he has found by publication of some sort or another that there are many other people who believe, think, and feel as he does" (3). *Real* writers, Don Murray seemed to say in 1968, don't have to think about audience.

In addition, we've complicated our sense of what pre-writing might be, including in our pedagogy Peter Elbow's work on freewriting. For Garrison, pre-writing was simple and easy: it was making a list of specific details. For Don Murray in 1968 and again in 1978, pre-writing was chiefly done off-paper. You'd think, and maybe sketch an outline, and then write. For all the "process" that there is in the first edition of *A Writer Teaches Writing*, it still foregrounds a think-then-write model—perhaps a result of the journalist's writing situation, in which the deadline is not two weeks hence, but today, at 11:00. Writing is, for Murray, discovery—but pre-writing for him did not include substantial free-writing, or talking with a peer or colleague. In 1991 Murray would write movingly of a "community of writers" (83) that helps sustain his writing, but in 1968 he presented writing as cerebral activity, rehearsal: "The writer has learned the importance of pre-writing, of knowing what he is going to do before he does it, of solving as many problems as possible off the page. The writer does not try to write too soon....the writer does not write until he has a good idea of what he has to say and how he can say it" (8).

We have also left behind Garrison's reliance on the "modes of discourse" as a framework for a semester's work. Garrison himself carefully undercut this framework even as he presented it, writing, "These are not forms of writing in any strict sense; they are simply convenient labels for the kinds of verbal expression most of us have to do often" (1973, 19). Yet the labels are there, and with them a grid of a-rhetorical writing genres much like the traditional modes of discourse: description, narration, summary, explanation, interpretation, criticism, persuasion, "research." Garrison's two-year college colleagues, Dawe and Dornan, in their *One-to-One* textbook, reified

Garrison's loose scheme and headed their chapters "Comparison and Contrast," "Classification," "Definition," "Cause-Effect," "Description," "The Deductive Essay," and "The Inductive Essay." Because of its Garrison connection we gave this textbook to our new teachers in 1982, but after finding that they were using these same "modes" as the goals of their writing assignments, asking their students to write a "Classification Essay" and then a "Comparison and Contrast" essay, we withdrew this book quietly from our library's shelves.

We've also modified our vision of the writer as an autonomous unit. Lisa Ede and Andrea Lunsford's work in collaborative writing, Karen Burke LeFevre's *Invention as a Social Act*, and articles such as Linda Brodkey's "Modernism and the Scene(s) of Writing," all works Berlin would classify as "Social Epistemic Rhetorics," have helped us understand that the autonomous author is a construction, not a fact. As acknowledgment pages attest, writers do not work entirely alone—any more so than physicists, for whom multiple authorship is a regular thing. So we've begun to see our classrooms not as "newsrooms," in which writers work in a one-to-one relationship with the teacher-editor, but as communities of writers—brought together, granted, by this rather strange custom called "Freshman English," but communities nonetheless. Student writers can, and will, read each others' work and respond to it; editing teams will work together to put out class publications. On occasion, our more adventurous teachers even assign essays that will be collaboratively written.

And in English 111, "Basic Writing," the first course on our writing program's sequence of courses, Marcia Curtis and her teachers have brought cultural critique into the center. Their syllabus is based on the assumption that basic writers' difficulty is not primarily a lack of practice and coaching, but an insufficiently-powerful sense of their own authority over texts—which itself stems from the students' academic and social marginalization and which no amount of editorial coaching and support will overcome. To help readers achieve this authority, Curtis and her teachers have introduced readings, carefully selected and managed so that students are seen as the experts. The students write in response to the reading, challenging the published work, arguing with it. In these classes students, Black, Latino, and white, who have experienced for themselves our cities' educational systems, may evaluate the assumptions behind visitor Jonathan Kozol's analysis of America's schools (*Savage Inequalities*) and, in doing so, critique too the learning situation with which they are currently involved (Herrington and Curtis). This powerful new agenda plays itself out in a writing workshop, filled now with networked computers but still a writing workshop. Garrison and Murray have given us a format that has at least permitted, and perhaps caused, our adaptation to new times and new students.

A Conclusion, and a Confession

I need to say that the Garrison/early-Murray model still lives deep in me, accounting for much that I consider good in my teaching and much that I now consider less-than-good. I close with a narrative that I hope makes this clear. In our freshman writing program we ask all our students to rate various elements of the course on a 1–5 scale, from "strongly disagree" to "strongly agree." Across our writing program, our students don't value their peers' comments as highly as they value their teachers' comments. Perhaps this is inevitable; perhaps it's OK—but, in any case, in spring 1992 I set out to change my own numbers, hoping to increase among students in my class the value we all place on peer editing and responding. To do this, I followed the practice of Nick Carbone, one of our teachers whose students highly value each others' comments. Nick does not give written comments on student writing at all. Peer comments are written; Nick delivers his comments orally, in a medium that he believes his students see as ephemeral. His reason: if he writes his comments, they will cancel the peer comments because his come from "the teacher" and have to do with evaluation. That's hard to argue with.

So that spring I followed Nick's model and refrained from writing comments on students' writing. This change gutted the enterprise of teaching for me. I *missed* writing comments on students' writing. I came to realize that I think myself a pretty good editor; I'm proud of my editing skills. So was Roger Garrison; so, to a lesser degree, is Don Murray. And perhaps the three of us are right. But it's more likely that I've internalized the teacher-as-editor model so thoroughly that change is not going to be easy for me. Though I'm pleased and proud when students don't need me, I also feel a bit lost. Roger Garrison said to us, when we read him in 1973, "It is the primary job of the teacher of writing to do himself out of a job as quickly and efficiently as he can" (1974, 56). Yet I'm reluctant, still, to get out of the center of things. I'm slouching, myself, toward a new, community-based classroom model, one in which I am a member of a community, a person who, *ex officio,* invisibly orchestrates the writing, reading, and publishing that take place. But the editor in me, the sense of myself as the best and most important reader in the room, the model of these two journalists-turned-writing-teachers, dies hard.

Works Cited

Addison, Joseph, 1979. *The Freeholder,* edited by James Leheny. New York: Oxford University Press.

Almasy, Rudolph. 1982. "The Nature of Writing-Laboratory Instruction for the Developing Student." In *Tutoring Writing. See* Harris 1982, 13–20.

Berlin, James A. 1987. *Rhetoric and Reality: Writing Instruction in American Colleges, 1900–1985.* Carbondale, IL: Southern Illinois University Press.

Brodkey, Linda. 1987. "Modernism and the Scene(s) of Writing." *College English* 49:396–418.

Carnicelli, Thomas A. 1993. Telephone conversation, 4 January.

———. "The Writing Conference: A One-to-One Conversation." In *Eight Approaches to Teaching Composition. See* Donovan and McClelland, 101–31.

Cleary, Linda M. 1991. *From the Other Side of the Desk.* Portsmouth, NH: Boynton/Cook.

Coles, William E. Jr. and James Vopat. 1985. *What Makes Writing Good: A Multiperspective.* Lexington, MA: D. C. Heath.

Collins, James L. and Charles Moran. 1982. "The Secondary-Level Writing Laboratory: A Report from the Field." In *Tutoring Writing. See* Harris 1982, 196–204.

Collins, James L. and Elizabeth A. Sommers. 1985. *Writing On-Line: Using Computers in the Teaching of Writing.* Portsmouth, NH: Boynton/Cook.

Connolly, Paul and Teresa Vilardi, eds. 1986. *New Methods in College Writing Programs: Theories in Practice.* New York: MLA.

Cooper, Charles R. and Lee Odell, eds. 1977. *Evaluating Writing.* Urbana, IL: NCTE.

———. 1978. *Research on Composing.* Urbana, IL: NCTE.

Dawe, Charles W. and Edward A. Dornan. 1981. *One to One: Resources for Conference-Centered Writing.* Boston: Little, Brown.

Donovan, Timothy R. and Ben W. McClelland, eds. 1980. *Eight Approaches to Teaching Composition.* Urbana, IL: NCTE.

Ede, Lisa and Andrea Lunsford. 1990. *Singular Texts/Plural Authors: Perspectives on Collaborative Writing.* Carbondale, IL: Southern Illinois University Press.

Emig, Janet. 1971. *The Composing Processes of Twelfth Graders.* Urbana, IL: NCTE.

Fisher, Lester. 1993/1994. Telephone conversations 6 January 1993 and 4 January 1994.

Fisher, Lester and Donald Murray. 1973. "Perhaps the Teacher Should Cut Class." *College English* 35:169–73.

Flynn, Thomas. 1983. "Promoting Higher-Order Thinking Skills in Writing Conferences." *Dynamics of the Writing Conference*, edited by Thomas Flynn and Mary King. 3–14. Urbana, IL: NCTE.

Foster, David. 1983. *A Primer for Writing Teachers*. Portsmouth, NH: Boynton/Cook.

Garrison, Roger H. 1981a. *How a Writer Works*. New York: Harper & Row.

———. 1981b. *Instructor's Manual to Accompany Garrison's 'How a Writer Works.'* New York: Harper & Row.

———. 1974. "One-to-One: Tutorial Instruction in Freshman Composition." *New Directions for Community Colleges* 2.1:55–83.

———. 1973. *Teaching Writing: An Approach to Tutorial Instruction in Freshman Composition*. Unpublished monograph. Westbrook, ME.

Hairston, Maxine. 1982. "The Winds of Change: Thomas Kuhn and the Revolution in the Teaching of Writing." *College Composition and Communication* 33:76–88.

Harris, Muriel, ed. 1982. *Tutoring Writing: A Sourcebook for Writing Labs*. Glenview, IL: Scott, Foresman.

———. 1986. *Teaching One-to-One: The Writing Conference*. Urbana, IL: NCTE.

Herrington, Anne J. and Marcia Curtis. 1990. "Basic Writing: Moving the Voices on the Margin to the Center." *Harvard Educational Review* 60: 489–96.

Hirsch, E. D., Jr. 1977. *The Philosophy of Composition*. Chicago, IL: Chicago University Press.

Judy, Stephen N. and Susan J. Judy. *An Introduction to the Teaching of Writing*. New York: John Wiley.

Kozol, Jonathan. 1991. *Savage Inequalities: Children in America's Schools*. New York: Crown

Laque, Carol F. and Phyllis A. Sherwood. 1977. *A Laboratory Approach to Writing*. Urbana, IL: NCTE.

LeBlanc, Paul. 1988. "How to Get the Words Just Right: A Reappraisal of Word Processing and Revision." *Computers and Composition* 5.3: 29–42.

LeBlanc, Paul, and Charles Moran. "Adapting to a New Environment: Word Processing and the Training of Writing Teachers at the University of Massachusetts at Amherst." *Computers in English and the Language Arts: The Challenge of Teacher Education*, edited by Cynthia L. Selfe, Dawn Rodrigues, and William R. Oates. Urbana, IL: NCTE. 111–29.

LeFevre, Karen B. 1987. *Invention as a Social Act*. Carbondale, IL: Southern Illinois University Press.

Leheny, James. 1992. "The Influence of Roger Garrison and Donald Murray." Talk given at the University of New Hampshire conference, "The Writing Process: Retrospect and Prospect," 9 October.

Moffett, James. 1968. *Teaching the Universe of Discourse*. New York: Houghton Mifflin.

Murray, Donald M. 1991. *The Craft of Revision*. New York: Harcourt.

———. 1985. *A Writer Teaches Writing*, 2nd. ed. Boston: Houghton Mifflin.

———. 1984. *Write to Learn*. New York: Holt.

———. 1980. "Writing as Process: How Writing Finds Meaning." In *Eight Approaches to Teaching Composition. See* Donovan and McClelland 3–20.

———. 1978. "Write Before Writing." *College Composition and Communication* 29:375–81.

———. 1968. *A Writer Teaches Writing: A Practical Method for Teaching Composition.* Boston: Houghton Mifflin.

Newkirk, Thomas. 1993. *Nuts and Bolts: A Practical Guide to Teaching College Composition*. Portsmouth, NH: Boynton/Cook.

North, Stephen M. 1987. *The Making of Knowledge in Composition: Portrait of an Emerging Field.* Portsmouth, NH: Boynton/Cook.

Olson, Gary A., ed. 1984. *Writing Centers: Theory and Administration*. Urbana, IL: NCTE.

Phelps, Louise W. 1991. "Practical Wisdom and the Geography of Knowledge in Composition." *College English* 53:863–85.

Reigstad, Thomas J. and Donald A. McAndrew. 1984. *Training Tutors for Writing Conferences*. Urbana, IL: NCTE.

Rodrigues, Dawn and Raymond J. Rodrigues. 1986. *Teaching Writing with a Word Processor, Grades 7–13*. Urbana, IL: NCTE.

Shaughnessy, Mina P. 1977. *Errors and Expectations*. New York: Oxford University Press.

Sheils, Merrill. 1975. "Why Johnny Can't Write." *Newsweek*, 9 December, 58–65.

Sommers, Elizabeth A. 1984. "A Writing Teacher Experiments with Word Processing." *Computers and Composition* 1.2:1–3.

Sudol, Ronald A. 1982. *Revising: New Essays for Teachers of Writing*. Urbana, IL: NCTE.

Young, Richard E. 1978. "Paradigms and Problems: Needed Research in Rhetorical Invention." *Research on Composing: Points of Departure*, edited by Charles R. Cooper and Lee Odell. 29–47. Urbana, IL: NCTE.

10

The Bad Marriage

A Revisionist View of James Britton's Expressive-Writing Hypothesis In American Practice

Mary Minock
Wayne State University

In a 1981 writing class in a community college in Flint, Michigan, I encountered one of my all-time favorite students, a nineteen-year-old auto mechanic named Jeff. Jeff wrote a perfect narrative of male bonding in a snowmobile trip to North Branch, one that netted him his first "A" ever, which he proudly displayed, along with the narrative, to everyone in class, in addition to members of his revision group, who had already been impressed with the narrative in draft form. His narrative, in fact, the first draft written in a trance of freewriting, warrants the same unmitigated praise that Ken Macrorie gives to other student narratives in his chapter, "Process, Product, and Quality."

Jeff's problem occurred in the next assignment, for even with his new-found interest in writing well he received a "C" for a paper calling for a generalized narrative—even after several revisions, several tutoring sessions, and several haunting conversations. Jeff had a habit of showing his confusion (and deep disappointment) in a facial twitch. And, as I tried to explain to Jeff what he was to do, drawing on his success story in the former text, I realized that each twitch of his represented a bad idea of mine. For I could see no real connection between his perfect narrative and the next assignment, an assignment that called for exploration, in James Moffett's terms, of "what happens?" rather than "what happened?" (1968, 35). I could see no way his perfect narrative, cast as a story and leaning toward the poetic, had anything much to do with my sly call for him to "invent the university" (Bartholomae, 1985), or, in this case, the college, on his own, in the next assignment. The rhetorical moves, which had lent suspense to the action, and which had created the humorous, understated Jeff of his story, appeared discursive and digressive in the next assignment. It was while instructing Jeff to explicitly state his logical connections, which had been deftly and *implicitly* rendered in Jeff's original story, that I found myself reciting the words I am sure he had heard before but could not fathom. "But here you've got to spell it out. Be specific."

My classroom drama of Jeff serves as a tangible introduction to my chapter, for it demonstrates the effect of a particular marriage of theory in practice. In America the linguistic philosophy of James Britton, along with the cognitive philosophy of James Moffett, came to be wedded to the expressionist pedagogies of Ken Macrorie, Peter Elbow, Donald Murray, and others, after Britton and his co-authors' *The Development of Writing Abilities* was published in 1975. The marriage was a bad one. The ideas of Britton and the expressionists were so combined in practice as to obfuscate the contributions of each. If this marriage sanctified the writing process movement, and allowed it to gather momentum in the mid-1970s and early 1980s, it nonetheless rested on the most vulnerable tenet of Britton's theory: the hypothesis that posits that expressive writing leads naturally and inevitably to other forms of writing. Writing abilities, according to the hypothesis, develop from writing close to the self and to speech, and gradually grow toward transactional writing on the one hand, and poetic writing on the other. The hypothesis, which practitioners of composition and rhetoric in America linked with expressionist notions of the composing process, made a marriage of expediency, for with this marriage they could battle the current-traditional paradigm. In the end, however, the marriage belied its own intentions. It ultimately served to formalize the theory of Britton and the pedagogies of the expressionists when practitioners tried to make a home for the marriage within American colleges and universities.

The marriage, enabled by the expressive-writing hypothesis, was a distinctly American integration of theory; the Language Across the Curriculum movement in England and movements elsewhere took other paths (compare Britton, Shafer and Watson; Mahala; Torbe). What I call a marriage was an interpretation, and from that a set of assumptions, that seemed to knit two strands of composition theory and served to order the curriculum and assignments in a reasonable way based on the contributions of the writers in question.

If my dialogues with Jeff introduce the vulnerability of the hypothesis—that expressive writing leads naturally and inevitably to other forms of writing—they also introduce a complication; the American interpretation was complicated by more than naive and literal formalism. For Jeff and I were both too smart, each with an intuitive sense of rhetoric, to think that the one text, with its audience and purpose, placed on the desk as product, would lead to the other text, with a different rhetorical construction. What makes this story of Jeff poignant is the cultural narrative we each shared in the office in Flint and the reason for Jeff's disappointment. We each subscribed to an American myth: we should be getting better and better. We, like the unemployed auto workers who were Jeff's colleagues, were caught in believing in fast and linear progress. And most courses and curriculum sequences in American colleges and universities are inextricably predicated on the same myth. What Britton envisioned as taking many years might be condensed by American practitioners to a quick curriculum sequence: journals in September, followed by narratives that moved, through the turning of the leaves, into the research paper of December. More was at stake in our applications than Britton's notion of development. We added our cultural myth of progress. The marriage of theory and practice was not only made in, but made *for*, the United States.

My chapter explores this marriage of theory in practice. I hope by my exploration to encourage a rereading rather than a representation of Britton, for the best of Britton, and indeed all of Britton, deserves a review. Britton's work resonates far beyond his developmental hypothesis sketched in *The Development of Writing Abilities*, and he is clear about what he wants to do. Britton wants the language of students, in which they think and convey ideas and collaborate to learn together, to stand on an equal footing with academic genres and registers in school. Even though he believes that expressive writing leads progressively to academic writing, he also believes in a plurality of genres of expression, with no insistence that the language of students will quickly metamorphose into ours. Britton urges the creation of a context where we all can learn from each other, and his project, although he does not use these words, is a call for a multicultural and multi-registered language curriculum. Agreeing with this call, but without Britton's belief in linguistic or cognitive progress, we may try again, within the current context of American colleges and universities, to apply the best of Britton.

My dialogues with Jeff ultimately provided the conclusion of this chapter. During the next semester, when I was able to switch assignment sequences, putting academic writing first, breaking away from academic writing later, and introducing poetic narrative as an opposition, I found good reasons for students to bring to school written texts out of their own linguistic, cultural and dialect registers, without wrenching those texts into the service of an unsupported notion of progress.

Tying the Knot: The Expressive-Writing Hypothesis as Countertradition

It is easy to see how the marriage of positions resting on the expressive-writing hypothesis came about. In 1975, when *The Development of Writing Abilities* was published, and until the early 1980s, the time was opportune to ally alternatives to the current-traditional paradigm. The "literacy crisis" of the early 1970s and the conservative calls for increased teacher authority threatened to alter the progressive changes made by expressionists and other writing-process advocates who had succeeded in providing a space for students to compose by *questioning* authority. Expressionist pedagogy, a romantic wave rising in the late 1960s, was still the most popular of oppositional pedagogies. Also, as Joseph Harris (1991) has recently reminded us, after the Dartmouth Conference of 1966 the conflict between several British participants who espoused "growth" theories, including Britton and also the American Moffett, and several American participants who advanced a formal curriculum, was left unresolved. Britton's hypothesis that expressive writing would lead to transactional writing provided a clear direction for sequencing the curriculum, and hence it served to legitimize the progressive activities of the expressionists being performed in many American classrooms. By 1975 more radical experiments of the late 1960s, such as the open-door policies at City University of New York, were already in the process of being dismantled.

For teachers of college composition, the 1970s showed a hopeful growth of composition theory around the process movement, initially an amalgamation of expressionist and other practices infusing the teaching of writing, but gradually drawing its breath from linguistics and rhetoric, with an uncertain relationship to science. Beliefs in process, "process over product," and beliefs in the promise of a new paradigm, were growing: Richard Young, along with Alton Becker and Kenneth Pike, linked rhetoric and change in 1970, reclaiming invention from classical rhetoric; Young in 1978, working from Thomas Kuhn, named the default tradition; and Robert Connors in 1981 traced the rise and heralded the fall of the current-tradition's arhetorical modes of discourse. By 1982 Maxine Hairston was predicting a new paradigm emerging for composition, based on process pedagogy and guided by principles of rhetoric.

In the late 1970s many of us could not predict additional rhetorical theories in opposition to the current-tradition, nor could we anticipate infusions from postmodern theories, with their non-rationalist epistemologies and their suppositions of decentered selves. In fact, in 1983 James Berlin identified only three theories as alternates to the positivist current-tradition: expressionism; the renewed classical rhetoric; and the new-rhetoric, the category into which he places Britton and Moffett.[1] The marriage based on Britton's hypothesis, in effectively allying two alternatives to the tradition, promised "a system of widely shared values, beliefs and methods," Young's definition of a paradigm (1978, 29). With that alliance, and in the climate of conservative retrenchment, the writing process movement might still gain momentum in order to secure its place as the authoritative force in composition practice. The marriage enabled it to do so.

History, of course, is told in hindsight. My marriage metaphor, in fact, serves as a conceit; it is a lens through which to view a particular consensus, a joining of theory in practice, from all the ideas that were in the air. And in reviewing the history of composition theories and pedagogies, I would now argue along with Harris, and others, that the curriculum "conflict has been less resolved than continually displaced" (1991, 640). Nonetheless, "process over product" seemed for many a useful enough slogan at the time. Moreover, the symmetry between Britton's hypothesis and the expressionists' process heuristic enabled another concept that was easy to popularize. If practitioners had created a slogan for the terms of the marriage, it would have been: "Expressive writing leads to transactional writing; expressive writing leads to any given text."

The marriage represented a peculiar blend of theory and an expedient interpretation. First of all, the marriage was undeclared by the parties involved; it was not a planned or mediated arrangement. Britton draws upon the ideas of many in citation, including Bruner, D. W. Harding, Langer, Moffett, Piaget, Sapir, and Vygotsky, among others, but he does not create the bond with the American expressionists. The expressionists often do not cite anyone; they argue from the personal and anecdotal. In *A Writer Teaches Writing* by Donald Murray (1968), *Telling Writing* by Ken Macrorie (1970), and *Writing Without Teachers* by Peter Elbow (1973)—the most influential books of the expressionists—we find few arguments from citation. These authors write eloquently about good teaching (Murray), or about a favored method of composing (Elbow). The expressionists, in fact, emphasized a part of the whole: the generation of ideas, or one mode of discourse, such as narrative (Macrorie). In an important sense, the expressionists served as resistance fighters. Many of their insights and much of their irreverence and play were directly opposed to the current-traditional emphasis on planning, correctness, and school exposition, or "Engfish" (Macrorie). They did not, in their most influential works, write directions for drawing up a curriculum. Moreover, although we can intuit a theory of rhetoric in their works, they do not state it. Not surprisingly, the expressionist contribution to the marriage would lead to problems in practice; after getting in place a curriculum based on self-expression, practitioners would still need to account for a *rhetoric* of self. A rhetorical concept of self would insure that when we viewed "self" in writing, whatever our notions about its existential construction, we would see it as one point on an axis embracing different presentations of self or ethos, depending on the audience, the purpose, and the context for the text.

It was Britton who provided the directions for drawing up a curriculum based on expressive writing. *The Development of Writing Abilities*, from which practitioners drew Britton's hypothesis, along with the most detailed of discourse taxonomies, reports the British Schools Council's findings about what adolescent students write in school. Britton and his co-authors circumvented the "somewhat mysterious orthodoxy" (1975, 3) of the modes of discourse by setting forth categories resting on the different purposes for writing. Their taxonomy at the first level is literally able to encompass the universe of discourse. It adapts the functional categories of language provided by Roman Jakobson (1960)—Jakobson who also influenced the taxonomies of Moffett and James Kinneavy, and who was himself influenced by Sapir and Aristotle (compare Jakobson 353; Moffett 1968, 11; Kinneavy 1971, 60). According to Britton and his co-authors, transactional texts show language directed toward participation, or "getting things done"; they may attempt to persuade or regulate, or may seek to inform or argue. Expressive texts are fluid, relatively unstructured, reveal the writer and her consciousness, and rely on implicit information and context. Functionally poetic texts, including prose and poetry, show language cast in the role of spectator or gossip, stepping back from participation in order to observe and offer comment on values (1975, 8). The basic divisions of Britton and his co-authors' taxonomy are represented in Figure 10–1.

Although Britton and his co-authors were influenced by the work of linguists and the rhetorician Aristotle, and accounted for the universe of discourse, they were nonetheless influenced just as much by what students wrote in school. That influence was exerted in two respects: most immediately Britton and his co-authors devised the taxonomy to catalog texts written by actual students in school. The second point of influence rested on speculations about cognitive

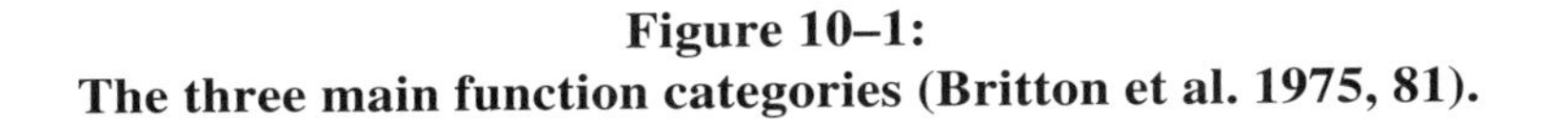

Figure 10–1:
The three main function categories (Britton et al. 1975, 81).

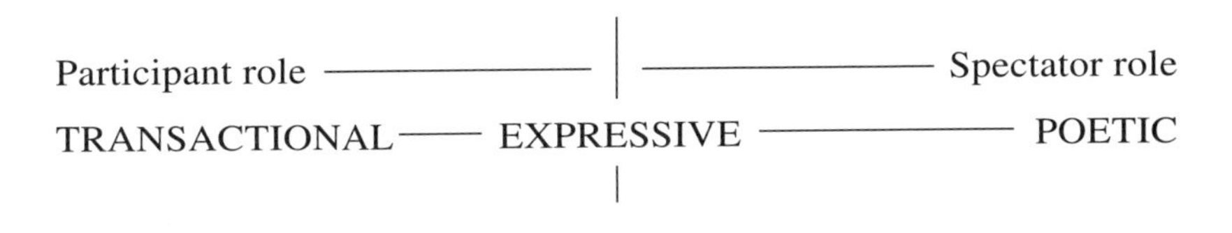

development from Bruner and Piaget (Britton et al, 1975, 202). For instance, the seven subcategories of informative and argumentative discourse, four of which are drawn from Moffett (compare Moffett 1968, 47), demonstrate that influence: record, report, generalized narrative, low level analogic, analogic, analogic-tautologic, and tautologic (94–98). Finding that most of their sample texts fit in these transactional categories, Britton and his co-authors discovered that of the many purposes for writing, precious few are engaged in school (1975, 146–61). Britton and his co-authors are aware, as is Moffett, that "taxonomy tends toward taxidermy" (1994) and argue against formalist interpretations of their schema.

Consequently, in American practice, Britton's contribution to the bad marriage was somewhat accidental. An overarching first problem involved the unresolved conflict in the American curriculum. Given the formalizing nature of the American curriculum, and our cultural commitment to progress, the vulnerability of Britton's hypothesis was partially based on it getting into the wrong hands, or more precisely, the wrong system at the wrong time. This vulnerability was especially manifest in the composition curriculum in the mid-1970s as conservatives sought to make order of the license of the expressionists and other progressives of the 1960s. That order, in a subtle way, would be contributed by Britton, specifically in Britton and his co-authors' seven categories of informative and argumentative discourse: record, report, generalized narrative, and so forth, advancing from sense observations to inductive reasoning, and culminating in hypothetical and deductive reasoning in tautological argumentation. These categories, in fact, replicate Piaget's stage theory of development, an ordering that splits and identifies logics according to a progression only discernable in testing and academic texts. And, whatever its faults or merits, it would be accelerated in America. In the words of Bob Samples on Piaget's schema, "'Let's speed it up' [was heard] on this side of the Atlantic and the cool, 'It doesn't matter' [was heard] on the far side...." (1976, 53). Thus, Britton's wish to draw upon a range of literacies would largely give way in America to

Fig. 10–2:
Function categories, adapted from Britton et al.

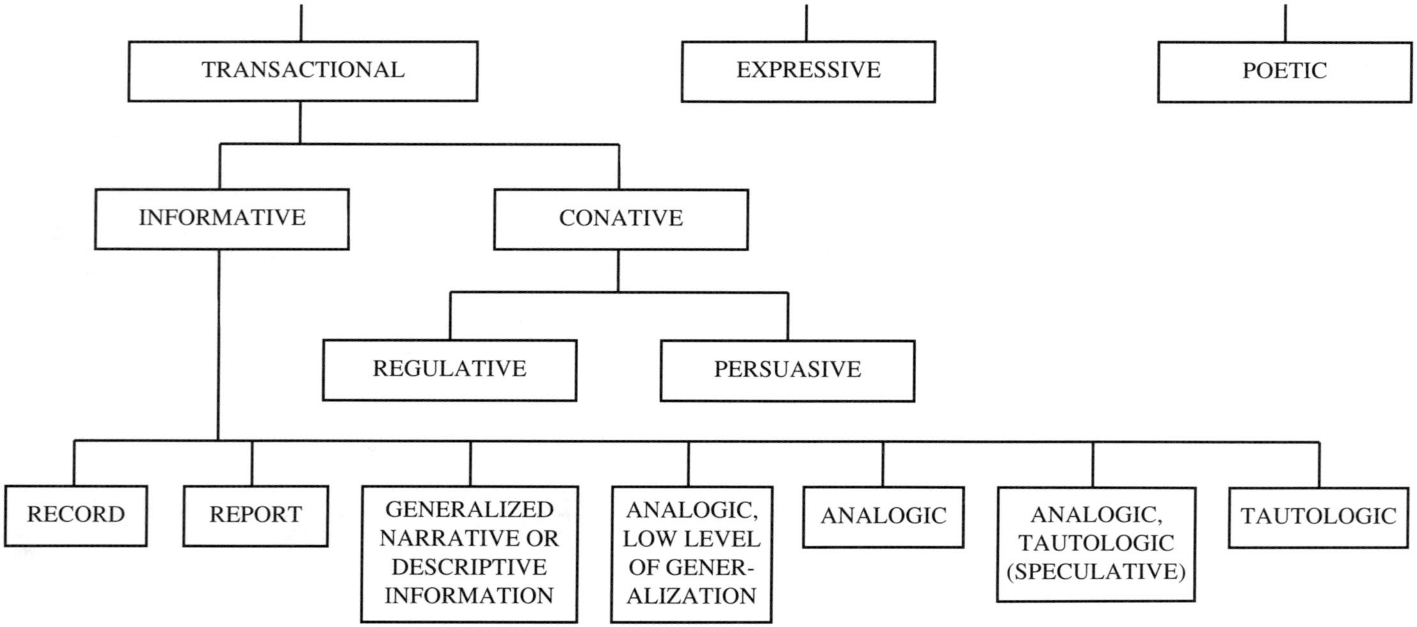

TRANSACTIONAL
EXPRESSIVE
POETIC
INFORMATIVE
CONATIVE
REGULATIVE
PERSUASIVE
RECORD
REPORT
GENERALIZED NARRATIVE OR DESCRIPTIVE INFORMATION
ANALOGIC, LOW LEVEL OF GENER-ALIZATION
ANALOGIC
ANALOGIC, TAUTOLOGIC (SPECULATIVE)
TAUTOLOGIC

his own progression toward academic literacy represented in his and colleagues' taxonomy. Figure 10–2 makes graphic the implied progression represented in Britton and his co-authors' function categories.

A second problem in applying Britton's hypothesis sprang directly from the American attempt to formalize the progression and speed it up: a linguistic error caused by our fast ordering of discourse along the continuum and our wish to get to "higher" literacies. While language, according to linguists, is ordered in registers and genres showing the influence of reoccurring situations or schemata, we often applied the hypothesis as though students would necessarily progress from one genre to another. Although I will suggest later that any notions of linguistic progress from orality to literacy may be unsupported, I also argue that it was largely in formalizing and accelerating Britton's hypothesis along the progression toward abstract logic suggested by the taxonomy that we belied the best of Britton. Britton, in fact, never shows in any of his many citations from students' expressive texts in many genres that these texts will promptly migrate to academic genres. We can, therefore, profit from rereading Britton.[2]

Britton's expressive-writing hypothesis itself attempted to incorporate an insight of Vygotsky, that writing, in whatever form, demands abstraction beyond speech, "as algebra is harder than arithmetic" (1962, 99). Britton and his co-authors suggest "that what children write in the early stages should be a form of written-down expressive speech, and what they read should also be, generally speaking, expressive" (1975, 82). They admit that not every child's first attempt at writing is expressive, but they go on to add:

> But it must be true that until a child does write expressively he is failing to feed into the writing process the fullness of his linguistic resources—the knowledge of words and structures he has built up in speech—and that it will take him longer to arrive at the point where writing can serve a range of his purposes as broad and diverse as the purposes for which he uses speech. (1975, 82)

Britton and his co-authors were also interested in discovering how students' views of their audience related to their purposes, and so they established a continuum of audience relationships for school writing. Along that continuum they grouped texts they perceived were written to the self as audience, to four increasingly distant versions of the teacher as audience, to peers or those less informed as audience, and to an unknown audience. Of the four pupil-teacher possibilities, ranging from child-to-trusted-adult to pupil-to-examiner, Britton and his co-authors were disappointed to find that students typically addressed a judge or examiner in their writing. That disappointment, I believe, in turn reinforced the hypothesis regarding expressive writing. If, in fact, a teacher functions as an examiner and is not trusted, that teacher cannot hope for writing "revealing the speaker, verbalizing his consciousness and displaying his close relation with a listener or reader" (1975, 90). Thus, behind Britton's theory is the hope that expressive writing may also encourage a more humane pedagogy, as it ultimately leads to transactional writing. The hypothesis, as Britton and his colleagues conceive it, presumes a rhetorical situation, an audience, and a purpose. It also lends itself to our ideal of a more personal pedagogy, a personal pedagogy that practitioners failed to differentiate from the personal pedagogy of the expressionists.

Moffett's theory, that I have subsumed in this discussion from *Teaching the Universe of Discourse* published in 1968, was influenced even more directly by Piaget, and Moffett argues even more forcefully for a progression "from the implicit, embodied idea to the explicitly formulated idea" (1968, 57) and the inevitable developmental progression from concrete to abstract logic. Moffett's theory influenced primary and secondary education in America from its publication in 1968, but it was not to influence curriculum planning in colleges and universities until after Britton and his co-authors' work was received in 1975. After that, practitioners in American colleges and universities conflated the linguistic speculations of Britton with the educational program of Moffett. Moreover, the most obvious point of the two merged theories, the continuum from expressive writing to transactional writing, was consonant with long-established assumptions about the curriculum. The notion that literacy would develop toward *academic* literacy reinforced the underlying influence of Piaget.

The direct terms that made the marriage between Britton and the expressionists were taken from Britton and his co-authors' observations about composing. They claimed that the expressive mode is also where we form the first drafts of new ideas. They write:

> Not only is it the mode in which we approach and relate to each other in speech, but it is also the mode in which, generally speaking, we frame the tentative first drafts of new ideas: and the mode in which, in times of family or national crisis, we talk with our own people and attempt to work our way towards some kind of a resolution. (1975, 82)

Britton and his co-authors also suggested, that in composing any given text, students should not abridge the expressive function, as they do when teachers prescribe outlines and formal planning. From these assertions, practitioners in America inferred that the hypothesis might apply to the composition of a text, as it applies to the development of a writer. The expressive-writing hypothesis then seemed to logically relate to the expressionist freewriting method of composition. Hence, the long-term development of writing abilities from expressive writing and the development of a single composition from freewriting could be seen in symmetry. Moreover, the humane pedagogy of the expressionists, with their Platonic notion that truth could be discovered as an individual vision (Berlin 1982, 771), could be seen as compatible with the humane pedagogy of Britton. The marriage was made. Perhaps the simplest emblem of the marriage, with its linear progression, was inferred in Britton and his co-authors' graphic representation of the developmental hypothesis in Figure 10–3.

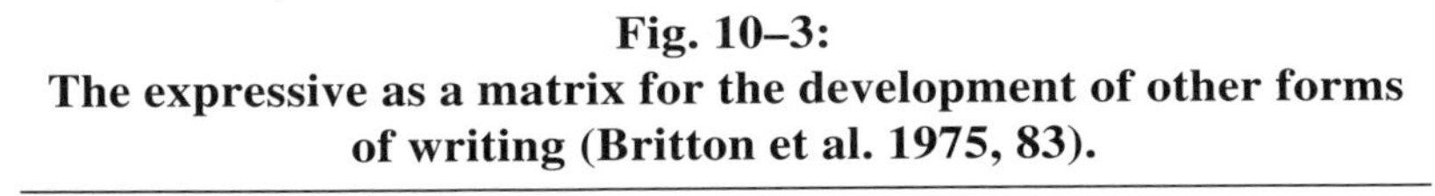

Fig. 10–3:
The expressive as a matrix for the development of other forms of writing (Britton et al. 1975, 83).

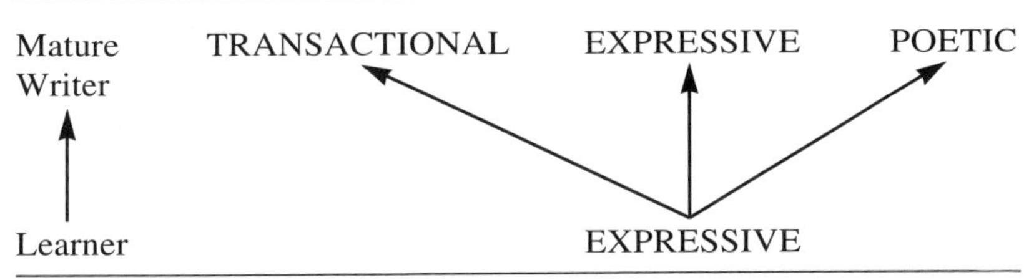

In the period following the publication of *The Development of Writing Abilities,* the braiding of these notions around the hypothesis guided curriculum planning. Many planned courses or course-sequences that were based on a developmental progression from free-written journals to narratives, to expository essays, to argumentation, to research papers. Many viewed the writing process as based on a similar progression, a progression from freewriting to discovered purpose, to purpose shaping form, to revision and editing—with a presumed notion that the self, discovered at earlier stages of the process, would eventually extend to an audience in revision. And for some of us, as my experience with Jeff indicates, the problems in the arrangement arose immediately.

Expression and the Rhetoric of Self

Problems in the marriage surfaced quickly in other ways, notably those arising from claims about the benefits of expressive writing and self-expression, coupled with the failure to address the question of a rhetorically constructed self. In attempting to enact the expressive-writing hypothesis within the composition curriculum, with its assumptions about progress, and advocating the miniature version of the hypothesis in freewriting, several went far beyond Britton's intentions in interpreting the concept of expressive writing. If Britton and his co-authors write, that without expressive writing, "it must be true that a child is failing to feed in his linguistic resources" (1975, 82), some were determined that if students did not get to tautological argumentation by December, they would at least discover and express their selves—sometimes, it seemed, discovering and expressing their selves while at the same time moving towards tautological argumentation. In my mind, this was the most dangerous application. In that application, many left unexamined the question of what linguistic resources were required for texts they assumed students would write if left to their own devices. Most importantly, many spoke of "self" and "self discovery" with the assumption that *one* self existed, that it could be found and captured in writing, and that once found it would not be lost, no matter what the genre or the audience for writing. This notion, cast into a formalized and fast-moving curriculum, was apt to result in a reductive and formalized notion of self.

Behind the marriage was an implied assumption. According to the consensus, one *discovers* meaning in freewriting, and *discovery* assumes meaning resides solely in the self to be found and can be viewed in expressive writing. Macrorie, in *Telling Writing*, puts it simply, positing a fixed core or store of truth: "It's a guaranteed activity: if you write fast—without thinking of spelling, grammar, punctuation, or form—and try to tell truths, sooner or later you will write something that moves you and others" (1985, 201). Although students with Macrorie as their teacher could intuit a good audience who would be moved, encouraging, and sympathetic, the notion, divorced from the concept of a rhetorically invented ethos, invited a dangerous judgement: teachers may identify the selves of students based on the *signs* of self they see in writing. As Sandra Schor puts it in 1979: "Aha! Now we see what you are. You are what you write" (76).

Formalism particularly intruded as practitioners assumed they might satisfy the needs for self-expression and "higher" literacies at the same time. Richard Beach synthesizes this assumption in a 1977 teaching manual for NCTE advocating personal writing. Beach asserts:

> AMP [autobiography, memoir, and portrait writing] can involve any of the kinds of writing in which students should be competent (expository, persuasive, expressive, narrative). Moreover, while the content may be personal, the process is the same, regardless of the mode. (6)

Beach's certainty that "subject matter need not dictate the mode of expression" (6) was supported in textbooks and shared by teachers who assigned a curious hybrid text, a text with expository structure and personal or expressive content. The products of "personal exposition" suggested the self could be wrenched into the hierarchy of typical expository essays. As students wrote these texts, they arranged content in hierarchical order, constructed "topic sentences" and a thesis to reinforce the hierarchy; they made logic parallel, and they constructed a conclusion that became an expository coda. At the same time, they were being asked to reveal their consciousness. Such a feat is hardly natural, and saying to oneself, for instance, "I have three problems currently troubling me in my life," calls for an unusual abridgement of expressive feelings.

Another hybrid text, a kind of expository-narrative presented in many textbooks, asked students to ruin the suspense of potentially good personal stories by writing expository introductions to them that explicitly stated a thesis. These narratives, like Jeff's, drew from linguistic resources gotten outside of school, and wanted to move toward the literary, but they were called back. The thesis gave it all away: "I learned that some friendships were meant to die." And belying the examples Britton provides in all of his writings—the authentic, spontaneous, delightful, and delighted voice of children and young people "who *practice* language in the sense in which a doctor 'practices' medicine" (Britton 1970, 130)—the voices we often heard in these personal essays and stories with hierarchical patterns were trivialized, teacher-pleasing, assignment-conforming revelations of the self. It is no wonder that many of our colleagues retreated back to impersonal essays.

Whatever the depth of self students expressed in free-written journals, or in personal-exposition, or in expository-narrative, when students attempted to translate that consciousness to more formal essays, it was often inappropriately applied or diminished. Many students simply had not enough experience of academic genres to know where they were going in their freewriting. Hence, the heuristic provided in expressive writing could not provide direction for the shaping of academic texts "at the point of utterance" (Britton 1982a). We were back where we started.

The Fall and Rise of the Modes of Discourse

The problems we encountered incorporating the marriage of theory into required college composition courses often seemed to be experienced in a time warp. If we were not naive, and many of us were not, we were at least unaware of how our point of resistance would affect the structure of our institutions. Or, more importantly, how the structures of our institutions were affecting our resistance. None of us, at least none of us that I know of, succeeded in eliminating academic writing, or the prototypic expository essay, from our repertoire. And most of us, knowing our students were capable and ready, and knowing literate ways with words and logic were as valid as experiential writing, did not want to. Whatever our visions for our courses, or however we wished to apply our theory, we were met with institutional expectations that composition courses were to end in prerequisite knowledge needed for more demanding content courses, or to give lessons for surviving the university. Students were not fooled. When expressive writing led to transactional writing, then the real agenda started, and they knew the fun would end around midterm.

In exploring the expectations that shape composition courses, we find ample evidence that they have fallen short of radical alteration in the last several years. Unfortunately, the expressive-writing hypothesis, and the assumption that students will promptly develop toward *our* language, often stands in the curriculum in its most reified form, serving to undermine the philosophy and the respect for students' language beneath it. The overriding expectation is that in composition courses we are to teach an applied skill. Moreover, the failure of our attempt at curriculum reform can be seen as grounds for retrenchment. Course descriptions from 1992 catalogs, in my random sample, often resort to the current-traditional modes of discourse, particularly exposition and argumentation, or all: "Contemporary and classic examples of the traditional modes of discourse are analyzed as models for writing."

Unfortunately for composition, competing pedagogies often share the spot in compromised course descriptions. Since the mid-1970s, according to Robert Connors, "there has been no clear ascendant; romantics and classicists coexist—usually amiably—in almost every English department" (1987, 180). Amiability verging on saintliness can be seen in the following description of a freshman writing class from a 1992–93 liberal-arts college catalog:

> An exploration of the process of writing, practice in discovering voice and in developing subjects. Emphasis on sustained work in diction, sentence patterns and paragraph development.

What is lost in such a compromise is a metatheory that would allow students to interpret the differing expectations and make coherent the differing advice from different teachers about the different writing they do and will do. In the rhetorically oppositional texts of Jeff is the start of such a theory, but students, harnessed to presumed linear progress, are hardly given such a metatheory from which to work. They often simply are left to figure out our prejudices.

Progress Beyond Progress: A Revisionist View of the Expressive-Writing Hypothesis

The excesses of our claims about expressive writing, and our assumptions about stages in composition of texts, led to new oppositional stances. And although I would do composition history a disservice by positing a linear progression from the hypothesis and its applications to all of the new oppositions, I nonetheless claim that the bad marriage within the writing process movement, with its assumptions about development, both spawned much of the opposition and continues in vestigial forms to influence a great deal of what goes on in the classroom. Opposition to the marriage, in some measure at least, informs the continuing history: for instance, the attempts of Linda Flower and John Hayes, among others, to describe a recursive generic writing process; the epistemic rhetorics of Berlin and Ann Berthoff; the postmodern theories of Sharon Crowley, Susan Miller and Louise Phelps; and the laments of Stephen North, among others, who are sad to see the pluralism that clearly demonstrates we have no synthesis to replace the default tradition.

The fate of other curriculum reform movements within the context of public education in America, coupled with the curious pendulum swings of public opinion, toughened many of us to consider a more openly political look at society and schools. Michael Katz (1975) for instance, shows us in the case of several reform movements that the innovations were incorporated into the bureaucracy in a way offering only the illusion of change. Cultural views of composition pedagogy, for various periods in American life, spawned several histories cutting across the boundary of the classroom,[3] and few of us were left innocent of the ideological contexts of our methods. At best, and I consider this one of its direct legacies, in presenting us with the compelling problem of "self" and self-expression, the marriage of theory around the expressive-writing hypothesis helped us move toward a more critical exploration of knowledge and how knowledge is constructed in schools.

Finally, although I have not attempted a proof, the hypothesis influenced us profoundly enough to spawn its own unexamined assumptions, reminiscent of the unexamined assumptions of the current-traditional paradigm that Young exposed in 1978. I make a speculative claim. If we could ask, we would find a clear majority of composition teachers start out their courses in September with more calls, in one way or another, for writing closer to the speaker and verbalizing his consciousness, and by December they will be asking for far more transactional writing from students. Moreover, I speculate that most of the expressive writing we ask from students serves directly as a heuristic for formal writing and is considered a first step—and not as an opportunity to liberate students to think and write in their own dialects. Or, as Daniel Mahala observes of invitations to write-to-learn in courses across the curriculum, expressive heuristics are construed as "methods that work" (1991, 773). I speculate further that, if asked, teachers would talk about questions of ease and confidence building, "self discovery," building on what is known, and many would render their explanations with language clearly showing their absorption of the consensus reading of Britton. I suspect that some would put the notion in a formalist way: "By December I should be preparing them for writing in disciplines." Or worse, "I should be preparing them for the exit exam."

Yet at the same time the writing process movement was taking its momentum from the expressive-writing hypothesis and unexamined concepts of self, elsewhere in composition theory was an insight enabling a revision of the hypothesis and a different approach to sequencing. If it took us a few more years to couch our observations in postmodern terms, or terms made popular by Kenneth Bruffee (1986), and others showing a clearer idea of self and writing from social constructionist theory, the germ of a better theory was there in 1971 in James Kinneavy's chapter on expressive writing in his *Theory of Discourse*. Kinneavy was later to give us another important model to solve the dilemma in his 1979 hermeneutic. In *Theory* Kinneavy draws from Sartre, Merleau-Ponty, and Cassirer to contribute a usable model to view self and self-expression. According to Kinneavy, the "I" that creates and is created through expression is a trinity of Being-for-Itself, Being-for-Others, and Being-in-the-World (1971, 405). Thus for Kinneavy self-expression is not the voice that emanates from speech as a starting point. It represents a dialectic rather than a monolithic concept. According to Kinneavy:

> A person achieves personality and, therefore, true self-expression when he has an authentic Being-for-Itself with an honest recognition and repudiation of his past, a vision of his future projects, an acceptance of his Being-for-Others, and an unillusioned picture of his Being-in-the-World. All of this will give him a unique style in his verbal expressions. (1971, 405–06)

If Kinneavy sees the possibility that the self arrives, or *achieves* self-expression, we may amend his model to include "arrivals" that are at interim stations. Self-expression is then a continuing and expanding dialectic—the self achieves *new* self-expression. The self is thus a dynamic of relationships, socially *and* individually constructed, and it will present itself differently in different kinds of writing.

Kinneavy's view of self allows us to look at expressive writing as a series of dialogues—with the self, or with others, and or with ideas.

We may consequently turn from the notion that expressive writing is a *first step*. We can then view expressive dialogue in context—with the self, with teachers and with colleagues, and with the intertext of the world represented in reading.

Embracing Contraries of a Different Sort: Literacy, Orality, the Best of Britton and Sequencing

What would happen if we tried again to apply Britton's ideas within current composition classrooms, without the expressive-writing hypothesis and its vestiges? For aside from the linguistic and rhetorical problems the hypothesis presented, it clearly caused us more problems in curriculum planning than it solved. And what would happen if we first of all disengaged from a notion of linear progress? For in committing to a linear notion of progress we steered development toward a goal: *our* goal of academic literacy. And up against the formalizing properties of courses and the curriculum, we encouraged students to leap along and get to it. I do not argue, of course, that writing abilities do not develop, and I do not argue against genres of expressive writing and genres of academic writing. I simply am not convinced that any one kind of writing can be said to systematically lead to another. I am not convinced that writing abilities develop solely from expressive speech and expressive writing. Finally, I am not convinced we can *know* how writer*s*, or "generic writers" (Miller 1982, 75), develop. We might speculate about how a particular writer develops, based on her experiences, based on her immersion in situations giving rise to *particular* spoken registers, and based on her knowledge of *particular* genres represented in what she has written and read. We must assume though, in the way language is appropriated, assimilated and organized in registers and genres, and with intertextual migrations across borders, including those between the written and spoken media, that the linguistic resources of our students, even before they come to our classes, are remarkably diverse and complex. Thus, if we should have no end point for development, we also may not be able to determine a particular knowable starting point. Moreover, aside from supporting a social context where several genres of writing are valued and demanded, and intervening to help in the process, we may not be able to *teach* the writing process. We simply cannot know, in any generic way, which of the many heuristics we suggest for composing are best.

Can we live, and can we teach, especially in America, with such uncertainty and without a notion of progress? I suggest we can live without the expressive-writing hypothesis, and I am suggesting we can assume, if we have faith, that we and our students who practice writing "in the sense in which a doctor practices medicine (Britton 1970, 130)" and without a single dummy-run are getting better and better. We simply may not be able to see that progress in a linear way because that progress across genres does not happen in a linear way. And we may find that without a linear notion of progress, we may help students learn more about the different choices they make while writing texts of different genres: choices they make intuitively if they know the lay of the land, and choices they make consciously, and even with guidance, imitation and intertextual travel, if they are unfamiliar with the customs and the ways. I am foremost arguing for a hermeneutic theory of growth, a theory where we encourage a constant look at the part-to-the-whole, and then the whole-to-the-part. The whole is a metatheory of rhetoric, that our students can and must hold against formalist prescriptions; a part is the composition of a text—a particular text, addressed to a particular audience, within a particular context, and taking up the customs of a particular genre. In writing texts of different genres and comparing their habits of writing texts of different genres, students may start a metatheory that informs their sense of rhetoric.

How then might we reread and reapply the best of Britton? One way to apply the best of Britton also applies the best of Peter Elbow and applies the best of what I learned from Jeff. Elbow (1993) currently argues for the advantages of binary thinking. He couches his oppositions in terms of generation versus editing, reading versus writing, form versus content, epistemology versus rhetoric, and so forth. Although he claims his thinking is ancient, resting on Boethius and other medieval scholars, and not postmodern (51), I would argue that his resolution about his oppositions—"not either/or, but both/and" (61)—is a strikingly postmodern way to put it. In fact, in Derridean terms, we may say a trace of the other is always already present in its opposition. Jeff taught me a great deal about the binary opposites of orality and literacy and a resolution. When I could see from Jeff's twitching that my notions of progress were wrong, I looked at it the other way. When I was able to switch sequences the next semester to disavow in practice the notion of linear progress, I was then able to see that the opposites could encourage a metatheoretical appreciation of both/and. I was also then able to incorporate one of the best strands of Britton: the opportunity for students to bring to school written texts from their own dialects. Those texts, especially those narratives addressed to intimates (more reasonable to expect in the climate of trust created towards the end of the semester), often (but not always) present oppositions to academic writing in linguistic and rhetorical choices. When these texts defer the rhetorical and linguistic choices that come to the surface in academic writing, they help students consider a metatheory. We find that speech and writing are continually displacing each other.

As example, all oppositions are fair game for metatheoretical analysis. For instance, a group of advanced undergraduate writers, African-American women writing long essays, break into a round of prayerful Black church rhetoric on a computer conference as they struggle to meet one of my deadlines (Minock 1992). Another advanced writer, also while writing a long essay, parodies her academic style in an expressive note to a friend. In each of the above examples none of the texts produced are strictly speaking "methods that work" for any of the others. The expressive texts are break-out texts, deferring the construction of self in the essays to take up the construction of self deferred in the first place. Other examples: two members of a collaborative group, veterans working on a project on Vietnam, are asked by the other members of the group to simply write their stories as ethnographic data, from which the other members quote as proof. A skilled academic writer, shifting to the genre of personal narrative, finds he has met his challenge. He hates writing the story and chronicles an unfamiliar writing process and a differing construction of his self as reason. Without a notion that any of one kind of writing can lead to another, all of these writers are developing a metatheory. The oppositions represented in their texts in different genres demonstrate a resolution toward both/and, both oral, "spoken" and expressive, *and* literate, written and transactional, and, in an important sense, an indeterminacy of either to capture the whole rhetorical self.

What seems to me what we also might gain from untangling the terms of the expressive-writing hypothesis marriage is recourse to another of Britton's ideas, the concept of shaping at the point of utterance, which modifies the freewriting prescriptions that we applied so liberally from the expressionists (Britton 1982a). If we understand Britton's notion of shaping at the point of utterance—complete with the understanding that an utterance implies a rhetorical situation—we should look more closely at how particular texts of particular genres are composed. We may then arrive at a clearer picture of the advantages of expressive writing, expressive talk, and collaborative learning. It may be that for particular writers in particular situations, expressive writing cannot serve as a heuristic. The "method-that-works" approach to journal-keeping; personal-exposition; written revision after written revision, replicating a long crawl from orality to literacy; a self that becomes less a self; and assumptions that expressive writing is always a good starting point and warm up for formal essays—all these curricular assumptions may slide into oblivion.

Finally, in the best of Britton is the answer, although he does not say it, to his own vulnerable hypothesis and to Piaget. Britton is always linguistically and sociolinguistically reasonable. Nowhere in Britton (and nowhere in Moffett, Macrorie, Elbow, and Murray, for that matter) do we see hybrid texts squinting across genres in unauthentic ways to advance a notion of advancing logic. No personal exposition. No academically structured stories. No incoherent dummy runs. In fact, perhaps the best of Britton is in his "Talking to Learn" (1990), where he presents transcripts of young women talking, notably without a teacher present. Not only do the transcripts support a feminist notion of collaborative and cooperative learning as the women travel freely back and forth between the personal and the public, helping each other build a hierarchy of logic and supporting each other in a democratic consensus, but they also show the young women capable of logic verging on the tautological. Within their dialect, without instruction, but also within school.

Notes

1. According to Berlin (1982), Neoplatonists or expressionists see truth as an individual vision; Neo-Aristoteleans or classical rhetoricians see an unambiguous connection between sign and signified; and the New Rhetoricians see truth as a dialectical relationship between what is discovered of the self and shaped for an audience and purpose during the writing process. By 1987 Berlin refined his taxonomy to allow for more competing rhetorics. He then lists objectivist or positivist theories, including the current tradition; subjectivist theories, including expressionism; and transactional theories, including the classical, cognitive and epistemic rhetorics. He places Britton and Moffett in the cognitive-transactional category.

2. A fuller representation of Britton's theory of development appears in *Language and Learning*, and in "Spectator Role and the Beginnings of Writing."

3. Among them Berlin's *Writing Instruction in Nineteenth-Century American Colleges*, and his *Rhetoric and Reality*; Sharon Crowley's *The Methodical Memory*; Susan Miller's *Textual Carnivals*; and David Russell's *Writing in the Academic Disciplines*.

Works Cited

Barnes, Douglas R., James Britton and Mike Torbe. 1990. *Language, the Learner and the School*. 4th. ed. Portsmouth, NH: Boynton/Cook.

Bartholomae, David. 1985. "Inventing the University." *When A Writer Can't Write*. Ed. Mike Rose. 134–65. New York: Guilford.

Beach, Richard. 1977. *Writing About Ourselves and Others*. Urbana, IL: ERIC and NCTE.

Berlin, James A. 1987. *Rhetoric and Reality: Writing Instruction in American Colleges, 1900–1985*. Carbondale, IL: SIUP.

———. 1982. "Contemporary Composition: The Major Pedagogical Theories." *College English* 44:765–77.

———. 1984. *Writing Instruction in Nineteenth-Century American Colleges*. Carbondale, IL: SIUP.

Berthoff, Ann E. 1981. *The Making of Meaning: Metaphors, Models, and Maxims for Writing Teachers*. Portsmouth, NH: Boynton/Cook.

Britton, James. 1990. "Talking to Learn." In *Language, the Learner and the School. See* Barnes, Britton and Torbe, 91–130.

———. 1982a. "Shaping at the Point of Utterance." *Prospect and Retrospect: Selected Essays of James Britton*, edited by Gordon M. Pradl. 139–45. Portsmouth, NH: Boynton/Cook.

———. 1982b. "Spectator Role and the Beginning of Writing." *Prospect and Retrospect: Selected Essays of James Britton*, edited by Gordon M. Pradl. 46–47. Portsmouth, NH: Boynton/Cook.

———. 1970. *Language and Learning*. London: Penguin.

Britton, James, Robert E. Shafer, and Ken Watson, eds. 1990. *Teaching and Learning English Worldwide*. Philadelphia, PA: Multilingual Matters.

Britton, James, et al. 1975. *The Development of Writing Abilities (11–18)*. London: Macmillan.

Bruffee, Kenneth. 1986. "Social Construction, Language, and the Authority of Knowledge: A Bibliographic Essay." *College English* 48:773–90.

Connors, Robert J. 1987. "Personal Writing Assignments." *College Composition and Communication* 38:166–83.

———. 1981. "The Rise and Fall of the Modes of Discourse." *College Composition and Communication* 32:444–63.

Crowley, Sharon. 1990. *The Methodical Memory: Invention in Current-Traditional Rhetoric*. Carbondale, IL: SIUP.

Derrida, Jacques. 1976. *Of Gramatology*. Trans. Gayatri Chakravorty Spivak. Baltimore, MD: Johns Hopkins University Press.

Elbow, Peter. 1993. "The Uses of Binary Thinking." *Journal of Advanced Composition* 13:51–78.

———. 1973. *Writing Without Teachers*. New York: Oxford University Press.

Flower, Linda, and John Hayes. 1981. "A Cognitive Theory of Writing." *College Composition and Communication* 33:371–87.

Hairston, Maxine. 1982. "The Winds of Change: Thomas Kuhn and the Revolution in the Teaching of Writing." *College Composition and Communication* 36:272–82.

Harris, Joseph. 1991. "After Dartmouth: Growth and Conflict in English." *College English* 53:631–46.

Jakobson, Roman. 1960. "Linguistics and Poetics." *Style in Language*, edited by Thomas A. Sebeok. 350–76. New York: Wiley.

Katz, Michael B. 1975. *Class, Bureaucracy and Schools: The Illusion of Educational Change in America*. New York: Praeger.

Kinneavy, James L. 1979. "The Relationship to the Whole to the Part in Interpretation Theory and in the Composing Process." *Linguistics, Stylistics, and the Teaching of Composition*, edited by Donald McQuade. 1–23. Akron, OH: University of Akron Dept. English.

———. 1971. *A Theory of Discourse: The Aims of Discourse*. Englewood Cliffs, NJ: Prentice Hall.

Macrorie, Ken. 1994. "Process, Product, and Quality." *Taking Stock: The Writing Process Movement in the 90s,* edited by Lad Tobin and Thomas Newkirk. Portsmouth, NH: Boynton/Cook.

———. *Telling Writing*. [1970] 1985. 4th ed. Portsmouth, NH: Boynton/Cook.

Mahala, Daniel. 1991. "Writing Utopias: Writing Across the Curriculum and the Promise of Reform." *College English* 53:773–89.

Miller, Susan. 1992. "Theory Writing: :Writing Theory." *Methods and Methodology in Composition Research*, edited by Gesa Kirsch and Patricia A. Sullivan. 62–83. Carbondale, IL: SIUP.

———. 1991. *Textual Carnivals: The Politics of Composition*. Carbondale, IL: SIUP.

Minock, Mary. 1992. "Intertext in ConferText: The Allusions of Adult Undergraduate Seniors on Computer Conference." 8th Annual Conference on Computers and Writing, Indianapolis, 2 May.

Moffett, James. 1994. "Coming Out Right." *Taking Stock: The Writing Process Movement in the 90s,* edited by Lad Tobin and Thomas Newkirk. Portsmouth, NH: Boynton/Cook.

———. 1968. *Teaching the Universe of Discourse*. New York: Houghton.

Murray, Donald M. 1985. *A Writer Teaches Writing*. 2nd ed. Boston: Houghton.

North, Stephen M.. 1987. *The Making of Knowledge in Composition: Portrait of an Emerging Field*. Portsmouth, NH: Boynton/Cook.

Phelps, Louise Wetherbee. 1988. *Composition as a Human Science: Contributions to the Self-Understanding of a Discipline*. New York: Oxford University Press.

Russell, David R. 1991. *Writing in the Academic Disciplines, 1870–1990: A Curricular History*. Carbondale, IL: SIUP.

Samples, Bob. 1976. *The Metaphoric Mind: A Celebration of Creative Consciousness*. Reading, MA: Addison-Wesley.

Schor, Sandra. 1979. "Style Through Control: the Pleasures of the Beginning Writer." *Linguistics, Stylistics and the Teaching of Composition*, edited by Donald McQuade. 72–80. Akron, OH: University of Akron Dept. of English.

Torbe, Mike. 1990. "Language Across the Curriculum: Policies and Practice." In *Language, the Learner, and the School. See* Barnes, Britton and Torbe, 131–66.

Vygotsky, Lev Semenovich. 1962. *Thought and Language*. Ed. and trans. Eugenia Haufmann and Gertrude Vakar. New York: M.I.T. Press.

Young, Richard E. 1978. "Paradigms and Problems: Needed Research in Rhetorical Invention." *Research on Composing: Points of Departure*, edited by Charles R. Cooper and Lee Odell. 29–47. Urbana, IL: NCTE.

Young, Richard E., Alton L. Becker and Kenneth L. Pike. 1970. *Rhetoric: Discovery and Change*. New York: Harcourt.

Section Four

Deconstructing the Writing Process

11

The Uses of Binary Thinking
Exploring Seven Productive Oppositions

Peter Elbow
University of Massachusetts/Amherst

Binary thinking—seeing things in terms of oppositions, contraries, dualisms—has become over the years one of my central habits of mind: a way of going at things I keep returning to. Central to me, for example, have been the oppositions between generating vs. criticizing, doubting vs. believing; teachers as allies vs. teachers as adversaries.

But in recent years, especially with the deconstructive reaction against structuralism, there has been strong criticism of this tradition of seeing things in terms of opposites. Hélene Cixous is one of many voices arguing that wherever there are polar oppositions, there is dominance: some classic terms are day/night, sun/moon, reason/passion—and of course lurking behind all of these pairs is usually gender: male/female. According to this critique, binary thinking almost always builds in dominance or privilege—sometimes overtly and sometimes covertly. (For a sharp critique of the use of binary oppositions, see LaCapra 1989, 23–24).

Even when people overturn or reverse the traditional dominance in a polar opposition—proclaiming for example that dark is better than light, passion than reason, female than male—it just means that the underdog is defined as overdog, and we are still left with thinking in

This article is a substanitally cut version of "The Uses of Binary Thinking," published in the Journal of Advanced Composition 12(1) Winter 1993. Reprinted by permission of the publisher.

terms of dominance or hierarchy. One side is privileged. Furthermore (so goes this critique), even when we work out a compromise or a Hegelian synthesis, difference and diversity are eliminated.

In this chapter, I want to argue that this critique is wrong—or at least to show that it only applies to one kind of binary thinking—the kind that I also am fighting against. Let me start with a trenchant summary of the critique of binary thinking. In "Paul deMan's Contribution to Literary Criticism and Theory" Jonathan Culler summarizes: "Deconstruction seeks to undo all oppositions that, in the name of unity, purity, order, and hierarchy, try to eliminate difference" (1989, 278).

Culler and deMan are complaining about oppositions but I can show that oppositional thinking, if handled in the right way, will serve as a way to *avoid* the very problems or conditions they are complaining about: "purity, order, and hierarchy." That is, binary thinking can serve to encourage difference, nondominance, nontranscendance, instability, disorder.

In short, there are really *two* traditions of binary or dialectical thinking. The better known is the Hegelian tradition, which uses binary thinking as a motor always to press on to a third term or a higher category representing a transcendent reconciliation or unity: thesis and antithesis are always harnessed to yield synthesis. There is always a single "answer" or "winner."

But there is another, perhaps older tradition of binary thinking that sees value in accepting, putting up with, indeed *seeking* the nonresolution of the two terms: not feeling that the opposites must be somehow reconciled, not feeling that the itch must be scratched. This is a tradition that goes as far back as the philosophy of yin/yang. In the West we see it as one theme in Socrates/Plato, and in Boethius, and in Peter Abelard's *Sic et Non*, and it continues down through the present. The goal is *lack* of resolution of opposites.

Boethius, operating in the Neo-Platonic tradition, believed that unity or truth often exists in a realm or form where human reason cannot grasp it either with logic or language—and that the closest we can come to the highest or deepest knowledge is to try to hold in mind propositions that are irreconcilable.[1]

Boethius influenced Chaucer, and I learned this tradition when I wrote my dissertation and book, *Oppositions in Chaucer* (1975). In studying *Troilus and Criseyde* I noticed that Chaucer was preoccupied with the ancient philosophical debate between freedom and necessity, so I decided to see whether the events of the poem were shown to be free or bound. What I found was that Chaucer seemed deliberately to show both: that everything happened by choice or free will, but also that everything was determined or bound by forces out of the characters' control. It's as though he gave us all at once two contradictory lenses through which to see human experience. Both lenses seemed wholly true and satisfactory. I pursued this way of seeing things and found it in many other places in Chaucer's poetry. (See my methodological chapter in the Chaucer book *The Value of Dialectic*—reprinted in my *Embracing Contraries* [1986a].)

Since then I've repeatedly seen the value of this approach: noticing oppositions or conflicts, even seeking them, but leaving them unresolved. Practice with this approach has led me to suspect that when we encounter something that is difficult or complicated or something that tangles people into endless debate, we are often in the presence of an opposition that needs to be made more explicit—and left unreconciled.

Though I am arguing for binary thinking, nothing here is arguing against framing issues in terms of *more* than two sides—just so long as there's *more than one*! If we can see *three* or *five* sides, that's good—as long as that multiplicity isn't a cover for letting one side be the real winner. For my real goal in this chapter is not to have pairs but to get away from simple, single truth—to have situations of balance, irresolution, nonclosure, nonconsensus, nonwinning.

And not only is binary thinking a powerful engine for producing difference and nonclosure, it is also inevitable in human perception and thinking. The easiest way to classify complex information is to clump it into two piles. Indeed the most instinctive and tempting clumps to use for complex data are the old favorites: like/don't like; ours/theirs; right/sinister; sheep/goats. This is why dichotomies tend to come packaged with positive and negative poles (see Smith 1988, 122). It may be that the very structure of our bodies and our placement in phenomenal reality invite us to see things in terms of binary oppositions, for example, right/left, up/down, front/back, near/far, male/female (see Lakoff and Johnson 1980).

The question, then, is not *whether* to deal with dichotomies but how to deal with them. There are basically five options:

1. Choose one side as right or better. This is "either/or" thinking.
2. Work out a compromise or a dialectical synthesis, that is, find a third term.
3. Deny there is any conflict (for example, "There is no difference between form and content" or "There is no conflict between teaching and research").
4. Affirm both sides of the dichotomy as equally true or necessary or important or correct. This is the approach I argue in this chapter.

5. Reframe the conflict so there are more than two sides. This is of course another good path. I don't particularly explore it here—but notice that I utilize it in making this very list.

The first three options are the most common and habitual ways we deal with dichotomy or conflict because humans seem to be uncomfortable with what is unreconciled or incompatible. Psychologists can explain the most diverse range of human thinking, feeling, and behavior in terms of our instinctive resistance to "cognitive dissonance": when we are presented with conflicting data, the organism seems to want somehow to find *some* kind of harmony or unity. Even at a sensory level we are constantly presented with contrasting views and shifting perceptions—but our brains always yield single, stable objects and categories (see Peckham 1967).

But even though binary oppositions tempt people to oversimple, black/white thinking, binary oppositions also present us with uniquely valuable occasions for balance, irresolution, nonclosure, nonconsensus, nonwinning. So I will celebrate and explore here the approach to binary oppositions that seems to go against the grain and require some conscious discipline: affirming both sides of a dichotomy as equally true or important—even if they are contradictory.

Of course I'm not saying we should balance *every* dichotomy we encounter. It sometimes makes sense to choose one side as right, the other wrong. Indeed when we *need* to make a difficult value judgment or sort out slippery distinctions, pairings are an enormous help. Opticians harness this process when they try to figure out a best lens for us: they keep giving us pairs and asking, "Which one is better," as they gradually zero in. I'm just asking us to notice the many situations where the easy, good/bad distinction gets us in trouble, and we need balance and irresolution.

Let me first illustrate the usefulness of this balancing kind of binary thinking by applying it to three examples: writing, teaching, and thinking/learning.

1. Writing

We cannot write well unless, on the one hand, we are able to come up with a plenitude of words and thoughts, and we do better if we cultivate a welcoming attitude and refrain from evaluating and criticizing. Yet on the other hand, we cannot write well unless we are able to evaluate, criticize and reject—an ability that is enhanced by an attitude of tough-minded skepticism. In short, skill in writing involves skill at generating and criticizing.

In recent years, some people have called this view an outmoded piece of dichotomous thinking, arguing that the opposition between generating and criticizing breaks down. The objection charges: "There *is no difference* between generating and criticizing. Every piece of generating is by the same token also a piece of criticizing—since the act of putting down one word is also the act of rejecting a host of other words we could have put down."

This objection is a logical quibble. That is, even though choosing X may seem *logically* the same as rejecting Y and Z in the realm of logic, as actions in the realm of human experience they are completely different. That is, when we choose X, we *may* indeed be rejecting Y and Z in the same breath, but often we are not rejecting anything at all. We simply write down X because it's the only thing that comes to mind. Y and Z were never there to be rejected. Writing down X when it's the only thing in mind is a very different act from writing it down when you also have Y and Z in mind—especially when you are torn between them. Generating and criticizing are very different activities. At any instant of writing we may be generating a great deal or not very much; or *criticizing* a great deal or not very much. What I'm pursuing here are two very different human abilities. People who can think of X and Y and Z are better at generating than those who can only think of X, but the ability I'm celebrating would lead one to think of many more than three—and not just write down one but write down lots of them. People can improve their ability to generate multiple options. Similarly people can improve their ability to criticize or see flaws in what looks plausible—and we also need that ability to write well.

If, instead of denying the difference between generating and criticizing, we look for it and honor it, we get a model with considerable explanatory power. By noticing how generating and criticizing tend to get in each others' way, we can better understand why writing tends to be so difficult, and why the process of writing tends to proceed in the variable ways that it does:

- When writing goes *very* badly, we are stuck or blocked. We are tied in knots by trying to be generative and critical at the same time.
- When writing goes passably but not very well, it is usually because we are having to *negotiate a compromise* between these conflicting mentalities: if generating gains the upper hand, we manage to pour out a lot of material but we cannot make it critically focused; if criticizing gains the upper hand, what we produce is good—but we produce very little because we see every potential fault in every sentence as we start to write it.

- When writing goes very well (as it occasionally does), we seem able at one and the same moment to reach out for just the right word and yet, (seemingly without effort or even awareness) put aside countless possibilities that aren't just right.

I make this same point in terms of *people*, not just writing sessions. For the characteristic method or style of going about writing that people develop often represents their way of negotiating the conflict between creating and criticizing:

- Some writers are characteristically blocked. They are balanced in their ability to find words and criticize them, so their writing method is the famous one of staring at the paper till blood breaks out on their foreheads.
- Others are characteristically undisciplined and loose; or characteristically cramped or tight.
- A few writers seem magically integrated. People have a hard time explaining what it is that these wonderful writers do—ascribing it to genius or to magic or to the muses. The writers themselves give remarkably contradictory accounts of what they're doing: "It's all inspiration!" "It's all perspiration!" "It's all system!" "It's all magic and serendipity!" Just what you might expect if people were explaining a complex skill that they happened to have learned, but that violates normal patterns of explanation. Their skill represents the ability to be magically extreme at both skills. Much of the traditional advice about writing is really advice to help with transcending opposites—for example, taking walks, waiting humbly, abnegating the self, paying homage to the muses, relinquishing some agency and control, meditating—or drinking.

But whatever the path one takes to good writing, notice that it is not the path of compromise or the golden mean. If we are only *sort of* generative and *sort of critical*, we write mediocre stuff: we don't have so much to choose from, and we reject only the worst. We need extremity in both directions. Instead of negotiating one point on the continuum between two extremes, we need as it were to occupy two points—near both ends.

Notice that I am introducing the dimension of time. What is paradoxical in logic—"being both generative and critical—occupying two spots on a single continuum"—is ordinary in time. Thus the most well-worn path for negotiating the conflict between generating and criticizing is by separating them in time. That is, even though it seems natural to try to *find* words and thoughts and *scrutinize* them at the same time to see if they are the right ones, this doesn't mean that we cannot become more skilled at separating these activities and doing them one at a time—thus separating the two mentalities. The time dimension helps us heighten the conflict, not minimize it—permitting us to clear an arena in which each side can operate unhampered to an extreme.

This, then, is the approach to heightening and separating opposites that I gradually learned—and I find I can teach it to students and teachers with helpful results. It is a skill. People often have an easier time taking risks, turning off all criticism, and thereby coming up with words and thoughts they didn't know they had, when they know they will have a time to be wholeheartedly critical and get rid of foolishness. And people often have an easier time being fiercely critical when they have gotten themselves to write too much—to generate too many ideas and hypotheses.

2. Teaching

The same kind of conflict lies at the heart of the teaching process. As teachers we too are inevitably asked to take two conflicting stances or engage in two opposed behaviors. On the one hand we are asked to be allies or helpers or hosts to students: to invite all students to enter in and join the learning community. And we can usually help them learn better if we take a somewhat positive or inviting stance and assume they *can* learn, that they *are* intelligent, that they *have* what it takes. (Teachers' expectations, positive or negative, probably have more influence on how well students learn than any differences in how they teach. See Rosenthal and Jacobson 1968.) Yet just as inevitably, we need to be on guard—to scrutinize, examine, test, reject. We have a loyalty not just to students but to institutions and to the body of knowledge we are teaching. We have to criticize what is wrong, reject what is unsatisfactory, be tough. In short, to teach well we have to be good hosts and good bouncers—we need skill both as ally and adversary. Teaching, like writing, may often be recursive, but it is a recursive blending or alternation of two conflicting dimensions: opening the gate wide and keeping the gate narrow.

We can heighten our awareness of this conflict of teaching stances or roles by noticing how students often skitter ungracefully between confiding in us as allies and guarding against us as adversaries. And they are right; we are usually both. Notice how these two teaching roles (like the two writing roles) are sometimes institutionalized as separate people. The tutor's function, for example in a writing center, is to be helper, and there is no need to be adversary at all. The examiner's function is to be adversary or critic and to provide no help. Oxford and Cambridge, like many European universities, have distinguished between teacher/tutor and examiner since the Middle Ages.

This conflict is unavoidable because, again, compromise or reconciliation is not the answer. Look at the options. It's no good *only* welcoming students and never critically examining their work. It's no good *only* criticizing wrong answers and never welcoming them and their risk-taking and their perplexity. And a happy medium or golden mean is no good: being only *sort of* helpful or inviting to students and only *sort of* vigilant as to whether they do decent work. Yet we seem to be stuck having to occupy only one point along the continuum that students know so well—from being "tough teachers" to being "easy teachers." We often vacillate: "This term, it's no more Mr. Nice Guy."

But really skilled teachers somehow find ways to occupy more than one point—to do justice to these opposites in all their irreconcilability. Again we see two ways to do this. The rarer path is one of mysterious finesse or transcendence whereby they simultaneously occupy more than one point. That is, a few remarkable teachers are extremely tough and inviting *at the same time*—remarkably welcoming to students yet remarkably discriminating in saying, "I won't take anything but the best."

The more ordinary path to good teaching involves finding ways to separate the two stances and moving back and forth between points on the continuum: finding times to be inviting and encouraging and other times to be especially vigilant. We tend to be more inviting at the beginning of a course or in our opening explorations and explanations of something; and more vigilant at the ends of courses and as we test. Somewhere toward the middle or end of a course, students often feel, "Hey, I thought this teacher was my friend. What happened?" (See my "Embracing Contraries in the Teaching Process, 1983.")

3. Thinking and Learning

We see the same contradiction at the heart of the intellectual process itself: a conflict between doubting and believing. The centrality of doubting is obvious. The ability to find flaws or contradictions has been foundational in the development of logic and in the critical tradition running from Socrates through Descartes and undiminished to now. Criticism and skepticism are usually identified with intelligence itself.

Less noticed, however, is the central need in the intellectual process for skill in believing: the ability to "try on," enter into, and experience ideas or points of view different from the ones we presently hold. Since "credulity," the tendency just to go along with whatever seems attractive or appealing or persuasive, is the main *problem* in the thinking of children or unsophisticated adults—and since schooling and careful thinking seem to consist of the process of *giving up* credulity and being instead more critical minded or skeptical—we have tended to overlook the fact that people are seldom skilled at thinking and learning unless they are also skilled at entering into and even believing ideas and points of view that are difficult for them. In short, we need skill both at doubting even what looks right, and at believing even what looks crazy or alien. This is one reason why good thinking and learning are so hard.

Of course most thinking involves some kind of combination or recursive intertwining of these mental activities, and it feels artificial to most people to try to separate. But that feeling is misleading and stems from the dominance or hierarchy of criticism in our culture's model of thinking and learning. For, by training, we are all perfectly accustomed to the process of trying to remove all believing or credulity in order to clear a space for uninterrupted, focused doubting or criticism. What we are less accustomed to is the effort to remove all doubting and criticism in order to clear a space for uninterrupted, focused believing.

So here is the same kind of dichotomy. Intellectual skill represents skill at opposites—accepting and rejecting, swallowing and spitting out, letting oneself be invaded and keeping oneself intact. And just as with writing and teaching, we see that at those moments of consummate skill in thinking, we seem to be able to manage what is paradoxical: we can get our mind around what is alien and odd and enter into unknown terrain—yet we are acute in our discriminating rejections.

Let me summarize before going on to the next examples. I'm arguing the benefits of one *kind* of binary thinking for understanding writing, teaching, and thinking: emphasizing dichotomies but holding them unresolved—giving equal affirmation to both sides. I think that this model for process explains the natural distribution of skills in these complex activities of writing, teaching, thinking, and learning. That is, people commonly negotiate a compromise between these conflicting skills or mentalities in a zero-sum economy: being strong at one side of things (generativity or openness or believing) and correspondingly weak at the other; or vice versa; or else middling at both—achieving a kind of compromise—but not excellence at either. Excellence is difficult because it requires doing justice to conflicting demands. Meeting those demands *simultaneously* is especially rare—and mysterious. It is easier to meet conflicting demands one at a time—though this leads to a less seamless, graceful, artful process; more bumpy, back and forth, and seemingly artificial. The process is thus recursive, though most people cannot become usefully extreme at both mentalities when they switch back and forth too rapidly.

In the three previous examples (writing, teaching, thinking, and learning), I have been engaged in emphasizing oppositions or conflicts that are often *unnoticed* or overlooked. In a sense I have been introducing dichotomies where some deny they exist. But now let me apply my approach to four *much-noticed* dichotomies—traditional and prominent. Here too, many people want to deny these dichotomies and call them wrongheaded and false—assert that they are the epiphenomena of traditional linguistic categories and that there is really no conflict or opposition. But when people deny these dichotomies, it seems to me they are engaging in wishful thinking or propping up a doctrinal position, or defending or disguising a dominance of one side by the other. My theme here—and in a sense throughout my whole chapter—is this: beware happy harmonies and mystical unions; look out for declarations of no conflict.

4. Teaching vs. Research

"No problem. They each reinforce each other." This is the latest doctrine—and a prime case of wishful thinking. Of course research *can* help teaching and vice-versa—just as generating can reinforce criticizing and so forth. But it is weak thinking to slide from there into the ever-recurring pious doctrine that there is no conflict between teaching and research. The two activities compete for our time, attention, and loyalty in the most concrete and obvious way. The extensive time I'm spending on this chapter is time I cannot spend on my teaching. I get completely involved in writing it and find myself putting off preparation or reading I ought to do for my classes. What I do here *may* make me a smarter, more thoughtful teacher, but I cannot really *apply* this work directly to my teaching. Few faculty members can bring their research directly into their undergraduate teaching.

But it's not just a matter of wishful thinking. When people claim that there is no conflict between teaching and research, they are usually—consciously or not—covering up or reinforcing the dominance of research over teaching. It's worth noticing that teachers and administrators at two-year colleges and in the elementary, middle, and high schools don't seem to be so tempted to proclaim that there is no conflict between teaching and research.

It's important to try to think carefully about this important political matter. It may be a good thing for teachers to do research—since it can make them more intellectually lively in their teaching (though do we really want to say that teachers who care most about research are always the most intellectually lively?). And it may be a good thing for researchers to teach—since it can help them be more aware of the relationships between what they are investigating and popular attitudes and the learning process. Nevertheless, it is nonsense to say you can't do one well without doing the other.

The theoretical point illuminated by my model is this: that teaching and research *don't* need each other—just as generating and criticizing don't need each other—indeed, the two sides of the dichotomy have a tendency to get in each other's way. It's only *writing* that needs both generating and criticizing. And it's only *a certain model of being an academic* that needs both teaching and research. Teachers can be good without doing research—just as researchers can be good without teaching. Editors can be good without doing any generating—just as draft writers or information gatherers or "leg-persons" can be good without doing any editing. (Before World War II, *most* academics didn't do much writing or research nor were they expected to do it. It was only at universities that there was a strong expectation to do research—not so much at colleges. Since then the "university" model has been spreading throughout all of higher education.)

So what does this dichotomous model tell us about how to improve the relationship between teaching and research? We can follow the same principles here as above. A few really gifted people can make teaching and research work together simultaneously. But most people need to take steps to keep the two from getting in each others' way—which usually means finding times to give *full* attention and commitment to each. Full attention is important because what we want is extremity in both sides: we don't want half-hearted teaching and half-hearted research, we want deep commitment to both teaching and research. Some people can give full attention to writing and research for a few hours each day and switch to give just as full attention to teaching for the rest of the day. Most people can't switch back and forth so quickly—and need longer periods to commit themselves to one or the other. And how can we improve what is usually the weaker side of the dichotomy, teaching? Clearly we can't improve it by blithely proclaiming that there is no conflict between the two and that research always helps teaching—meanwhile continuing to give all the incentives to research and very few to teaching. We have to decide whether we are willing to give the incentives to teaching without which it can never thrive.

The trickier and more politically sensitive question is whether we can or should save the "university" model of what an academic is: someone who necessarily teaches *and* does research. The model of binary thinking I am arguing for does not imply any answers to this essentially political question. (One suggestion comes from Carnegie

Commission: a conception of "research" that isn't so much at odds with teaching because it doesn't necessarily involve conventional competitive publication.)

5. Form vs. Content

The objection: "They are indissoluble. We can't distinguish them or judge one apart from the other. Surely you don't want to be associated with old fashioned school teachers who give split grades!" Of course form and content are *linked*—are often *functions* of each other. A change in one will likely make some change in the other. But the notion that we cannot distinguish or talk about or evaluate them separately flies in the face of common sense and common practice.

Here, as in the other oppositions I've discussed, opposites *do* fuse or magically interact when everything is going perfectly. That is, in the ideal poem, form and content function just as the doctrine proclaims they should: we can't tell the dancer from the dance. But in ordinary sublunary texts, we have no trouble telling which is the dancer. The reason the text is not magical is that dancer and dance *don't* perfectly realize each other. We can tell, for example, that the content is working better than the form—or vice versa. When we talk about imperfect texts or texts in progress or nonliterary texts—for example, about student texts, about our own texts, or about university guidelines for tenure, as opposed to Keats' poems—our statements almost invariably imply a clear difference between form and content. Yes, in the last analysis, theoretically, any change in wording causes a change in meaning (at least fractionally). But the point is we make changes in wording *because* we can palpably feel and distinguish gaps between form and content.

This doctrine of the indistinguishibility of form and content serves to *enshrine* literary language as special and desirable—and also, oddly enough, to hold up literary language as paradigmatic of all language. The doctrine seems to give special honor to *form*.

6. Reading vs. Writing

The idea that there is no conflict here is a classic case of pious doctrine serving to cover the privilege or dominance of one spouse over the other. (This is a large subject that I have treated elsewhere at length [1993]). For many reasons, often political, it is crucial to recognize the difference between the act of trying to fit your mind around words someone else chose, and trying to choose your own words and get others to fit their minds around them. Again it's a case of resorting to a kind of *logical* equivalence that covers up a fundamental opposition in the realm of human experience—especially with regard to human agency.

At the overtly political level, we see this dominance in the vastly superior working conditions given to teachers of reading or literature in higher education compared to teachers of writing (Slevin 1991). At the theoretical level, we see a clear conflict of interest between readers and writers in deciding on the meaning and interpretation of a text: it's in the interest of writers that they should decide what their own text means; it's in the interest of readers to say that only readers can decide what a text means. Clearly there's no right answer: either/or, zero-sum arguments are a trap, and so is a compromise: both points of view must be given full or even extreme validity. At the present critical moment (a moment that has lasted rather a long time), authority is tipped more toward readers than writers.

Of course reading and writing *can* serve or reinforce each other. Input can serve output and vice-versa. But (just as in teaching/research), the reinforcement is one-sided unless it is built on a recognition of conflicting interests between the two sides and the current privileging of one side. When harmony is just spouted as a pious doctrine, it tends to support the dominance of reading in the current academic world. It tends to be used in support of proposals to scrap the only writing course in college and make it into a reading-and-writing course—while the majority of reading (literature) courses are tacitly invited to remain as they are, namely, committed primarily to reading. We must view with suspicion any pronouncements of happy harmony when the status quo serves one side more than the other.

7. Private vs. Social

The current conversation seems to have foundered on the polarity itself. Participants in the current private vs. social debate seem to assume the incompatibility of the two and celebrate one or the other—condemning the opposite. But as so many thinkers have recognized (notably George Herbert Meade and John Dewey), *either/or* thinking is the problem here.

Clearly humans are both: inherently connected and intertwined with others, yet also inherently distinct and separate. Language comes to us from outside, neverthelesss the language that we speak and write also comes to us from the inside—as early as age three or four. We can focus on either dimension of how humans exist with each other: from an ultimate point of view, everything we say or write comes from outside—we don't make up words; but from a proximate point of view, all the language that comes to our lips or our pens comes from the inside.

If we take the trouble to step outside the doctrinal bickering, we can easily see that it is a good thing to be *more than usually social*—but also to be *more than usually private*. The more we connect and communicate with others, the more . . . well, who needs to argue this point these days? But a moment's thought will also show us that we are clearly better off the more we can hold commerce with ourselves, pursue trains of thought through inner dialogues even if no one else is interested, resist or tune out the pressures of others, keep our selves separate. ("All the unhappiness of men arises from one single fact, that they cannot stay quietly in their own chamber" Pascal *Pensee* # 139.) We have good reason to value social discourse—and see social interrelatedness everywhere, even where we don't notice it at first; but we have equally good reason to value the cultivation of private, desert-island discourse and individuation.

So again, my argument is for affirming both sides equally—not to compromise but to push for extremity in both directions—*and* to resist attempts at priority or hegemony by either side. The best way to achieve this goal, to fight clear of the trap of partisans on each side fighting to stamp out the other, is to remember what rhetoricians sometimes forget though it was Aristotle's favorite phrase (not so much in the *Rhetoric*, however): "*There is one sense in which. . . .*" There is a sense (currently much publicized) in which all language is social. But just as clearly, there's a sense in which all language is private: the tapping on prison walls by individuals in solitary confinement, with only slight chances of being heard much less understood. The situation is not either/or but both/and.

When both/and is the goal, it follows that the weaker or neglected dimension needs to be strengthened. Thus, it's obviously a problem when persons are *only* private and always hold themselves apart and unrelated to others and don't know how to connect or function socially. But it's equally problematic when people are *only* social and can only think and use language when there are others around to interact with, and can only think those thoughts that others agree with or are interested in. Such people are too subject to peer pressure; we use the expression that they "have no mind of their own."

As with the other dichotomies I've considered, the opposed sides *can* work together and reinforce each other when all goes well. The more of a social life one has, the richer one's private life can be. As Vygotsky and others point out, our private life is often a folding in of what was first social. But it goes the other way too: the more private life one has, that is, the more one is able to have conversations with oneself and follow thoughts and feelings in different directions from those of people around one, the more richly *social* a life one can have.

We can see this same political dynamic in the earlier dichotomies

I explored (in writing, teaching, thinking, and learning): when people claim that there is no real dichotomy or no real conflict, their arguments serve (whether consciously or not) to cover up and reinforce an ingrained power imbalance. For example, when people argue that there is no conflict between generating and criticizing in writing, or between believing and doubting in thinking and learning, they are reinforcing the present dominance of criticism and critical thinking in the academic or intellectual realm. They are reinforcing the prevailing set of assumptions that tell us that it is a good thing to clear space for nonstop, unrelieved criticism or doubting while people write or think; but it is a bad thing to clear space for nonstop, unrelieved generating or believing or making a mess. Periods of extreme control and planning are currently felt to be fine, but not periods of nonplanning or relinquishing control. Extremity in doubting is fine, but extremity in believing is bad. This attitude toward belief is so ingrained in our academic and intellectual culture that people don't realize that what they are afraid of—namely, fanaticism or closed-mindedness—represents not extremity of belief but poverty of belief: the ability to believe only one thing.[2]

The Epistemology of Lived Experience vs. the Epistemology of Logic or Propositions

The *kind* of binary thinking I'm advocating here—an approach that tries to heighten dichotomies and affirm both sides equally—involves, it seems to me, a special link or even commitment to experience. There is a phenomenological bias; perhaps even a bias toward narrative.

My own story is paradigmatic. That is, I came to this approach through my *experience* of writing—primarily an experience of perplexity or even bafflement. I quit graduate school when I got so blocked I couldn't write. When I finally came back five years later I was scared and self-conscious about writing, so for four years I scribbled notes to myself—short ones and long ones—about what was happening to me as I wrote, especially when things went particularly badly or well. It was from these experiential, often narrative notes that I developed the hypothesis that writing was hard because of the conflicting needs to generate but criticize, control but let go, say *Yes* but say *No*. My thinking grew out of a process of trying to be true to my experience and to find a theory that didn't violate it.

I've come to think that this approach to dichotomies honors the complexity of one's experience and the wandering narrative of events. The approach invites experience to precede logic. And here too of course there is a tradition: an empirical, inductive, pragmatic tradition that favors Aristotle's science over Plato's, Bacon over Descartes—and that we see in William James and John Dewey.

You can't say what I've just said, however, without someone quickly objecting, "But there is no such thing as experience without theory. That's naive American Romanticism. Theory is always already in everything we do. No act can be innocent of theory." But here again this claim—and it has become a doctrinal chant—papers over another binary distinction: theory vs. practice. (Boethius pictures Dame Philosophy with two prominent letters embroidered on her robe, Theta and Pi.) For the claim that there is no dichotomy or conflict between theory and practice tends to champion theory over practice.

Of course it's true that no act is innocent of premises and implications. But it is a failure of clear thinking to let that fact blind us to a crucial difference: between coming at a piece of experience with a conscious and explicit theory in mind vs. coming at it as openly as possible—making an effort to try to hold theory at bay—and then trying to notice what happens.

It is true that trying to hold theory at bay and not articulate our tacit theories serves to open ourselves to self-deception: we tend to "find" theories that we are already pre-disposed to believe. But when people spend all their time wagging their finger at this danger, they tend to miss a crucial experience. We can increase our chances of seeing more complexity and contradiction in our experience—and finding new theories or theories that surprise us—if we make an effort to honor and attend to experience as closely as possible. This process can even lead us to theories we are predisposed *not* to believe—theories we don't like. We usually notice this difference, for example, between two textures of research—for example in classroom research: one where the observer starts with a position and consciously looks at everything through that lens, and another where the observer tries to take notes about what she is seeing and feeling from moment to moment, and waits to see what gestalts emerge.

There is in fact a strong tradition of trying to pay good attention to one's experience, which we now see in the discipline of phenomenology—involving what is called "bracketing." One can get better at it. Like the discipline of holding off critical thinking or holding off awareness of audience, people mustn't say it can't be done just because they haven't learned how to do it. If we want to get better at attending to experience, it helps to notice the competing demands of theory and logic.

Let me stress again that my enthusiasm for experience and induction is not a claim that they are superior or prior or priviledged. I don't claim that induction is better than deduction, Aristotle than

Plato, Bacon than Descartes, Dewey than Derrida. I am simply resisting a *counter* claim of priority, an assumption of privilege. I'm simply jostling for 50 percent of the bed. I am trying to maintain a balanced and unresolved opposition in order to prevent *either* side from being slid into the margin by means of a haughty denial of oppositional thinking.

In fact I acknowledge that the view I am presenting in this chapter has attained such a degree of generality as to become a theoretical bulldozer itself. To the degree that I fall in love with my theory of opposites, I'm liable to use it to bludgeon experience. But I don't shrink from this possibility. That is, I have no hesitation about turning around and celebrating theory too. Sometimes it is only by bludgeoning experience—for example through being obsessed with something—that we can make experience give up secrets that we don't get by innocent observation. But to the degree that I am committed to experience, then I will struggle—*in addition* and on certain occasions—to try to keep my eyes and pores open and *hold off* my preoccupation with opposites.

I want to call attention to a connection between this emphasis on experience and the work of some of the earlier figures in the field of composition: Macrorie, Britton, Murray, myself, and others. What these figures had in common—and what seems to me to characterize that moment in the history of composition—was a burgeoning interest in the *experience* of writing. There was a mood of excitement about talking about what actually *happens* as we and our students write. Thus, there was a lot of first person writing and informal discourse. And thus the overused term for the movement: the "process approach." People wanted to talk about experience during the process of writing—not just about the resultant text or product. "Process" connotes experience.[3]

I see a correlation between this emphasis on the experience or process of writing and a willingness to articulate contraries and leave them unresolved. To be open and honest about experience leads to unresolved and conflicting propositions. This opening period of the "process" movement in composition corresponds, I'd say, to the moment when literary critics were interested in reader response criticism: "Let's try to tell what actually happens to us as we read." (I called this "giving movies of the reader's mind" in *Writing Without Teachers* in 1973). But since then, scholars in both literature and composition (with the notable exception of some feminists) have tended to back away from this interest in talking honestly and personally about their own experience. An autobiographical openness about one's own experience doesn't seem to fit comfortably with our current model of academic scholarship.

Thus I call the approach to binaries that I'm talking about an epistemology of experience—whereas an insistence on logical coherence is more an epistemology of propositions.

Epistemology and Rhetoric

The kind of binary thinking that I celebrate here would seem to lead to skepticism about knowing or epistemology: a distrust of language and of the possibilities of knowing (Gibson 1962). Yet this same approach seems more affirmative about being or ontology: it implies a faith that we live in a world consisting of more than just our minds and language and logic—and that we can have a *kind* of commerce with them. But once I put it this way, I have grounds for being less epistemologically gloomy: the implication is that if we can sit there and hold the two irreconcilable propositions in mind—at least if they are the right ones—we can get *some* sort of knowledge about the complexity of things.

What's interesting to me here, however, is the paradoxical relationship between this epistemology of contradiction and *rhetoric*. Even though I'm arguing throughout for more difference, more contradiction—more of what Boethius called "war" between truths—I think I'm opening a door to a rhetoric that is less warlike or adversarial.

Look at how rhetoric or persuasion or argument usually work. When people argue and call each other wrong, they tend to assume that only one of them is right. Graff (1987) explores this link between epistemology and adversarial rhetoric. If there is only one truth or right answer, then people need to fight for supremacy; those with the wrong answer must be suppressed or brought around.

But if we celebrate binary thinking of the sort I've been describing, there's every chance of discovering that *both parties to the argument are right*—despite their disagreement. Their two claims, even though completely contradictory (X and not-X), might *both* be accurate and useful views of the complex phenomena they are fighting about. If they were more open to the epistemology of contradiction, they might come closer to a full description and understanding of the issue under discussion by affirming and entering into each others' propositions (without having to give up allegiance to their own). There is less need to try to bludgeon people into agreement. Thus John Trimbur's (1989) essay celebrating dissensus or the limits of consensus has been extremely fruitful and influential in the profession—coming as it does out of the tradition of Bruffee and his concensus-based model of social construction.

My interest in affirming oppositions, then, connects with my interest in nonadversarial, nonviolent, nonoppositional rhetoric: rhetoric as believing game (see my "Metholodological" 1986b). More and more people are noticing the problems with either/or rhetoric (as opposed to both/and rhetoric): the assumption that in order to argue *for* a position we must argue *against* the contrary position as wrong. Thus the conventional strategy in most persuasive essays is to start out by trying to show that the other view is wrong. Of course I'll do better at getting you to see the strengths of my view if you don't first have to confess your error or cry uncle. And I'll increase my chances of success if *I*, in turn, am able to see the truth of *your* view. For feminist explorations of non-adversarial rhetoric, see Frey 1990; Lamb 1991. See also the extensive exploration of "Rogerian rhetoric," for example in Brent 1991; Teich 1992. Ong (1981) is interesting on the history of the adversarial and irenic traditions in culture. Lakoff and Johnson (1980) show how deeply enmeshed our culture is in the assumption that "argument equals war"—through their exploration of the tacit "metaphors we live by."

Some readers may want to accuse me of not practicing what I preach. For if I am so interested in nonadversarial rhetoric and the believing game, why am I fighting so hard throughout this chapter? And why in my career have I so often seemed to take partisan stands?

But we have more options than just (a) fighting (which means trying to exterminate the enemy or her position) and (b) falling into a kind of nonviolent limpness. There is a third option: to fight with someone to try to get them to listen to us or to consider our view—fight hard—and yet nevertheless not push them at all to give up their view. That is, there are two kinds of fighting: fighting to be heard and fighting to keep the other person from being heard; fighting to create dialogue and fighting to insist on monologue. I am fighting here more to be heard than to wipe out the other view.

For I have been partisan. I've always written more excitedly about generating than revising, and been preoccupied if not obsessed with freewriting. I've certainly celebrated private writing and the ability to turn off awareness of audience during certain points in the writing process. I've made more noise about teachers as allies than as evaluative adversaries. And I've campaigned my whole career for the believing game.

But I've always made it clear that the goal of my enthusiasm or partisan behavior was to right the balance or bring about equal emphasis, never to try to stamp out the other side. Because there has been such a one-sided tradition in teaching and theorizing about writing—a tradition that says, "Always plan; always maintain vigilance and control, always use critical thinking"—I've seen a clear need to make a louder noise in favor of periods of non-planning, generating or freewriting, and holding off critical consciousness. But in all of my pushing for the generative, I've never argued against critical consciousness or doubting or criticism; only for an equal emphasis on both sides—a stronger contradiction—what D. H. Lawrence called the "trembling instability of the balance" (1985, 172).

Despite my enthusiasms on one side, I have never wavered in making clear my commitment to those very members of the pair that I'm trying to push over to their side of the bed—out of positions of dominance: I've always confirmed my commitment to revision and critical consciousness in writing; to subject matter and even evaluation in teaching; and to doubting in thinking and learning. And when it comes to the opposition between the private vs. the social dimension in writing, I helped get the profession interested in the first place in the social and collaborative dimension of writing with my *Writing Without Teachers* in 1973.

Thus I would invite readers to compare the rhetorical shape of my writing with that of people who are extremely critical of my work (for example, James Berlin, Jeanette Harris). Even though I allow myself unabashed enthusiasm and open partisanship where they use tones of alleged judiciousness, compare the rhetorical goals. My goal has never been to wipe out the enemy but to strengthen the weaker and neglected side—to keep two sides alive and equal—to push for a dialogue among equal voices—to make room for a situation of balanced opposition.

In fact, what really needs explaining is why there has been such a tendency to see me as one-sided and extreme—to see me as someone only interested in generating, making a mess, and the private dimension—to be blind to my support for critical thinking, revising, doubting, and the social dimension in writing—when I preach over and over this theme of embracing contraries and of trying to get opposites into unresolved tension with each other. That is, I'm criticized for being narrow or one-sided, and on epistemological grounds, but really the criticism itself represents an epistemological narrowness: an inability to understand that someone can argue for balanced contraries by championing the weaker side, even though this is my continually announced and clearly explained point—a seeming inability to see an epistemological argument for contraries. The current academic world likes to celebrate indeterminacy and epistemological doubt, yet even radical theorists often seem to fall into assuming that if anyone says anything in favor of X (especially if X smacks of feelings, private discourse, or the relinquishing of control), they must by definition be *against* the opposite of X (thinking, analysis, logic, and the social dimension)—whatever they say to the contrary. I can't help believing, then, that a more dialectical or contradictory epistemology can lead to more large mindedness.

And how do we learn or develop this large minded epistemology or habit of dialectical thinking? One important way we learn it is through interaction with others: through dialogue. After all, that's the original link that Socrates and Plato had in mind in their original conception of "dialectic": bring people into conversation in order to create conflict among ideas. Dialogue leads to dialectic.

So just as we learn to talk privately to ourselves by internalizing social conversation with others (as George Herbert Meade and Vygotsky tell us); so we can learn the kind of binary or dialectical thinking I'm interested in from conversation. That is, our greatest source of difference and dichotomy is when people of different minds come together to talk. So in addition to calling for an "epistemology of contradiction," I could also call it an "epistemology of dialogue" or (to be fashionable) a "dialogic epistemology." But it's not enough to have dialogue between opposing views if the dialogue is just adversarial. The question is whether the participants learn how to internalize *both* views—enlarge their mind and their assumptions—instead of just digging in and fighting harder for their own view. So it's a question of what *kind* of dialogue we have. Does it represent a collaboration between conflicting views? We learn rhetorical warfare from dialogue with rhetorical warriors, but we learn dialectical large mindedness from dialogue with people who have learned an epistemology of dialogue or contradiction.

The reigning epistemology among scholars and academics today is dialectical *in a sense*, but not the large minded sense we most need. It is too skeptical or unhopeful. This epistemology says, in effect, "I believe X and you believe Y, and there is no real truth or right answer in the back of the book to tell us who is right. So we can keep on fighting." What I'm looking for is a dialectical epistemology that is more hopeful. It says, "I believe X and you believe Y, and by gum we may well *both* be right—absolutely right. So we should figure out ways to work together." Notice the crucial difference of relationships here between epistemology and rhetoric. In the former case (the ruling paradigm we currently live in) we have eternal warfare between people (rhetoric) because the people don't have eternal warfare between concepts in their individual minds (epistemology). In my vision of how things *can* be, we have the opposite situation: eternal warfare between concepts in the mind—resulting in more cooperation and less zero-sum warfare between people.[4]

Notes

1. Boethius questions: "What cause of discord breaks the ties which ought to bind this union of things? What God has set such conflict between these two truths? Separately each is certain, but put together they cannot be reconciled. Is there no discord between them? Can they exist side by side and be equally true?" (V, Met 3) For more on the background of binary thinking, see my version of this chapter in the *Journal of Advanced Composition.*

2. It had become more or less commonplace in rhetoric of the eighteenth and nineteenth centuries to say, "We can't really teach invention. It's too much of a mystery to describe where words and ideas come from. But we can teach about the other divisions of rhetoric." These latter were matters of product (for example, style and arrangement). But starting in the 1960s some people began to say, "Well let's *do* talk more about invention. We *can* say something about the experience of finding words and ideas and what it's like when we write." More recently, figures in composition (such as James Britton) have begun to be referred to as "expressive" or "expressionists." That term seems to me a problem and I sometimes wonder if the term is not hostilely motivated. For the prime originators and theorists who use the term (for example, James Berlin and Jeanette Harris) have tended to use it as a term of disapproval. None of the "expressionists" use the term "expressive" with any centrality except Britton—and one could never sum up his views or his work with the label "expressive." I rarely see the term used except by people who identify themselves as *not* expressive. I don't think I used the term until I began to reply to its hostile uses. Chris Burnham is one of the few scholars who has shown himself willing to take on the job of trying to analyze and defend expressive writing. See his "Expressive Rhetoric: A Source Study (1992)."

3. For the exploration of yet another productive binary opposition see my essay, "The Shifting Relationships between Speech and Writing (1985)."

4. Omitted here is a long final section on the relationship between rhetoric and dialect. I am very grateful to Charles Moran, John Trimbur, Robin Varnum, and Elizabeth Wallace for helpful responses and suggestions on this paper.

Works Cited

Abelard, Peter. 1976. *Sic et Non: A Critical Analysis Edition,* edited by Blanche B. Boyer and Richard McKeon. Chicago, IL: University of Chicago Press.

Boethius. 1926. *The Consolation of Philosophy,* edited by R. K. Root. Princeton, NJ: Princeton University Press.

Berlin, James. 1987. *Rhetoric and Reality: Writing Instruction in American Colleges, 1909–1985.* Carbondale, IL: Southern Illinois University Press.

———. 1982. "Contemporary Composition: The Major Pedagogical Theories." *College English* 44:765–77.

Burnham, Chris. 1992. "Expressive Rhetoric: A Source Study." *Perspectives on Twentieth Century Rhetoric: Essays Toward Defining the New Rhetorics*, edited by Theresa Enos and Stuart Brown. Los Angeles, CA: Sage.

Brent, Doug. 1991. "Young, Becker and Pike's 'Rogerian' Rhetoric: A Twenty-Year Reassessment." *College English* 53:452–66.

Burke, Kenneth. 1969. *A Rhetoric of Motives*. Berkeley: University of California Press.

Coleridge, Samuel Taylor. 1907. *Biographia Literaria*, edited by John Shawcross. 2 vols. Oxford: Oxford University Press.

Culler, Jonathan. 1989. "Paul deMan's Contribution to Literary Criticism and Theory. *The Future of Literary Theory*, edited by Ralph Cohen. 268–79. New York: Routledge.

Dewey, John. 1919. *Democracy in Education*. New York: Macmillan.

Elbow, Peter. Fall 1993a. "The War between Reading and Writing." *Rhetoric Review* 12.1:5–24.

———. 1993b. "The Uses of Binary Thinking." *Journal of Advanced Composition* 12(1):51–78.

———. 1986a. *Embracing Contraries: Explorations in Learning and Teaching*. Oxford University Press.

———. 1986b. "Methodological Doubting and Believing: Contraries in Inquiry." In *Embracing Contraries*. *See* Elbow 1986a. 254–300.

———. 1985. "Shifting Relationships Between Speech and Writing," *Conference on College Composition and Communication* 36:283–303.

———. 1983. "Embracing Contraries in the Teaching Process." *College English* 45. Also in *Embracing Contraries*. *See* Elbow 1986a.

———. 1981. *Writing With Power*. New York: Oxford University Press.

———. 1975. *Oppositions in Chaucer*. Wesleyan University Press.

———. 1973. *Writing Without Teachers*. New York: Oxford University Press.

Frey, Olivia. 1990. "Beyond Literary Darwinism: Women's Voices and Critical Discourse." *College English* 52:507–26.

Gibson, Walker, ed. 1962. *The Limits of Language*. New York: Hill and Wang.

Graff, Jerry. 1987. *Professing Literature: An Institutional History*. Chicago, IL: University of Chicago Press.

Harris, Jeanette. 1990. *Expressive Discourse*. Dallas, TX: Southern Methodist University Press.

Kuhn, Thomas. 1962. *The Structure of Scientific Revolutions*. Chicago, IL: University of Chicago Press.

LaCapra, Dominick. 1989. *Soundings in Critical Theory*. Ithaca, NY: Cornell University Press.

Lakoff, George and Mark Johnson. 1980. *Metaphors We Live By*. Chicago, IL: University of Chicago Press.

Lamb, Catherine. 1991. "Beyond Argument in Feminist Composition." *College Composition and Communication* 42:11–24.

Lawrence, D. H. 1985. "Morality and the Novel." *Study of Thomas Hardy and Other Essay*, edited by Bruce Steele. Cambridge, England: Cambridge University Press.

Ong, Walter. 1981. *Fighting for Life: Contest, Sexuality, and Consciousness.* Ithaca, NY: Cornell University Press.

Peckham, Morse. 1967. *Man's Rage for Chaos: Biology, Behavior and the Arts*. New York: Schocken.

Rosenthal, Robert and Lenore Jacobson. 1968. *Pygmalion in the Classroom.* New York: Holt Rinehart Winston.

Slevin, James. 1991. "Depoliticizing and Politicizing Rhetoric and Composition." *The Politics of Writing Instruction*, edited by Richard Bullock. 1–22. Portsmouth, NH: Heinemann.

Smith, Barbara Herrnstein. 1988. *Contingencies of Value: Alternative Perspectives for Critical Theory.* Cambridge, MA: Harvard University Press.

Teich, Nathaniel, ed. 1992. *Rogerian Perspectives: Collaborative Rhetoric for Oral and Written Communication*. Norwood, NJ: Ablex.

Trimbur, John. 1989. "Consensus and Difference in Collaborative Learning." *College English* 51:602–16.

12

Who's Afraid of Subjectivity? *The Composing Process and Postmodernism or A Student of Donald Murray Enters the Age of Postmodernism*

Robert P. Yagelski
Purdue University

Who—or what—is the "I" that is ostensibly writing this chapter?

Until recently, such a question was not especially troubling to teachers and scholars in the field we call rhetoric and composition. Our interest lay more clearly in *what* and *how* "I" was writing—the decisions and processes that seemed to define the writing—than in "who" was writing. But of late we have become more interested in how to understand and define the "who" inherent in this chapter. We have begun to see this "who" as constituted by a bewilderingly complex array of forces, largely beyond any semblance of his or her (or my) own control. We have become interested, that is, in redefining the "subject" or "self" that is ostensibly writing this chapter.

This problem of defining the self is an old one, "caught up," as Paul Smith points out, "in the set of philosophical terms and problems which are familiar from Descartes, Locke, Hume, Hegel, Heidegger, Sartre, and many others" (1988, xxvii). But the postmodern version of this old problem has presented a peculiar challenge to teachers and scholars in rhetoric and composition, for it raises difficult questions about the idea of writing as process, an idea that has become our orthodoxy. What is most troublesome about the postmodern critiques of the process orthodoxy is that they call into question the assumption that as I write this—and as my students write their essays—"I" and "they" have significant control over the processes by which this writing comes to be. In other words, these critiques question the very notion of the agency of the writer, a notion that lies at the center of the enterprise of teaching writing as process. That enterprise has depended on the assumption that a "subject" or "self" or "individual" engages in the process of writing in a way that determines the shape of the text that is ultimately produced. If the self or subject or individual does not exist as agent, the process approach to teaching writing would seem to be a sham.

In short, our postmodern notions about knowledge and subjectivity complicate the widely held conception of composing as a process and raise a difficult question for teachers of writing: Does "the composing process," steeped as it is in a view of writing as an individual, cognitive activity, adequately describe writing as it has come to be understood in recent years? Or to state it differently, how might we reconcile our conception of the composing process with our evolving understanding of writing as discourse, as a socially and culturally grounded activity?

The question is important in part because, as Charles Kostelnick has put it, "the process approach has emerged as the new composition 'paradigm'" (1989, 267). As postmodern critiques of the work of Donald Murray, Peter Elbow, and other "expressivists" proliferate, writing pedagogies in schools at all levels continue to be shaped by the idea that writing is a process and should be taught that way. And despite growing acceptance of postmodern notions of discourse and socially constructed knowledge, we still routinely speak of *planning*, *drafting*, and *revising*—terms that suggest individual agency—in our conversations about writing and teaching writing.

Such a state of affairs may simply underscore the complexities of an inherently interdisciplinary field that is in transition. But my hunch is that "process" remains viable because much of what it represents fits quite comfortably into a postmodern environment; that is, "process" pedagogies—as distinct from what James Berlin has called "expressionistic rhetoric" (a distinction I'll explore momentarily)—are not entirely incompatible with our emerging postmodern notions of knowledge and discourse. I'd like to explore the connections between process and postmodernism by sorting through some postmodern critiques of "expressivism." In doing so, I'll suggest that the key to reconciling process with postmodern thinking lies in reconceptualizing the self, an effort that can help us redefine the composing process and the way it is taught.

Process as Paradigm: The Postmodern Critique

My own development as a teacher of writing parallels to some extent the evolution of our disciplinary thinking about what it means to write and how best to teach writing. My story begins in 1983, in Durham, New Hampshire, when I walked into Don Murray's office as a brand-new teaching assistant in the M.A. program at the University of New Hampshire. Like so many new TA's at UNH, I was struck by Don Murray's openness and the generous way he gave good advice about writing. But I was more taken by what he said about writing. When, at that first TA orientation, Don began to talk about "the writing process," he was describing what *I* had been doing as a struggling professional writer. And when he and his colleagues criticized the way schools typically taught writing, they were describing *my* education. It wasn't any sort of epiphany for me to realize that I'd learned to write by writing for a living, not by writing essays in schools. But no one had ever pointed that out in quite the straightforward and convincing way that Don Murray did. And when I began to teach my own composition classes, I found that "process" as an approach to teaching, as a way to think about what writers do, worked.

And here I think is the key: the idea of composing as a process is a powerful way to understand what writers actually *do*. The beauty of "the composing process" is in the way it makes simple this complicated activity of writing. It allows us to talk about, study, and teach writing in ways that make the complexity of the act manageable.

And yet the powerful simplicity of the idea of composing as a process and its widespread acceptance as a way to understand and teach writing can obscure the fact that it is, after all, an *idea*, a framework for understanding writing, a set of assumptions about writing. It is often easy to overlook the fact that the composing process as a concept is a convention employed by teachers, scholars, and researchers to enable them to understand and discuss the complicated activity of writing. And it is with this *idea* that we run into trouble in these postmodern times.

Before surveying the various critiques of what we might call "process-oriented pedagogies" that have appeared in recent years, I should point out that there is no such thing as "*the* process approach," a phrase that inaccurately implies some sort of monolithic pedagogy or theory of teaching writing. As Don Murray has often pointed out, there is no such monolith. Moreover, it will be necessary for my purposes here to distinguish between "process" and "expressivism." Although the two terms are sometimes used synonymously, the latter term has come to refer to a theoretical perspective on writing, usually associated with Elbow and a few others, that, according to some critics, is founded on certain (problematic) epistemological assumptions. At the same time, expressivism is also associated with specific pedagogical strategies (for example, student-teacher conferences and peer editing groups), and here the distinction between "process" as a way of understanding writing and expressivism as a theoretical paradigm begins to blur. The problem is that "process" has at least three overlapping meanings. For many, "process" refers to the same student-centered pedagogical strategies usually associated with "expressivism".[1] "Process" is also used synonymously with "expressivism" to refer to a *theory* of writing and/or teaching.[2] And, third, "process" is used as a description of how writers write. This third definition is closest to my use of the term here: "process" refers to a way of describing and understanding what writers *do* when they write; "process-oriented" pedagogies grow out of that understanding. By contrast, I use "expressivism" to refer to a theoretical perspective on writing that focuses attention on the writer as meaning-maker and on writing as self-expression and self-discovery. As several critics have pointed out (see especially Faigley 1986), expressivists as well as those with other theoretical perspectives (cognitivists, social constructivists) see writing as *process*; the key differences between these perspectives lie in the way that process of writing is defined (for example, as self-discovery or as cognitive process).

With that in mind, consider briefly some of the criticisms leveled at "expressivist" approaches to teaching writing by three critics who share broad postmodern assumptions about language, discourse, and power. I choose these three critiques largely because they seem typical of the critiques of expressivism that have been appearing recently. Although each critic cited here approaches his or her task with a different agenda, all three see problems in the ways in which expressivist theories and pedagogies construct the student writer as a subject.

Perhaps the best-known critic of "expressivism" is James Berlin. Berlin critiques what he calls "expressionistic rhetoric," identified most closely with Don Murray and Peter Elbow, on the basis of what he sees as problematic ideological implications, arguing that "expressionistic rhetoric" locates "the existent with the individual subject" (1988, 484). Such a move, according to Berlin, obscures the fact that "each of us is heterogeneously made up of various competing discourses, conflicted and contradictory scripts, that make our consciousness anything but unified, coherent, and autonomous" (1992,

18). This exclusive focus on the individual in expressivist approaches to teaching cannot work: "It will not do to say [to our student writers], 'Be yourself,' since all of us possess multiple selves, not all of which are appropriate for the particular discourse situation" (1992, 19). For Berlin, this approach plays into the hands of the dominant ideology within our capitalist system in the way its rhetoric "can be used to reinforce the entrepreneurial virtues capitalism most values: individualism, private initiative . . ." and so on (1988, 487).

Like Berlin, John Clifford attacks process-oriented pedagogies for their apparent focus on individual writers and for their questionable assumptions about who those writers are. He asserts that "traditional and expressivist rhetorical theory . . . unproblematically assumes that the individual writer is free, beyond the contingencies of history and language, to be an authentic and unique consciousness" (1991, 39). Drawing on Althusser's famous essay, "Ideology and Ideological State Apparatuses," Clifford argues that "apparently trivial conventions and rituals of teaching composition . . . help to install us as subjects within society" (42). Here I take Clifford to be referring to classroom techniques, such as peer editing, that have become standard in many composition classrooms. The problem with these "traditional and expressivist" practices, according to Clifford, is that they construct a subject position for students that "denies identity, represses class conflict, negates the way ideas originate in specific social configurations" (44).

Susan Jarratt also criticizes "process approaches" for concealing conflicts within the classroom that reflect larger conflicts in society. She complains that in the "expressivist" pedagogies of Donald Murray and Peter Elbow, "the complexities of social differentiation and inequity in late-twentieth-century capitalist society are thrown into the shadows by the bright spotlight focused on the individual" (1991, 109). Jarratt asserts that the pedagogies of Murray and Elbow are structured around the "ideal of the harmonious, nurturing composition class" (113) and, echoing Clifford, she complains that the pedagogical practices associated with these approaches to teaching writing represent ways of "avoiding confrontations over social differences" (109). For Jarratt, students are constituted by their gender, race, and class affiliations, which often conflict with each other; to play down such conflict by focusing too narrowly on the individual is to deny the "uneven power relations resulting from these differences" among students (113).

What these critiques have in common is an implicit questioning of the assumption that writing is primarily an individual, cognitive activity; they problematize the notion of "individual" or "subject" as often conceived in expressivist discussions, and they share the view that writing is profoundly social. Interestingly, however, these critiques of expressivism have less to say about the composing process per se than about the political implications of particular "expressivist" approaches to teaching that process. These critiques, in fact, are critiques of epistemological stances associated with particular (popular) pedagogical strategies, of various versions of process as practice; they are not critiques of the *idea* that writing is a process. Berlin tacitly acknowledges this in a description of his version of a freshman classroom that is constructed around what he calls "social-epistemic rhetoric": "This effort locates *the composing process* within its social context . . ." (1992, 26; my emphasis).

My point here is that the idea of writing as process remains essentially intact even as postmodern critics attack so-called expressivist pedagogies and theories. I think there are several reasons for this. First, the notion of writing as process fits in well with evolving postmodern ideas about language and meaning. Berlin writes that "language is . . . a pluralistic and complex system of signifying practices that construct realities rather than simply presenting or re-presenting them" (1992, 19). To "construct realities" through the use of this complex system of "signifying practices" is an ongoing process of negotiation through language. Thus, to see writing as a recursive activity in which meaning is somehow made is to underscore the constructive and constructed nature of language and language use. In addition, the idea that writing is a process lends itself to countless adaptations in classrooms: freshman composition, business writing, technical writing, creative writing; indeed, to structure classrooms around process is also to help students come to understand the constructive, interested nature of language and language practices. But the most important reason is that the *idea* of writing as process, with its assumption that writing is always in progress, remains the most compelling and useful way to describe what writers actually seem to *do* when they create texts. Process provides a workable framework that enables me to describe adequately what I do when I write this chapter and what my students seem to be doing when they write theirs.

Nevertheless, recent postmodern critiques of "expressivist" pedagogies do raise troubling questions—questions that I think can often be overlooked by teachers who become excited by the possibilities that process-oriented pedagogies can offer students. Indeed, the apparently exclusive focus on the individual writer that critics like Berlin, Clifford, and Jarratt bemoan in their critiques of expressivist pedagogies is one of the attractions of those pedagogies for many classroom teachers who have become frustrated by the ways in which students' voices are squelched by traditional pedagogies. Like so many teachers, I can testify to the power of expressivist pedagogies in giving voice to students in school-based writing. I felt this power after I left UNH and took Don Murray's ideas about teaching writing into my own classroom in a small high school in Vermont. What Murray had taught me about teaching writing served me well in that classroom, for it seemed to empower my students in ways that they had not previously experienced. And I have my share of stories about students whose newfound voices seemed to validate my commitment to a process-oriented pedagogy. Perhaps the most telling story is that of Trevor, a remarkably bright young man who expended considerable energy devising ways to resist the educational system—and the individual teachers who represented the system. I remember the end of a difficult and trying year with Trevor, then a junior, when he suddenly seemed to catch fire in his writing and produced not only some of the angriest and most engaging indictments of schools I had yet seen from a student but also some well written and entertaining adventure stories. To me, Trevor had found his voice in writing. I have similar stories about the college freshmen I taught at large state universities and about the men I taught in a state prison in the midwest.

But over time my excitement about students like Trevor was tempered as I began to wonder what my version of process might imply about who my students were and how they used language to make meaning. Like Murray, I viewed my students as writers, each with his or her own ideas. My purpose was to help them explore those ideas and express them effectively in writing. Accordingly, I encouraged them to "discover" their ideas, to "know what they think by seeing what they say," to find meaning by looking within. At the same time, however, I was coming to see that writing might best be understood as something other than self-discovery. I can remember a discussion surrounding an essay I had shared with one senior class, an essay written by an angry first-year African American student in an open admissions community college. The essay was a powerful indictment of a racist educational system and its effect on this young man; it was also full of spelling and punctuation errors, unconventional phrases, and features of Black English Vernacular. I had thought the exercise would drive home to my students the arbitrariness of rules of grammar and the power of voice in writing. I hadn't expected the discussion to degenerate into biased criticisms of racial and ethnic groups by my mostly middle-class and upper middle-class white students. I hadn't expected my class to mirror the unsettling racial and class divisions that existed outside my classroom. Susan Jarratt might point out that my focus on individual voice tended to obscure the conflict that grew inevitably out of my students' class, race, and gender, and she would be right.

The experience led me to question assumptions that seemed to lie beneath my version of the writing process. As I came to see my teaching as inevitably ideological, I began to wonder how I might reconcile the apparent power of process as an approach to teaching writing with my sense of the inherently social and political nature of writing and the ideological nature of teaching writing. In his text *Write to Learn* (1987), Don Murray states, "We write alone to discover meaning" (3). He goes on to say that "once that meaning is discovered . . . then we want or need to share it with other people" (3). That statement seemed to describe how I had been writing for years, but my experience as a teacher and a great deal of research in the field convinced me that meaning did not reside within the individual, but rather, as Deborah Brandt (1990), Martin Nystrand (1989), and many others have pointed out, within the interactions between individuals. Writers, that is, did not really "discover" meaning within themselves so much as they constructed meaning through their transactions with others within complex social and cultural and political contexts.

Process and the Socially Constituted Self

How, then, might we conceive of the individual student writer within a realm of social and cultural discourse? Is it possible to retain in our teaching what is most useful about the idea of writing as a process at the same time that we account for the inherently social and political nature of writing? Obviously I think the answer to that question is yes. But the answer requires that we reconsider our notions about the "individual" writer—a project well under way in postmodern discussions of writing and discourse.

It is a curious postmodern paradox that we've come to value individual difference even as we now deny the validity of individuality as an idea. But even if, as Paul Smith writes, "the term 'individual' is ideologically designed to give the false impression that human beings are free and self-determining, or that they are constituted by undivided and controlling consciousnesses" (1988, xxxv)—I would argue that some conception of the individual is necessary if we want to understand how writers write and how to help students learn to write effectively in various contexts. As Tom Newkirk once said to me, "The 'self' might be a construct, but it's a useful construct." I agree. The problem is how to define the "self" in a way that enables us to talk about "individual" student writers at the same time that we highlight the profoundly social nature of writing.

One way to get at the answer, I think, is first to understand "self" *as* a construct. Such a move might seem painfully obvious, but American culture and its educational institutions are imbued with assumptions of individual agency and autonomy that are specious at best and downright destructive at worst. A quick look at our obsession with standardized testing and ability tracking in schools should confirm that schools tend to see students as individuals with varying kinds and degrees of abilities and disabilities that must be assessed and fostered or remediated. Furthermore, our methods of assessment grow out of a set of assumptions that hold that students' individuality can best be understood in terms of cognitive abilities that can be objectively measured. I'm afraid that adopting "process" pedagogies doesn't necessarily challenge such notions, in part because the apparent focus of such pedaogies on the individual, as Berlin suggests, allows these pedagogies to be co-opted by school systems in ways that perpetuate this narrow cognitive perspective on students and writing (1988, 487).

What's missing here is the idea that individuals are configurations of a dizzying array of social and cultural interconnections and relations. I am Polish, American, male, white, middle class, a former Catholic, a father, an educator, a high school and college graduate, a teacher, a native of the East, a resident of the Midwest, a former resident of New England, and so on, living at a particular historical moment. In other words, the "self" that defines "me" is a socially constituted self, and the social and cultural aspects of that self may have much more to do with how I write than some set of "cognitive" skills. As psychologists Scribner and Cole have concluded,

> Cognitive skills . . . are intimately bound up with the nature of the practices that require them. From this perspective, inquiries into the cognitive consequences of literacy are inquiries into the impact of socially organized practices in other domains (trade, agriculture) on practices involving writing (keeping lists of sales, exchanging goods by letter). (1981, 237)

By now this notion of socially defined cognition is nothing new,[3] but Scribner and Cole's conclusion suggests that understanding writing may have more to do with understanding its social uses than with understanding the "cognitive" abilities of individual writers.

A redefinition of the self as socially constituted as opposed to cognitive provides a useful way to reconceive writing as process. A conception of a socially constituted self at the center of the writing process allows for a profound sense of the social nature of writing at the same time that it retains process as a framework for teaching and for understanding how students write. It highlights the notion that, as Kathryn Flannery writes, individual "'needs' and 'desires' are not simply part of a cognitive, or, for that matter, individual domain, but are themselves manifestations of the dialectic between the individual and her social circumstances" (1991, 705). Berlin reinforces the need to conceive of the individual within an inevitable and unavoidable "network of intersecting discourses" (1992, 21). According to Berlin, to understand this is not

> to deny that all of us display a measure of singularity. As Paul Smith [1988] argues, the unique place of each of us in the network of intersecting discourses assures differences among us as well as possibilities for originality and political agency. This does not mean, however, that anyone can totally escape the discursive regimes, the power/knowledge formations of the historical moment. (1992, 21)

In other words, while we can—and should—in our teaching create space for the differences among our students and provide each of them with "possibilities for originality and political agency," we must do so in ways that highlight their connections to the broader discourses that help constitute them. I'm thinking here of my former student, Trevor, and of the ways in which his powerful voice was a result of the connections between him and the discourses of schools and social control that so deeply affected his life. "Finding his voice" was not a matter of some sort of self-exploration but rather a result of his emerging realization of his relation to the various discourses shaping his life and his engagement with them. His "voice" was enabled only within those contexts.

Don Murray underscored this social perspective on process in his keynote address at the 1992 UNH Conference on the Composing Process. In his talk, "But What Do Writers Do?", Murray shared with his listeners several drafts of a poem he had written about his experiences as a paratrooper in World War II. In discussing how the poem came to be, Murray showed how the reactions of his poetry group to his evolving drafts shaped his revisions; he described his complex interactions with Mekeel McBride, a poet and member of Murray's poetry group, regarding one stanza in the third draft of Murray's poem. Murray clearly showed that the version of this stanza that appeared in his subsequent drafts was a result of a form of collaboration between him and McBride. "How much of this stanza," he asked, "is mine? How much is Mekeel's?"

Murray's collaborations with McBride profoundly shaped his text, yet the text itself does not seem to reveal either the inherently social nature of the process by which it was created or, more to the point, the social forces that helped shape the various individual writers who collaborated on that text. But the social nature of the act of writing a poem goes beyond the kind of collaboration Murray engaged in with McBride and the other members of his poetry group. At one point, as he explained "his" reasons for changing the title of the poem-in-progress from "Peace in Time of War" to "My Battlefield Deferment," Murray said that he had felt compelled to write about war in part because he believes that veterans should testify to the horrors of war. Referring to the 1991 Gulf War, he said, "Desert Storm showed that we have a president [George Bush] who doesn't know what war is. I think veterans have to speak out about what war is really like." He added that his revised title "may have been inspired by the ridiculous debate about Bill Clinton's draft record," a reference to the public controversy during the 1992 presidential election surrounding Democratic candidate Bill Clinton's student deferment during the Vietnam War.

Murray's comments highlight the notion that he is writing within a broad social, cultural, historical, and political context—a context that inevitably shapes the creation of his poem. The very idea for his poem can be seen as a product of the dialectic between his personal experiences in World War II, which provide some of the images in the poem and which are in some sense his alone, and the contemporary political and cultural scene, a broad, shared context that provided the impetus to write the poem and helped shape the very content of the poem. Murray's reference to the political controversy about Bill Clinton's draft record not only explains the wording of the revised title, but it also reveals the way in which Murray's highly personal poem is inextricably bound up in the cultural and political context in which it is being written; moreover, Murray's comments also highlight the complicated ways in which what we might call his "self" is socially constituted. And, as Berlin might point out, the various discourses—political, personal, poetic—in which Murray participates constitute who he is and what he might say: "Only through language do we know and act upon the conditions of our experience" (Berlin 1991, 21).

Murray's discussion of his poem thus suggests that the writing and revising of his intensely personal poem is a decidedly social act, not only in that the contexts within which he writes inevitably shape his writing but also in that he himself is shaped by those contexts. His revising, an apparent result of the careful and idiosyncratic decisions he has made as a writer struggling to express personal ideas, is thus also a social act. But he *does* revise. That is, he, as a writer at his desk, engages in some set of literate activities that alter and shape the text he is developing. And of course he also plans and drafts, other sets of literate activities in which he engages as he completes his poem. *Planning*, *drafting*, and *revising* are useful terms to help us conceive of what Murray is doing as he writes the poem. Constructs that they are, they nevertheless enable us to identify, understand, and talk about what writers do. They help us account for, in Deborah

Brandt's words, how "literacy is actually accomplished by everyday readers and writers in everyday life" (1990, 34). And they do not invalidate the vital notion that what he does is a social act or that he is socially constituted or that the "truths" he reveals do not reside solely "within" him. In this sense, process as a way to think about writing is not at all incompatible with postmodern notions of subjectivity, knowledge, and discourse.

Writing as Social Process and the Writing Classroom

What this social perspective on process means for my classroom is subtle but, I think, profound. Students still focus on their own work in the course and their texts are still the primary texts. But unlike earlier versions of my writing classes, my present versions take *writing*—really, *discourse*—itself as a primary topic: not simply the process that we as individuals seem to go through as we write essays, but the very nature of writing as an activity and its connection to our social, political, and cultural selves. In other words, each student explores his or her own writing process within the broader framework of writing as a social activity—so that planning, drafting, and revising are not simply individual activities with idiosyncratic twists but individual manifestations of inherently social activities that underscore each writer's connection to the broader contexts within which he or she writes. The class thus becomes, to borrow John Clifford's description, an "interactive writing workshop imbued with a sense of the writing process as multifaceted, evolving, and exploratory" (1991, 47) as well as inherently social, political, and cultural.

As a practical matter, such a focus means that students do not simply write personal essays on any topics that might interest them; rather, the students write to explore their experiences within broader contexts. Like the course James Berlin (1992) describes, my course is thus structured around a common theme—usually education—which provides the subject matter that students explore through their individual and collective experiences. In addition, we write to participate in the discourse of our class as well as in the broader discourses surrounding educational reform in American society. In writing about educational issues of concern to them, the students not only examine their own writing processes, but they also examine the forms and conventions of various kinds of discourses about education—academic, popular, governmental—in order to become more aware of the connections between those forms and broader social, political, and cultural forces. In addition, students are urged to see themselves as part of what Berlin calls the "network of intersecting discourses."

Like Susan Jarratt, I want my writing courses to become places where I help students "to locate their personal experience in historical and social contexts—courses that lead students to see how differences emerging from their texts and discussions have more to do with those contexts than they do an essential and unarguable individuality" (1991, 121). At the same time, understanding their writing as process enables me to understand what they, as individual students, do as they participate in these broader discourses. I thus construct a writing pedagogy that accounts for and intersects with the individual and idiosyncratic *processes* in which my students engage as *writers* at the same time that it grows out of postmodern conceptions of subjectivity that define those students as socially constituted *authors* participating in situated discourses.[4]

It occurs to me as I conclude this essay that my classroom looks and sounds very much as it always has: students scattered about the room engaged in a lot of open-ended discussion, a lot of collaboration, a lot of one-to-one conferences, and a lot of writing and reading. It also occurs to me that this is the look and sound of the classrooms of so many of my colleagues. No surprise, since much of what we have come to associate with "process" remains familiar and central to our teaching. I'd argue that that's because the idea of writing as process not only continues to be perhaps the most effective means by which to describe how writers write, but it also remains a valid way to understand what writers do even as postmodern notions of language and discourse challenge the way we understand writing itself.

Notes

1. For one useful example, see Deborah Brandt's definition of what she calls the "process-centered workshop" (1990, 121).

2. Of course part of the problem here is defining "expressivism." Susan Jarratt (1991) seems to use it to refer to a set of pedagogical stategies founded on certain assumptions about writing and writers. James Berlin uses the term "expressionistic" to refer to what he calls a "rhetoric," or coherent theory of writing. Some critics use the term quite broadly; Stephen Fishman and Lucille McCarthy, for instance, have defined expressivism as "the view that creating text involves exploring personal experience and voice" (1992, 647).

3. Linda Flower (1989) has recently argued for understanding cognition in terms of social context. Glynda Hull and Mike Rose (1989) have attempted to explore the connections between cognition and social and cultural factors. See Barbara Rogoff (1990) for a useful "constructivist" perspective on cognition.

4. See Sharon Crowley's (1985) essay, "writing and Writing," for a discussion of the distinction between *author* and *writer*. My thanks to James Porter

(1994) for helping me clarify these terms as well as the distinction (and overlap) between "pedagogy" and "process." Porter's bibliographic essay is a good source for those interested in understanding postmodern conceptions of the author.

Works Cited

Berlin, James A. 1992. "Poststructuralism, Cultural Studies, and the Composition Classroom: Postmodern Theory in Practice." *Rhetoric Review* 11 (Fall):16–33.

———. 1988. "Rhetoric and Ideology in the Writing Class." *College English* 50 (September):477–94.

Brandt, Deborah. 1990. *Literacy as Involvement: The Acts of Writers, Readers, and Texts.* Carbondale, IL: Southern Illinois University Press.

———. 1986. "Toward an Understanding of Context in Composition." *Written Communication* 3 (April):139–57.

Clifford, John. 1991. "The Subject in Discourse." *Contending With Words*, edited by Patricia Harking and John Schilb. 38–51. New York: MLA.

Crowley, Sharon. 1985. "writing and Writing." *Writing and Reading Differently: Deconstruction and the Teaching of Composition and Literature*, edited by G. Douglas Atkins and Michael L. Johnson. 93–100. Lawrence, KS: University Press of Kansas.

Faigley, Lester. 1986. "Competing Theories of Process: A Critique and a Proposal" *College English* 48 (October):527–42.

Fishman, Stephen, and Lucille P. McCarthy. 1992. "Is Expressivism Dead? Reconsidering its Romantic Roots and its Relation to Social Constructionism." *College English* 54 (October):647–61.

Flannery, Kathryn T. 1991. "Composing and the Question of Agency." *College English* 53 (October):701–13.

Flower, Linda. 1989. "Cognition, Context, and Theory Building." *CCC* 40 (October):282–311.

Hull, Glynda, and Mike Rose. 1989. "Rethinking Remediation: Toward a Social-Cognitive Understanding of Problematic Reading and Writing." *Written Communication* 6 (April):139–54.

Jarratt, Susan C. 1991. "Feminism and Composition: The Case for Conflict." *Contending With Words*, edited by Patricia Harking and John Schilb. 105–23. New York: MLA.

Kostelnick, Charles. 1989. "Process Paradigms in Design and Composition: Affinities and Directions." *College Composition and Communication* 40 (October): 267–81.

Murray, Donald M. 1992. "But What Do Writers Do?" UNH Conference on the Composing Process: Retrospect and Prospect. October 9.

———. 1987. *Write To Learn*, 2nd ed. New York: Holt Rinehart.

Nystrand, Martin. 1989. "A Social-Interactive Model of Writing." *Written Communication* 6 (January):66–85.

Porter, James E. 1994. "Selected Bibliography: The Concept of 'Author' in Rhetoric/Composition and Literary Theory." *Rhetoric Society Quarterly*.

Rogoff, Barbara. 1990. *Apprenticeship in Thinking: Cognitive Development in Social Context*. New York: Oxford University Press.

Scribner, Sylvia, and Michael Cole. 1981. *The Psychology of Literacy*. Cambridge, MA: Harvard University Press.

Smith, Paul. 1988. *Discerning the Subject*. Minneapolis, MN: University of Minnesota Press.

13

On the Critical Necessity of "Essaying"

Thomas E. Recchio
The University of Connecticut

> Luck and play are essential to the essay. It does not begin with Adam and Eve but with what it wants to discuss; it says what is at issue and stops where it feels itself complete—not where nothing is left to say. Therefore it is classed among the oddities. T. W. Adorno, "The Essay as Form"

Starting this chapter has been more difficult than any writing I have done for years, probably because I am writing about something that will not stand still. My subject is the essay, but I am not concerned with the essay as product, as a configuration of words with particular formal features, stylistic characteristics, and rhetorical topoi. I am not concerned with the essay as a method of writing, the appropriate means through which one may render experience. Rather, I would like to discuss the essay as a writing practice whose fundamental ground is a critical orientation toward the object of inquiry and towards the subject, that is, the self. As Graham Good argues in *The Observing Self*, "The essay is an act of personal witness. The essay is at once the *in*scription of a self and the *de*scription of an object" (1988, 23). In other words, in essaying, the writer and the object of inquiry (an experience, an institution, a text, a disciplinary practice, or even one's self as that self is rendered in language) define and transform themselves reciprocally, aspects of each becoming understood in relation to the other (Good 1988, 8). My object of inquiry is the place of the essay in the teaching of writing; in writing this I hope to work toward a reconciliation between my professional commitments and personal values and between the conventions of academic writing and my desire to be heard as an individual. In exploring the relation between myself and our profession, I will be critical of both, my purpose less to draw a conclusion than to claim with Montaigne the privilege to "speak as one who questions and does not know . . . not [to] teach [but to] relate" (cited in Good 1988, 5).

I.

It is mid-winter in 1971. A twenty-year-old Marine sits in a windowless room on an American air force base on the northern tip of the main island of Japan. The Marine's F-4 Phantom jet squadron has been assigned to fly air cover for Navy spy ships off the Korean coast. The planes are launched infrequently, so the Marine's main job is to wait. He and his fellow Marines (all enlisted men with high school educations at best) spend most of their time playing pool, drinking beer, and smoking grass; service to country seems analogous to his capacity to tolerate high levels of alcohol and extended periods of boredom. Upon his enlistment he had been given a National Defense Service Medal, the Vietnam conflict still being "operative" (to borrow a Watergate word). Two and a half years later, he will feel that a Certificate of Merit from the Anhauser-Busch Brewing Company would have been more appropriate. Today he waits, somewhat queasy, fighting sleep.

In a moment of idle thoughtlessness, he reaches down and picks up a book from the end table next to his chair. The book is *The Brothers Karamazov* by Fyodor Dostoevsky. He recognizes the author's name as Russian, probably a commie, he thinks. He remembers having read histories and biographies voraciously when in high school, anything but the books assigned for class. He is out of the habit of reading, but he is also bored and out of beer. He opens the book and reads. He finds moments of hate-filled love between fathers and sons, spiritual desire mired in earthly passion, the "Grand Inquisitor" speaking for the military-industrial complex. The inarticulate stirrings of his intellectual and imaginative desires reawaken under the shaping pressure from the words on the page. The book seems to be reading his mind, to be, in fact, giving him a mind to read. He knows instinctively that his life will never be the same.

Over the next year, he reads nineteenth-century Russian literature with a passion; he is much taken with Dostoevsky's *Notes from Underground*, inwardly affirming the "underground" man's defiant "twice two makes five." He culls authors' names (from Gogol to Goncharov) and novel titles (from *Dead Souls* to *Oblamov*) from the introductions to every novel he reads. He begins to write too, first poetry (mawkishly philosophical stuff about village idiots, despite having never read Wordsworth) and later the beginning of a novel (embarrassingly autobiographical). After his return to the States and his release from the military, he spends his next ten years in college and graduate school, from North Carolina to California to New Jersey, his goal to understand what he later learns to call his epiphany. He stops writing "creatively" and starts writing "critically." He begins to understand his life as a kind of essay, a continual restless effort to compose a self in relation to his experience of the world and of language. Subsequently, he thinks of this effort in self-composition as an open-ended process, aspects of which are describable in retrospect but which do not culminate in a final product. He feels fortunate, even blessed, to have found a kind of work that seems to offer possibilities for wholeness, where his personal and professional lives can become one. He recalls the alienation of his military experience when wholeness was an illusion conceivable only through numbing both body and mind. He remembers his working-class father who always seemed either tired or drunk, emotionally distant because of his inarticulateness. He feels saved by words, by stories, by writing. He looks forward to future epiphanies.

It is mid-winter in 1991. A fortyish professor of English Literature and teacher of writing is standing behind a podium under the irritating florescent lights of a run-down classroom. Wires dangle from the wall where a clock had once been. The professor holds a cheap paperback copy of Mary Shelley's *Frankenstein* in his hands. He talks about creation myths; he mentions feminist discussions of how Mary Shelley's anxieties about being a mother colored the language she used in describing the creation of the monster. He mentions William Godwin, the notion of *tabula rasa*, and John Locke's theories of education. He offers, he thinks enticingly, fragments of Shelley's biography: the circumstances of her marriage, the birth of her children, the early death of her husband. He quotes Percy Shelley's "Alastor" and parallel passages from *Frankenstein*, and suggests that Percy's wife Mary may have been trying to re-write "Alastor" to correct her husband's naive faith in the radically creative powers of language and the renovating powers of the imagination. He describes the story-writing contest among Byron, the Shelleys, and a man whose name escapes him, which was the catalyst for the writing of *Frankenstein*. He tries to be witty, interesting, engaging. His students, many feeling queasy from the previous night's parties, are fighting sleep. They are more than tired; they are bored, waiting for class to end. They have better things to do.

When the class ends, the students rush from the room, one leaving his copy of *Frankenstein* on the floor next to his chair. The professor stuffs his notes and his book into his bookbag and walks briskly to his office, not bothering to bend down to retrieve the student's book. He sits at his desk, glances at the book-covered walls of his office, packs his pipe, and tries not to think. He thinks anyway. He's been trained to. His thoughts carry him to the past. He recalls his youthful intoxication with texts. He remembers midnight discussions in graduate school when he and his fellow students would sip wine, talk philosophy, and read Walt Whitman, T. S. Eliot, A. A. Milne. ("I contain multitudes." "I have shored these fragments against my ruins." "Half way down the stairs is the stair where I sit. There isn't another quite like it.") He remembers wanting to share the excitement of such talk, its poetic quality, its surprising juxtapositions of images, writers, and ideas. He recalls how hard he worked to grow as a teacher, to have a system of reading, to develop a coherent line of thought for every book and every poem he taught, to design writing assignments with clear, formal guidelines in order to help his students write with precision and power. He remembers his desire to become expert, as reader and writer, to be worthy of his profession. He thinks he has achieved that; he knows his stuff. He feels worthy. But his students are beginning to make him feel the opposite. He is tempted, as he has heard so many of his colleagues do, to blame his students, to construct them as intellectually incorrigible, to consign them to the damned of the unlettered. His imagination is teased with apocalyptic visions, the decline of education, the decline of the West, the death of literate culture. He pushes those visions aside and resolves to do better. He wishes he knew how.

II.

One way to construe those two scenes (other than as epiphany and anti-epiphany) is to see them as marking central moments in my progress from novice to expert, from one who wants to know to one who thinks he knows (which is, in a sense, true), but I cannot avoid recognizing in that "progress" an obvious sense of diminishment and loss, a version of the literary trope of the movement from innocence to experience. More specifically, that loss could be understood as the result of a change from personal commitment to professional performance, from exploration to consolidation. In the first scene, reading and writing provided an intellectual site where I could work on the human task of becoming, of forming and reforming a self; in the second scene, reading and writing provided a means of confirming what I thought I had become. While it is true that performance and consolidation do not necessarily involve a diminishment of commitment or serve as roadblocks to one's becoming, I felt stalled. Perhaps the loss is related to a change in my attitude toward language; that is, I was losing a sense of the eventfulness of language, beginning to treat language as a kind of information. The loss signals a change from openness to closure, from a process to a product orientation toward language—toward learning, toward life.

Such a loss seems at times inevitable given the pressures toward specialization in the university and the fragmentation of personal and professional life. In that context, it would not be much of an exaggeration to say that my task of becoming has been turned into a ritual; in playing the role of teacher, of professor, I simply perform an institutional function. The dissatisfaction evident in the second scene is both a sign of alienation from my work and a stimulus for change. But what form might that change take? How might it be conceptualized? In what medium might it begin to be realized? How possible is it to bridge the gap between the personal and professional, to begin to affirm one's humanness through one's work with others?

Reconsidering the essay as a critical orientation towards self and other can provide a starting point for exploring those questions. Consider the following, for example.

> In German scholarship the essay is linked constantly to *Wissenshaft,* that is, "science," in the root meaning of "knowledge." It is the meeting ground between "pure literature" and "pure science," the mediator between "poetry" and "science." It is the means of overcoming the isolation of specialists, of bridging the gap between science and the rest of society, between natural sciences and humanities. It can provoke a synthesis of science and art at a "common third level," and on that level can seek to restore the "lost unity" of culture; to recapture a world-view *(Weltbild);* and to counteract the fragmentation of culture, the proliferation of isolated disciplines of learning—in a word, the disintegration of the mind. At this level it goes well beyond criticism in the ordinary narrow sense to become the criticism of life *(Lebenskritik).* (Chadbourne 1983, 142)

Note the key terms in that passage—*mediator, overcoming isolation, bridging the gap, synthesis, counteract fragmentation, Lebenskritik*—which, taken as a whole, suggest a working definition of the essay and, following Bruno Berger, what we might call the "essayistic spirit" (Chadbourne 1983, 142). Reflecting a critical orientation toward self and other, the essay, as both attitude and writing practice, is Janus-faced; it looks inward and outward simultaneously, implicitly and/or explicitly registering the relationship between the person writing and the object and the context of the writing. The "essayistic spirit" is self-conscious, aware always of the provisional nature of any discourse and the situatedness of any writer. On this latter point, Max Bense observes that "whoever criticizes must necessarily experiment; he must create conditions under which an object is newly seen" (cited in Adorno 1984, 166). And those conditions, despite the pre-determined "intentions" of various discourses (Bartholomae 1985), are already implicit in the particular situation of the writer.

In creating such conditions through a recognition of one's personal situation, writers are not isolated from their objects; they establish a connection, albeit arbitrarily. Instead of masking arbitrariness through a putatively objective formal discourse, however, the essay takes "arbitrariness reflectively into its own procedure" (Adorno 1984, 166). The essay, then, provides a means through which our personal sense of and commitment to our professional lives can find expression in a public space; our texts can begin more openly to reflect our sense of self at the time of writing. Somewhat akin to Bakhtin's notion of the novel as an open form that offers a "distinctive social dialogue among languages" (1981, 263) rather than a genre as such, the essayistic spirit can shape writers' fundamental sense of their task whether or not the completed piece of writing is overtly reflexive.

III.

Change for me as a teacher of writing is beginning to find a conceptual center in the idea of the essay as a writing practice where self formation and cultural formation proceed together in a dialogical relation, with self dependent on culture for its potential forms and culture dependent on many selves for its composition. The idea of the essay hints at the possibility of realizing the potential interanimation of life and language, of one's person and one's work, as each informs the other in continually shifting configurations, a vague sense of which I have in retrospect constructed, somewhat naively and nostalgically, from my Marine experience. Realizing the potential of the essay in the Freshman English classroom, however, is a thorny problem, for writing pedagogy has been dominated by formalized, self-contained systematic thought where play, discovery, and recursiveness are squeezed out of discourse, and subordinated to a misleading, formalist consistency and clarity. This essay has survived in name only, its pleasures and dangers avoided, its spirit nearly dead. The pedagogy of rhetorical modes and of thesis-then-demonstration-argument still dominate the teaching of writing. Such a formalist pedagogy is hard to resist because it appeals to our desires for clarity and the minimization of risk. Nonetheless, I will add my voice to some others in order to suggest that writing instruction can be infused with the essayistic spirit.

Recently, I reviewed twenty years of *College English* issues to see how the "essay" has been addressed in the professional literature. Two articles in particular, Keith Fort's "Form, Authority, and the Critical Essay" (1971) and William Zeiger's "The Exploratory Essay: Enfranchising the Spirit of Inquiry in College Composition" (1985) discuss the essay in terms similar to my own. Fort concerns himself with what he calls the "prescribed structure" of critical essays on literature. "In the essay," he argues, "it would seem that [the] key rule is that there be a thesis which the essay proves" (1971, 631). He characterizes that key rule as the "[f]ormal tyranny of essay writing," a tyranny that "is based on the need of those who are in control to make the appearance of the expression confirm a desired idea of which there is *no doubt*" (1971, 631, my italics). Skepticism, uncertainty, openness to possibility have no place in such a form.

Zeiger echoes Fort on the tyranny of form in his discussion of the notion of "proof" in the expository essay. To *prove*, in the expository writing taught in Freshman English, he argues, is to demonstrate "a truth or [establish] the validity of a proposition," whereas for Montaigne (and other Renaissance writers) it is "to examine [an idea] in order to *find out* how true it [is]" (1985, 455). The former is the art of "demonstration," the latter the art of "inquiry" (1985, 456). Zeiger closes his article with the following: "Teaching the exploratory essay would contribute to the larger effort of revitalizing the humanities by restoring the spirit of inquiry to a place of currency and honor, and by educating people to communicate freely with one another" (1985, 464). While I share a concern about the potential continued tyranny of a rigid formalist pedagogy, and while I would dearly love to help to restore "the spirit of inquiry" throughout the university curriculum and, by extension, professional and social life, I am not convinced that the problem can be addressed by teaching the "exploratory essay." By bracketing the notion of exploration in a separate form, inquiry is ghettoized, the rigidity of other forms remains unchallenged and unchangeable, and the processes through which writing in any form is done get short-changed. As the boundaries between and among academic discourses continue to blur (Geertz [1983] and Elbow [1990]), it seems more useful to consider the points of contact between the person writing and the available and changeable discourses within the writer and at the writer's disposal.

In other words, there is no neutral language available for purely personal expressive purposes, nor does any person writing merely deploy and transcribe an absolutely pre-configured language. As David Bartholomae puts it, in part, "I would not say . . . that the person is erased in professional discourse. The person writing can be found in the work, the labor, the deployment and deflection (willed or otherwise) of the languages and habits of academic writing. The person . . . can be found in the figuring, not in the figure" (1985, 130). I would add, however, that the figuring can change the figure, though it does not always. Discourses, academic or otherwise, do not remain constant; figures (that is, conventions of discourse) change over time through an accumulation of nuance and inflection. People write. Boundaries blur. We shape language even as language shapes us.

At this point, I would like to evoke the work of Mikhail Bakhtin, not simply because his work helps to explain the relation between stability and change in the life of language, but also because his work has been emerging as a significant link between my past and my present personal and professional life.

I first encountered Bakhtin's work in 1974 in a shabby used book store called Olde York Books in New Brunswick, New Jersey. Books were piled everywhere in no particular order; the smell of canned spaghetti cooking on a hot plate and the sight of ratty rattan chairs with ripped, overstuffed seat cushions randomly placed throughout the shop gave the place an aura of literary naturalism. George Gissing would have been at home there (I think now). My reading of Dostoevsky was still fresh, so when I saw the title *Problems of Dostoevsky's Poetics* I couldn't resist. Though confused by the title (Dostoevsky hadn't written poetry, had he?), I bought the book (the 1973 Rotsel translation published by Ardis). When I tried to read it, however, I was stumped. Sentences that now speak to me with clarity seemed nonsensical. "The new artisitc position of the author vis-a-vis the hero in Dostoevsky's polyphonic novel is a *consequent* and *fully realized dialogical position* which confirms the hero's independence, inner freedom, unfinalizedness and indeterminacy" (Bakhtin 1973, 51). While I understood "independence" and "inner freedom," I did not know enough about Bakhtin's (or anyone's) theory of language to get a grasp on the nuance of those common terms, much less on the whole meaning of the passage. I felt, nonetheless, that somehow reading and writing must be essential in one's struggle to attain independence and inner freedom, and I now see that the struggle has something to do with one's individual effort to construct a voice for one's self, even if that effort can never be absolutely successful. For in language there is space for individual effort in a medium that by its nature depends on many individuals for its existence.

In "Discourse in the Novel" (1981) Bakhtin discusses this tension between the idea of a common language and the reality that individuals speak both as representatives of groups and as unique, unduplicatable beings. Bakhtin uses the term heteroglossia to define "languages that are socio-ideological: languages of social groups, 'professional' and 'generic' languages, languages of generations and so forth" (1981, 272), in short, the full range of particular jargons that distinguish one social group, profession, or whatever from another. He goes on to claim that a common language "makes its real presence felt as a force for overcoming this heteroglossia, imposing specific limits to it, guaranteeing a certain maximum of mutual understanding and crystallizing into a real, although still relative unity—the unity of the reigning conversational (everyday) and literary language, 'correct language'" (1981, 272).

Since social groups are composed of individuals, the nuanced language conditioned by personal experience injects another level of heteroglossia within social and professional languages. Language, in this view, always mediates between the life-world of the individual and the large and small unifying pressures of public and professional life. Although Bakhtin tends to value heteroglossia over a common language (for personal and historical reasons related to Soviet life in the first three-quarters of the twentieth century), he claims that every utterance reflects both. But rather than dichotomizing those forces, Bakhtin argues that they constitute another kind of unity. "It is possible," he argues, "to give a concrete and detailed analysis of any utterance, once having exposed it as a contradiction-ridden, tension-filled unity of two embattled tendencies in the life of language" (1981, 272). Such a unity has little to do with conformity to conventions even as it does not reject conventions. It is a "tension-filled" unity, played out in the consciousness of particular speakers and writers, an effort to reconcile contradictions that result not from some failure of internal coherence within a discourse (or from within a life) but from the very conditions of language in a fragmented, heteroglot world.

Bakhtin's theory of language outlines a context where the essayistic spirit can thrive, where almost every written utterance can contribute to the inscription of some aspect of the self through the disclosure of something "other" in a discourse. If we imagine the heterogeneous nature of contemporary culture manifested within individuals in addition to being diffused among various social and professional groups, we can understand the failure of formalist writing pedagogy as a failure to impose a unitary linguistic practice onto multilinguistic (heteroglossic) consciousness. That is, the boundaries between and among the multidisciplinary and nondisciplinary verbal worlds we inhabit continually shift and blend in the mind; to use a key term from Bakhtin, the languages we experience and use in the world continually "interanimate" each other. Despite the compartmentalization of contemporary life, the various discourses at play in our consciousness tend to fuse together as we inevitably essay to construct a provisional coherence in the face of fragmented experience. Written products, then, carry traces of the linguistic, cultural, institutional, and personal contexts that surround and partially determine their composition. No writing is *sui generis*. It is deeply embedded in the history of language and of discursive practices. Writing products thus carry traces of personal and impersonal (or transpersonal) intentions, that is, the desires of the writer and the constraints of a discourse and/or discourses.

I would like to "read" the following passage, written by a student in freshman English, in order to locate some of those traces and to speculate about what they might reveal about the interplay of the language of the student's social world and classroom discourse. The assignment asked for an interpretation of Clifford Geertz's "Deep Play: Notes on the Balinese Cockfight" in the context of Stanley Fish's argument about "interpretive communities" in "How to Recognize a Poem When You See One."

> Last week, while this assignment was plaguing my mind, I was listening to a particularly loud and obnoxious song whose lyrics reminded me of my own personal image of Stanley Fish. The lyrics to this song, "Eye of the Beholder" by Metallica, are strikingly similar to what I felt inside about Stanley Fish, but I just could not place those feelings into words. The song that helped me put this image to paper reads as follows: "Doesn't matter what you see, or into what you read, you can do it your own way, if it's done just how I say. Independence limited, freedom of choice is made for you my friend, freedom of speech is words that they will bend, freedom with their exception."
>
> Who says heavy metal songs are useless conglomerations of satanic, destructive, and immoral lyrics? I do not want to appear to be digressing from the assignment by talking about my personal interests in music. The point I want to make is that the lyrics to this song helped me focus my perception on the ideas being discussed in the assignment. Similar to what the song says, Stanley Fish makes his students see what he wants them to see. To Fish, texts and objects do not exist. Rather the interpreter creates objects. It is here that Stanley Fish is wrong in his assumptions on interpretation and Clifford Geertz is wrong in his methods of interpretation of the Balinese.

The two most striking features of that passage are intelligence and anxiety: intelligence in the student's suspicious interpretation of Fish's argument and anxiety about the source of the student's insight, the heavy metal band Metallica. The writing reflects an uneasiness in its crossing of the boundaries separating the student's social language from classroom language. The language of rock music, defined by Michael Moffat as an emergent medium of "a common, classless, internationally defined youth culture," that "unmistakenly state[s] their antielitist sentiments" (1989, 50–51), and the language of the classroom reflect, though uneasily, a characteristically essayistic engagement, connecting the personal and the cultural in enacting their points of contact in the individual consciousness. What I call the personal here, however, is also, as suggested by Moffat's observation, cultural. Thus the passage reveals a clash of cultures, which the writer struggles to mediate. In this light, we might say that the personal is less a pure, contextless subject position, some domesticated version of Emerson's transparent eyeball, and more a multi-cultural construct, the configuration of which is unpredictable and subject to change. We can see traces in the passage of the student's effort to construct an authoritative position for himself, based on his "local knowledge," even as he simultaneously resists a discourse (the discourse of interpretive communities) that would give him a prefabricated authoritative position.

The authority in the passage, and essayistic authority more generally, is paradoxical. The apologetic moments ("I don't want to appear to be digressing . . . The point I want to make is that . . .") imply a distrust of personal authority, just as the judgment offered on Fish ("It is here that Stanley Fish is wrong") asserts a distrust of academic authority. This double distrust, a version of what Paul Ricoeur has called "hermeneutical suspicion," marks the writing as essayistic. The passage, in being critical of self and other, achieves the authority of a mind at work.

The sense of the essay that I am trying to approximate suggests that "essaying" is, at least implicitly, a subversive activity, for in its tentative and suspicious inscription of the self through an encounter with an object, the essay simultaneously stabilizes and destabilizes both. That subversive quality, I think, tends to give teachers of writing pause. By emphasizing the centrality of a critical orientation toward self and the texts of the academy, we fear that we may misrepresent the writing that students will have to do in other courses. They simply will not *need* to be critical in the introductory courses in the various disciplines, and it is questionable whether they will *need* to be critical, in the essayistic sense, in their major courses. To borrow Richard Rorty's terms, by encouraging an essayistic spirit in all student writing we may prematurely encourage students to produce an "abnormal discourse" when, in fact, they will be asked to write in the "normal discourse" of the academic disciplines (cited in Bruffee 1984, 647). To tilt the emphasis slightly: is it not necessary to know a discipline from the inside, to master its conventions in order to learn its possibilities and limitations, before earning the authority to be critical of it and of one's place in it?

I felt the force of that question recently in a discussion with a student who had asked me to read a paper she was writing for an education school graduate course. When I pointed out the lack of a critical dimension in the paper, she explained that her professor had told her that since she had not generated the statistics in the study she was responding to (or replicated the study to gather her own statistics), she had no grounds to be critical. Her task was simply to report. Of course, one can never simply report, for in reporting one has to select, and in selecting one judges relative value; one interprets. But I suspect her professor meant that in reporting, students have to mask the interpretive component of their work through a putatively objective language. Even though the student had studied statistics and knew how to interpret them, she was not permitted to exploit the knowledge she brought to her task. She had to hide what she knew and suppress her interpretive authority. Not surprisingly, the student was frustrated; she felt demeaned. From such a professor's point of view, to teach the essay in the terms of this chapter is to ask students to do too much too soon. But to begin with the simple is merely to put off an encounter with the complex, and as Adorno puts it, "Such a postponement of knowledge only prevents knowledge" (1984, 162). If the fundamental goal of freshman writing courses is to empower students as critical thinkers through writing, critical about their objects of study and about themselves, we need to invite them not just to look but to think, not simply to perceive but to probe, not to accept but to question, all qualities of the essay as a record of the mind at work.

There are a couple of questionable assumptions implicit in the idea of a necessary deferral of criticism until a student has fully entered a discourse. One is that knowledge is something that one acquires (rather than makes) in an orderly, linear way, beginning with the simple and building up to the complex—as if in learning how to write we begin with individual sounds linked to letters, build to words, to phrases, to clauses, to sentences, to paragraphs, to papers. The other is that criticism can only be generated from within a discipline, by those who have mastered disciplinary practices and who accept the values of those practices—as if, for example, in criticizing the Catholic church we should look to priests to lead the way. If we grant that such assumptions underlie the idea of a normal discourse, the implications for what constitutes education are disturbing, for education would have to be in the service of the *status quo*, suffused with complacency. Its main task would be socialization in the most limited and narrow sense: socialization as uncritical conformity.

Of course, one could object that the very fact that I am writing this belies my point. Aren't I criticizing from the inside? Hasn't the institution given me a place from which to write, the authority to write, even, on some level, the words to write? And as a necessary consequence, haven't I already been co-opted? I feel the force of those objections, but to credit them as definitive would be to lapse into silence, and it would grant the institution a power that I don't think it has. While my language is both enabled and constrained by my insitutional context, the institution does not totally determine what I write. As my discussion of Bakhtin's theory of language reveals, there are other, pre and post-institutional languages at play in my consciousness, social languages from my experience and the languages of the students I have worked with. Thus, pressures for institutional change have complex sources that converge at points of intersection between institutional and non-institutional life. The precise contours of change are open, the future always an unanswered question.

If there is even a degree of truth in what I have claimed in my criticism of a necessary deferral of knowledge (and I grant that I have overstated the case, but not by much), it is imperative, I think, that the essay, understood as a critical orientation toward the object and the self, have a central place in writing instruction and in the university curriculum as a whole. Essayistic writing—writing as inquiry, writing as a way to understand—requires, as Adorno has it, that we begin "with the most complex . . . which is in every case the habitual" (1984, 162). The habitual, our habits of thought and the matter-of-course presentation of texts/objects of study, should themselves be the first objects of critique. In essaying to understand an object, a text, a discourse, we need to examine ourselves in relation to the object, to bring out in the open our assumptions about the object. Only after we have worked out what aspects of the object our assumptions and intentions toward it enable us to see can we begin to uncover our blind spots, to see more, to see differently, to come to a new understanding in establishing a new relation to the object.

This critical orientation, this essayistic spirit, enables a writer to work self-consciously within the margins of difference between subject and object, and, in confronting that difference, to change the relation between the two. Through the essay, subject and object interanimate each other dialogically; they do not exist in stasis. The knowledge that comes through essaying unfolds; knowledge is not simply there, a given. The essay, in its very contingency, in its sensitivity to its specific contexts, and in its resistance to prescribed forms, is the most powerful means through which writers can negotiate an entry into the discourses of specific disciplines. (N.B.: Janus, in addition to looking before and behind is also the god of doorways.) As a flexible, unmethodical orientation, the essay can exploit and animate any number of verbal formulations (discourse forms) without surrendering its critical dimension to the "normality" of a given discourse. The essayistic spirit carries the promise for writers to participate in and to change a discourse; it can thrive on the meeting ground between the person and the discipline where individual people participate in the work of understanding. Whether the writing practices of particular academic disciplines implicitly reject the essay or not—and I would argue that most, ideally, would not (although most on the introductory level assume a walk-before-run idea of learning)—should not constrain the highest pedagogical ambitions of freshman writing programs.

IV.

It has been a rather long (and I hope not too tedious) passage from my rendering of my Marine Corps epiphany to my grand claims for the place of the essay in writing instruction. My impulse now is to focus on the relation between the two, to draw a conclusion (for example, that the moments of personal narrative and of academic analysis and application in this chapter are equally essayistic); to make a detailed recommendation about, say, teaching practices (how can I do better as a teacher?); or, at the very least, to make a stylistic gesture that would create some sense of aesthetic closure. Even though I take on the tone of the teacher in the latter part of this essay, recall that with Montaigne my intent is to relate, not to teach. So I would like to back off from my effort to "recommend" the essay as *the* most desirable approach to writing instruction and relate something of my effort at self understanding through both writing this essay and reading texts I hoped would help me in my task. I was not sure (and still *am* not completely) what the particular relevance of my Marine experience was to the idea of the essay as I started writing. The sentences in my Marine anecdote that address the idea of the essay are clearly imposed. I did not think in those terms at the time. The anecdote is a reconstruction, not a "true" rendering of thought and experience. I wanted to believe that the experience could be understood in the context of the essay because, quite simply, I wanted this chapter to be as much an essay as it is an academic argument. That is, I wanted to inhabit what I like to think *is* my own writing. But perhaps the idea of the essay I have been struggling to articulate is simply too utopian to be of much use. Perhaps not.

Let me draw on a short section from Robert Musil's three volume *The Man Without Qualities* (1985) to help me out of this impasse. In a chapter with the wonderful title, "The earth too, but Ulrich in particular, pays homage to the Utopian idea of Essayism" (the source of my utopian reference in the previous paragraph), Musil charts a change of perception in the thinking of his character, Ulrich. "From the earliest times of the first self-confidence of youth, which it is often so touching, even moving, to look back upon later, all sorts of once-loved notions lingered in his memory even today, and among them was that of 'living hypothetically'. This phrase still expressed the courage and the involuntary ignorance involved in a life in which every step is an act of daring without experience behind it" (296). For Ulrich, "living hypothetically" involves "[a] thrilling sensation of being destined to something" (296). Experience, however, changes his sense of destiny. After having desired to have "a character, a profession, a definite mode of existence," Ulrich "tries to reach a different understanding of himself." Musil renders that "different understanding" as follows:

> Later, as his intellectual capacity increased, this gave rise in Ulrich's mind to a notion that he no longer associated with the indeterminate word "hypothesis" but, for certain reasons, with the peculiar concept of the essay. It was approximately in the way that an essay, in the sequence of its paragraphs, takes a thing from many sides without comprehending it wholly—for a thing wholly comprehended instantly loses its bulk and melts down into a concept—that he believed he could best survey the world and handle his own life. The value of an action or of a quality, indeed their essence and nature, seemed to him dependent on the circumstances surrounding them, on the ends they served, in short, on the whole complex—constituted now thus, now otherwise—to which they belonged. (297)

As I read those lines, I felt, as I had with my reading of Dostoevsky, that I was reading myself. I too dreamed of a profession and of forming a stable "character." I too looked back at my "involuntary ignorance" with some affection and recognized a quality of "daring" in my lack of experience as a reader and writer. Dreams change; the desire for "large terms of reference" (296) and the utopian dream of free and full self-expression become transformed by experience, changed by circumstances, revised through interactions with others. "The peculiar concept of the essay" offers another kind of utopian dream, a dream where everyone can speak and write from where they are, where everyone has the authority of experience and of the workings of their own minds. In the essay, we have a notion that refuses to see wholly, a notion that invites us to confront our situatedness, to look from where we are and then to shift, to move, to see partially, and to look again ("constituted now thus, now otherwise"). The essay invites writers to resist absolutes, and it bestows on us the authority to write and rewrite in an effort to understand and, through understanding, to remake ourselves, our work and our lives.

Works Cited

Adorno, T. W. 1984. "The Essay as Form." Trans. Bob Hullot-Kentor and Frederic Will. *New German Critique*, 32:151–71.

Bakhtin, M. M. 1981. "Discourse in the Novel." *The Dialogic Imagination*. Trans. Caryl Emerson and Michael Holquist. Ed. Michael Holquist. 259–422. Austin, TX: University of Texas Press.

———. 1973. *Problems of Dostoevsky's Poetics*. Trans. R. W. Rotsel. Ann Arbor, MI: Ardis Publishers.

Bartholomae, David. 1990. "A Reply to Stephen North." *PRE-TEXT* 11.1–2: 122–30.

———. 1985. "Inventing the University." *When a Writer Can't Write*, edited by Mike Rose. 134–65. New York: The Guilford Press.

Bense, Max. 1947. "Uber den Essay und seine Prosa." *Merkur* 3:414–24.

Bruffee, Kenneth A. 1984. "Collaborative Learning and the 'Conversation of Mankind.'" *College English* 46.7:635–52.

Chadbourne, Richard M. 1983. "A Puzzling Literary Genre: Comparative Views of the Essay." *Comparative Literature Studies* 20:133–53.

Cohen, J. M., trans. 1958. *Montaigne: Essays*. Harmondsworth: Penguin.

Dostoevsky, Fyodor. 1957. *The Brothers Karamazov*. New York: New American Library.

———. 1968. "Notes from Underground." In *Great Short Works of Fyodor Dostoevsky*. New York: Harper & Row.

Elbow, Peter. 1991. "Reflections on Academic Discourse: How It Relates to Freshmen and Colleagues." *College English* 53.2:135–55.

———. 1990. "Forward: About Personal Expressive Academic Writing." *PRE-TEXT* 11.1–2 (1990):7–20.

Fish, Stanley. 1993. "How to Recognize a Poem When You See One." In *Ways of Reading*, edited by David Bartholomae and Anthony Petrosky. New York: St. Martin's Press.

Fort, Keith. 1971. "Form, Authority, and the Critical Essay." *College English* 32.6:629–39.

Geertz, Clifford. 1993. "Deep Play: Notes on the Balinese Cockfight." In *Ways of Reading*, edited by David Bartholomae and Anthony Petrosky. New York: St. Martin's Press.

———. 1983. "Blurred Genres: The Reconfiguration of Social Thought" *Local Knowledge: Further Essays in Interpretive Anthropology*. 20–35. New York: Basic Books.

Good, Graham. 1988. *The Observing Self: Rediscovering the Essay*. London: Routledge.

Kauffmann, R. Lane. 1989. "The Skewed Path: Essaying as Unmethodical Method" *Essays on the Essay: Redefining the Genre*, edited by Alexander J. Butrym. 221–40. Athens, GA: The University of Georgia Press.

Lukacs, Georg. 1974. "On the Nature and Form of the Essay." *Soul and Form*. 1–18. Cambridge, MA: The MIT Press.

Moffatt, Michael. 1989. *Coming of Age in New Jersey.* New Brunswick, NJ: Rutgers University Press.

Montaigne. 1971. *Selections from the Essays of Montaigne*. Trans. and Ed. Donald M. Frame. Arlington Heights, IL: AHM Publishing Corp.

Musil, Robert. 1953. *The Man Without Qualities*. 3 Vols. Trans. Eithne Wilkins and Ernst Kaiser. London: Secker and Warburg.

Torgovnick, Marianna. 1990. "Experimental Critical Writing." *Profession 90*. The Modern Language Association of America. 25–27.

Zeiger, William. 1985. "The Exploratory Essay: Enfranchising the Spirit of Inquiry in College Composition." *College English* 47.5:454–66.

Section Five

Narrating the Writing Process

14

"Where Your Treasure Is" *Accounting for Differences in Our Talk About Teaching*

Susan Wall
Northeastern University

"Where your treasure is," says the Biblical proverb, "there will your heart be also" (Mt. 6:21; Lk. 12:34). So it goes in our discipline too: the economic metaphors of wealth and possession that regularly appear in our scholarship signify the opportunities for power and unalienated work that we find in our professional lives. And these opportunities, in turn, reciprocally shape the values and agendas we have brought to the reform of literacy in our nation's schools over these last several decades.

In what follows I examine a set of these economic metaphors in their connections to both our theories and our practices as teachers of writing. My project is to try to account for some of the often-contested differences in how we talk about what it is that we do. I am particularly concerned with enduring debates over theoretical language that often seem linked to divisions within the profession among levels and kinds of teaching. For there continue to be contentiously different ways with words among the two groups that produce much of the scholarship of our profession: teachers at the elementary and secondary levels (and some professors who work closely with them), for whom progressive practice continues to define itself in terms of the

I would like to thank those who read and responded to earlier drafts of this chapter, especially Lad Tobin, Tom Newkirk, and Peter Elbow.

expressivist theories that have characterized the "writing process" movement from the 1960s on; and those who teach and publish on writing at the college level, for many of whom some version of what James Berlin calls social-epistemic theory has replaced expressivism as the dominant language of our pedagogy.

"Replaced," however, may be too mild a word. I think it's fair to say that a great deal of recently published work by college-level composition scholars (many but not all from departments of English) has engaged in a concerted and almost relentlessly negative critique of expressivist pedagogy. Especially singled out for condemnation has been expressivism's emphasis upon the writer—her intentions, her choices, the meaning that the process and product of writing have for her, her "personal growth"—at the expense, the critics say, of the other two parts of the rhetorical triangle: audience (that is, readers, or, more broadly, society) and text (or, more broadly, language). James Berlin, whose 1987 book, *Rhetoric and Reality,* has been especially influential in shaping this argument, puts his issues with expressivists this way:

> Their position, in both theory and practice, conceives composing in personal terms, as the expression of an isolated self attempting to come to grips with an alien and recalcitrant world. This view accordingly denies the social nature of language and experience and has students respond to external conflicts through such activities as keeping a journal and writing personal essays, rather than by engaging in public discourse to affect the social and political context of their behavior. (185)

Berlin here is specifically responding to Cy Knoblauch and Lil Brannon's 1984 book, *Rhetorical Traditions and the Teaching of Writing*, an important contribution to the "process" movement in writing. But a similar critique could be made, indeed *has* been made, of others identified with expressivism such as Donald Murray, Peter Elbow, and Ken Macrorie, by scholars such as Lester Faigley, Susan Miller, and Sharon Crowley.

Berlin suggests that we might consider this latter group of theorists under the general category of "social-epistemic" rhetoric. Despite important differences among them, these theorists share the assumption that there are limits and constraints on the freedom and autonomy of the author to control the meaning of her work. In this view,

> . . . knowledge is always knowledge for someone standing in relation to others in a linguistically circumscribed situation. That is to say, all elements of the communication act are linguistically conditioned: interlocutor [that is, speaker or writer], audience, and reality are all defined by language and cannot be known apart from the verbal constructs through which we respond to them. Language

> forms our conceptions of our selves, our audiences, and the very reality in which we exist. Language, moreover, is a social—not a private—phenomenon, and as such embodies a multitude of historically specific conceptions that shape experience, especially ideological conceptions about economic, political, and social arrangements. (Berlin 1987, 166)

Despite Berlin's claim that he is basing his critique of expressivism on "both theory and practice," I see his work as an invitation to the reader to make an abstract, theoretical response, to take up his taxonomical project on its own terms. And in many ways I have found and continue to find that invitation attractive. Reading passages such as the ones I have quoted above, I am drawn to Berlin's argument, seeing my own values in his description of a pedagogy that directs students' and teachers' attention to social and political contexts, to the ways that our writing is constrained (even, in a sense, authored) by the discourses that precede us, to our identities as they are socially constructed by class, gender, race, and other "historically specific conceptions." I want also, at the same time, to question the either/or categorizations on which Berlin's argument depends, to recognize that in the expressivist works that he critiques (publications of the sixties and seventies), the authors do not generally define the self as isolated or knowable apart from language, even if that self is located in the social setting of the writing workshop or conference without much reference to the larger "economic, political, and social arrangements" to which Berlin refers. In my graduate seminars at Northeastern, for example, it's not hard to ask students to apply Berlin's taxonomy to the works we are reading *and* to invite them to question the dichotomies to which his definitions are pushed.

Yet I find myself increasingly reluctant to do these things—to define my work or the work of other teachers primarily in terms of theoretical categories or, more broadly, to write or teach the history of the process movement and our discipline's more recent social turn as predominantly a history of ideas. Even though I ally my own work more with Berlin's social-epistemic position than with an expressivist one, I am especially uneasy with what Berlin and other critics of expressivism seem to be claiming: that expressivism is somehow a "naive" theory that our profession has "outgrown." Accounting for differences in our talk about teaching seems to me more complicated than such a history of ideas can account for, more located in the specific politics and material consequences of the contexts in which we teach.

I prefer to argue here (as some other scholars also are beginning to do) that we need to reread expressivism through a critical frame that contextualizes the historical development of expressivism so as to ask for whom it remains a popular approach, and why. Such an analysis would be, I believe, actually *more* social-epistemic than many of the theoretical critiques that we've seen so far, since it would take seriously the claim that we cannot understand the terms of expressivism (or any pedagogy for that matter) without locating them (as Berlin suggests) in the "linguistically circumscribed situation[s]" in which they arose, looking for the "historically specific conceptions" that shaped their metaphors, "especially ideological conceptions about economic, political, and social arrangements."

In the last section of this chapter, I describe some of the ways that we might approach such a revisionist project and how, in fact, it is already happening. But I want to begin with the story of my own efforts at such a critique, as a way of arguing for the local politics of teaching that such a revisionist project entails. And I do this because I believe that the impact of experience upon a teacher's theoretical understanding—what Louise Wetherbee Phelps (1988) calls "theory disciplined by practice"—has been and should continue to be the particular strength that composition scholarship has to offer the discipline of English.

On "Ownership" and "Riches": Metaphors and Teaching

It was early in the summer of 1983, and the exotic blue flowers blooming all over the Berkeley campus were almost as bright and pure as the late-afternoon California sky. As coordinator for a new National Writing Project site, I was making the expected pilgrimage to the Bay Area project's summer institute to see what I could learn from the place where it all had started. Five or six of us were off in a small group, sharing ideas and experiences about responding to writing. The conversation echoed others I'd been in before—until I heard Mary K. Healy, the project co-director, vehemently object to the behavior of a teacher who had taken a paper *out of a student writer's hands* to read it. I was astonished and dismayed. I thought: Why, I do that all the time! After all, it was the job of a reader to read and respond to a written text; isn't that what we were talking about—response? Yet Mary K. had treated what that teacher had done as a serious violation of the student's rights concerning his own work, a step over an invisible property line. What was going on?

I encountered many other surprises and puzzles that year and in subsequent summers, first as a writing project director and then, more recently, in my work with Northeastern's Institute on Writing and Teaching. But no discovery was so troublesome as the gulf of interest and understanding I felt when I talked with elementary and secondary teachers—especially elementary teachers—about reading student writing. What concerned me was what happened when we talked about how to respond to students' texts—or, rather, my sense that we were talking right past one another. We simply weren't speaking the same language. And this was true as well of the scholars whose works we were reading, writers whose discussions served to define the key terms and metaphors for our teaching. One pair of tropes served, more than any others, to express our differences: "ownership" and "riches." Here are two examples—both from colleagues at the University of New Hampshire—to suggest how central and contentious these metaphors have been in our field.

The first is from Donald Graves's book, *Writing: Teachers and Children at Work*, published the same year I began to work with teachers, 1983. Graves writes: "The data show that writers who learn to choose topics well make the most significant growth in both information and skills at the point of best topic. With best topic the child exercises strongest control, establishes ownership, and with ownership, pride in the piece" (21). This sense of ownership, he concludes, directly affects the text produced: "Many eight- and nine-year-old children can do extensive revisions of a single selection" when they "are writing to find out what they mean for themselves. . . . The data are very clear that children . . . take ownership and control of the writing at the point of knowing their subject" (4).

Now let me set in opposition to Graves a second quotation. This one comes from Tom Newkirk's 1989 essay, "The First Five Minutes: Setting the Agenda in a Writing Conference." He writes: "I see the writing conference as a dialectic encounter between teacher and student, in which both assume complex roles. The teacher, in particular, cannot escape the difficult choices between praise and support, suggestion and silence, each choice carrying with it a risk. For that reason, I am uncomfortable with some of the metaphors increasingly used to describe this complex relationship, many of which echo private property and contractual law." Here Newkirk cites as an example Graves's metaphor of "ownership," as well as Cy Knoblauch and Lil Brannon's claim in *Rhetorical Traditions* that the student text should not be "appropriated" by the teacher, that choices about revising that text should be governed by the writer's intentions rather than the reader's expectations. Taking a stance against these writer-centered positions, Newkirk goes on to argue:

> Ownership implies clear property lines guaranteed by legal statutes that are (at least to lawyers) clearly spelled out. For the most part, those who own property can do what they want with it. . . . [But this] metaphor of ownership is not slippery enough [for our purposes]. To a degree the student owns his or her paper, but the paper is *intended* for others in the way property isn't; and so to a degree, the

> writing is also owned by its readers. . . . The expectations of the teacher, the course, and the academy must interact with the intentions of the student. Intention, in other words, cannot be an absolute, a 'God-term.' (329)

Newkirk's interactionist position on responding to student texts was mine too when I began my work with elementary and secondary teachers, and it still is. I believed that writing originates (if it is now possible to use that term at all) in prior texts or uses of languages, and that new meanings, further "texts," are composed when the writing is read—whether the reader is the writer, the teacher, or anyone else. I valued the sense of mutual enrichment that comes when writers and readers share what Newkirk calls "complex roles," a "complex relationship." Why, I wondered, didn't these teachers see that writers don't "own" a text's meanings? Why didn't the issue of "intentions" seem as vexing to them as it did to me? Whenever we talked about sample student papers, the conversation always went immediately to the writer: what was *she* thinking, feeling, experiencing, learning? What did *he* intend to write? Trying to get teachers to see it my way failed miserably, of course. (After all, my comments and course materials were every bit as open to interpretation as any other "text.") No matter how much we discussed Reader Response theory or examined our own variant readings of texts, the discussions and papers from these seminars continued to echo Mary Ellen Giacobbe's dictum that what beginning readers and writers need most is "time, ownership, and response." When I think now of those first summer workshops and the bafflement and frustration I felt, I am reminded of my fifth-grade French teacher, an unfortunate woman who knew too little about either speaking English or teaching American children to be effective. "Look your book!" she would sputter helplessly as we ignored her. "Look your book!"

We all are apt to do badly at work that is new to us, and my teaching that first year or so was no exception. But I did attempt some explanation for the differences of focus and interest those classes had revealed among teachers at various grade levels. My first strategy was to turn to the different pedagogical theories that we had learned through our educations as writing teachers—hardly a surprising move for someone fresh out of graduate school! My own schooling in composition had led me to think of reading as well as writing as a form of composing, each reading of a text, including a student's text, constituting a "rewriting" of the original. This kind of theoretical emphasis on textuality and the generative power of reading has come into college-level composition *via* literary theory, both American versions such as Louise Rosenblatt's, which describes reading as the opening up of new meaning-producing "transactions," and continental theories that celebrate the "polysemous" text indebted to the texts that precede it and endlessly open to interpretation. An important corollary of these assumptions for teaching writing is that even when the writer is present and in dialogue with the reader, any statement of a writer's "intentions," whether made before or after a text is composed, is simply another text to be interpreted, not to be confused with whatever readers make of the original text in question.

Expressivist process pedagogies, of course, also emphasize the importance for writers of getting other readers' responses to their work and the crucial role of revision, just as the text-and-reader centered pedagogy I had learned also emphasized invention and the writer's choices. Yet the difference in emphasis placed on these concerns could make all the difference to how one defined what was important in teaching, especially when it came to the contextual constraints on writers and whether these were to be regarded as primarily a help or a hindrance. Consider how, for instance, David Bartholomae concludes an essay that he published in 1982 on the subject of what enables students to write well ("Writing Assignments: Where Writing Begins"). He brings forward a passage by the poet William Stafford in order finally to name what he, Bartholomae, values in the act of teaching. You will probably find the passage familiar; it is widely anthologized:

> A writer is not so much someone who has something to say as he is someone who has found a process that will bring about new things he would not have thought of if he had not started to say them. That is, he does not draw on a reservoir; instead, he engages in an activity that brings him to a whole succession of unforeseen stories, poems, essays, plays, laws, philosophies, religions, or—but wait!
>
> Back in school, from the first when I began to try to write things, I felt this richness. One thing would lead to another; the world would give and give. Now, after twenty years or so of trying, I live by that certain richness, an idea hard to pin, difficult to say, and perhaps offensive to some. (Stafford 1970/1990, 915-16)

To live by that idea as a teacher of writing, Bartholomae argues, is to acknowledge that while students may have memories that shape their writing, we as their teachers have no access to these memories in any unmediated way. Rather, what we can know and attend to are the texts that students write and the occasions we create for their composing—occasions in which (as poststructuralist theory argues) we and they are both constrained and enabled by what others have said before. While we may speak of writing producing ideas, we must also recognize, he argues, that writing is an act of self-location within discourses that precede us. Indeed, it is reading and writing within *and against* the "already said" that affords students—or any reader and writer—the opportunity to make new meaning.

It is telling, then, that the article in which Bartholomae quotes Stafford is entitled, "*Writing* Assignments: Where *Writing* Begins" (my emphasis), and that the broad context of writing that Stafford defines is immediately relocated by Bartholomae in the academy: "A sequence of assignments," Bartholomae writes, "is repetitive. It asks students to write, again, about something they wrote about before. But such a project allows for richness; it allows for the imagination that one thing can lead to another, that the world can give and give. This is an idea hard to pin, difficult to say, and, perhaps, offensive to some" (1982, 45).

Donald Graves, I soon realized, was one of those who might find that idea "offensive." Assigned topics, he has argued, put young writers on "writer's welfare," taking away the "ownership" they should exercise over their work. Children will not grow if they remain dependent upon adults to tell them what to do. "Ownership," in other words, names more than issues of reader response for Graves—just as for college-level scholars like Bartholomae "richness" broadens out very quickly to questions of the writer's position within a given discourse. In Graves's work and the work of others associated with him such as Giacobbe, Atwell, and Calkins—all major influences on the teachers I've worked with—assumptions about the relationship of experience and thought to the production of written text are interwoven with other key assumptions that define terms such as "voice," "self," and "authorship." These assumptions taken together and applied to teaching have been labelled "expressivism" because (it is said) they tend to treat writing as the self-expression of the writer's thoughts and feelings.

"Expressive," however, is a term that ironically fails to see what Graves is so struck by when he observes young writers: the *loss* of meaning when thoughts are turned into marks on the page. In *Writing: Teachers and Children at Work* (1983) in a key chapter also tellingly entitled "See the *Writing Process* Develop" (not, as Bartholomae might put it, "See where *Writing* Begins"), Graves defines writing as a drawing upon a "reservoir" of memories in order to transform remembered experience into text. This transformation, as he sees it, inevitably entails a "process of reduction" for all of us (220), but most of all for beginning writers whose abilities with verbal thought and speech far outstrip what they can capture of these in writing. When young learners come to see the huge gap between their memories and their words on the page, the realization of what has been lost can be so powerful as to block their composing. "They feel," Graves writes, "the lack in their words, which have been reduced from richer images and intentions" (220). He then recalls from his own research the memorable example of a child named Alison who is trying to write about the death of her dog, Muffin. Alison's memories "swirl" in her mind: images, smells, textures, words. But all she finally can write is: "I felt him on the bed next to me." Last year, Graves notes, Alison would have been unaware of this reduction; she "would have poured a torrent of words and sentences onto the page." This year, however, she is "paralyzed," not having learned yet how "*to add* what is naturally subtracted through the very process of writing itself" (220).

In his reading of Alison's experience and other like hers, Graves develops an approach to writing that might be more accurately labeled "recuperative" than "expressive," foregrounding the retrospective process of remembrance rather than the prospective one of reading a text. But while his analysis acknowledges the gap between intention and text that also informed my own pedagogical concerns, in the end the focus of his work remains on the writer and her intentions, so that the teacher becomes a facilitator but not a co-creator of meaning.

Graves does not ignore the fact that school writing is public writing, and that writers will have—and will need—other readers, responders who may directly affect the composing of their work or, more indirectly, read it in ways that the author did not intend. Yet there is no question that when it comes to the metaphor of "ownership," the term carries very different meanings than it does for Newkirk, Bartholomae, or myself. We might say that Graves is more concerned with the *production* of written discourse and with the difficulties attendant on that production for inexperienced writers, while the latter group is more concerned with the *reception* of written discourse—or, perhaps more accurately, with claiming a role for readers and for culture in the production of meanings.

Accounting for Our Differences: The Limits of Theory

Since I don't believe that people pull philosophies of teaching out of the air, when I tried to account for teachers' different allegiances to student/process-centered or reader/text-centered pedagogies, I attributed them at first to differences in development between the two groups of students we teach. Elementary researchers were teaching me that young children acquire a wealth of spoken language at an astonishingly early age, but that it takes a long time for their written texts to catch up. As Susan Sowers observes, "With the young writer the experience reflected in talk will be much fuller than the text reflected back to the student" (1982, 77). For many college writers, however, the speech/text relationship often becomes reversed: the sentences they come to produce (like those in the academic texts they read) are actually longer, more complex, "richer" than their speech—a way of holding together more predication, more "thought," in a single utterance. So, I reasoned, it makes sense for teachers at different levels to attend differently to talk and to writing—at least those teachers who believe that literacy instruction needs to begin with the learner's linguistic abilities, to "begin with where they are" as language users, as Ann Berthoff likes to say (1981, 9–10).

And it makes sense too, given the retrospective emphasis of expressive pedagogy, that scholars of elementary and secondary education might turn their attention to experiences *outside* of school, not only as sources for their students' writing topics but for metaphors about the values associated with reading and writing. I think, for example, of Nancie Atwell's central metaphor for reader response in her reading/writing workshop: the literate conversations she remembers enjoying with her husband and friends around her dining room table. There, she says, the talk about books "isn't sterile or grudging or perfunctory. It's filled with jokes, arguments, exchanges of bits of information, descriptions of what we loved and hated and why" (1987, 19). This is a remarkable metaphor: traditional symbols of wealth and privilege—the dining room, the literary salon, the trading exchange—are here transformed into a method that will empower the sons and daughters of lobster fishermen and gas station attendants. But notice that the metaphor locates wealth (being "filled" and productive) *outside* of school; it's not created *by* academic reading and writing.

The question of *where* wealth and power were located by these tropes was a signal that more than development defined our differences—as well as other experiences I was having that pointed away from both speech and text to context. Graves, for instance, reminds us that a child's developing skills with language are profoundly affected by social attitudes enacted at home and in the schools. Most children, he says, are allowed and even encouraged to "acquire spoken language through experimentation, repetition, and errors," whereas they soon discover that acquiring written language means "a concern for early correctness and proper etiquette, with little attention given to content. In speech it was the other way around—content was primary, conventions secondary. Children have more ownership of their speech; they rent their writing" (1983, 162).

I began to pay attention to passages like that because I was learning more about the contexts in which so many elementary and secondary teachers teach—contexts in which they, too, often "rent" their curricular materials, have decided for them the books or topics they are to teach, are required to pretend in statements of "behavioral objectives" that they can predict the "returns" on their instruction; and, of course, will in all cases be held "accountable" for these results. When education is imagined in terms of bookkeeping rather than what Stafford calls the "give and give" of engaged literacy, even the introduction of reading and writing "process" instruction often comes to seem a limited freedom in a system that reproduces in microcosm the inequities of choice and opportunity outside of the schools. As Lynda Feldman, one of the teachers in our summer institute, wrote—in an echo of Freire's famous "banking" metaphor of education: "The teaching population mirrors society as a whole. Elementary school teachers are like the bank tellers of our communities. Their secondary school counterparts are the junior loan officers. Neither has much in the way of power; both have much in the way of regulation (that is, curriculum) to follow."

Freire warns us that "banking theory and practice, as immobilizing and fixating forces, fail to acknowledge men as historical beings; problem-posing theory and practice take man's historicity as their starting point" (1983, 71). My own initial explanations for the gulf I felt between my pedagogy and that of the elementary and secondary teachers I knew failed in just the way that Freire defines. In construing our differences as matters of either pedagogical *theory* or a response to universal patterns of human *development*, I was mystifying the conflict by idealizing and naturalizing teachers' values, not understanding that their metaphors named political positions arising from their social and economic situations. When Don Graves writes of how a mandated curriculum keeps children on "writer's welfare" or how isolating writing from the rest of the learning that goes on in school makes even the best writing workshop a "ghetto," when Nancie Atwell and Mary Ellen Giacobbe insist that the first step in effective literacy instruction is to grant students "ownership" of their reading and writing, when Mem Fox, Tony Petrosky, and Jerome Harste condemn the basal readers, workbooks, and standardized tests that "strip" away the metaphors and complexities of texts and distort and "impoverish" language for young readers and writers, these scholars are not just describing the constraints under which many children and adolescents experience schooling. They are describing the professional lives of too many teachers as well.[1]

This is not to suggest that college instructors never face similar problems. The hierarchy of status and privilege in universities means that we who hold positions as professors all too often exploit part-time instructors and teaching assistants by giving them too much work and too little training. We then attempt to compensate for the problems that follow from these decisions by squeezing choice and creativity out of the curriculum, mandating workbook exercises, formulaic prose forms, short, decontextualized readings, and standardized testing. But the majority of college level composition scholarship is not being written by those instructors but by professors (like me) who possess more freedom and control in our professional lives, who can take "time, ownership, and response" much more for granted. No wonder, then, that the economic metaphors of our scholarship speak of *producing* multiple interpretations from texts in which, through new "transactions," we always discover "supplementarity" and payback is endlessly "deferred," or that we discuss reading and writing in terms of metaphors associated with colonization ("discovering" new "territories of language"), leisure ("playing" the "polyphonic" text), or self-reproducing wealth.

Berlin, for example, in an essay entitled "Rhetoric, Poetic, and Culture: Contested Boundaries in English Studies" (1991), borrows the metaphor of "cultural capital" from a work by the French critic Pierre Bourdieu, *Distinction: A Social Critique of the Judgement of Taste*. Bourdieu looks at the way that differences in social class and political power are reproduced by upbringing and by education, since these teach the next generation the specific forms of manners, taste, attitudes towards art, and other markers that reinforce class distinctions. "It is the role of English teachers," Berlin argues, "to serve as the bankers, the keepers and dispensers, of certain portions of this cultural capital, their value to society being defined in terms of its investment and reproduction" (37). It becomes quickly obvious, however, that by "English teachers" Berlin means English professors. His concern is the hierarchical division within the large majority of college English departments, where the emphasis upon a highly aesthetic version of literary studies and simultaneous denigration of work in rhetoric (including composition) "serves the interest of a privileged managerial class while discriminating against those who are outside of this class" (33). Berlin's proposed solution? Place literature and rhetoric on a par, examining their codes, the "reading and writing practices appropriate to each."

> This will mean an end to the invidious valorization of the literary because of its rich organic complexity and its satisfaction of the aesthetic need, and the dismissal of the rhetorical because of its purported practicality and mechanical simplicity. Both are rich and complex in their expression of meaning and both are necessary in the continued health of a society. The work of English Studies will be to study the discursive practices involved in generating and interpreting both. The English classroom will then provide methods for revealing the semiotic codes enacted in the production and interpretation of texts, codes that cut across the aesthetic, the economic and

> political, and the philosophical and scientific, enabling students to engage critically in the variety of reading and writing practices required of them. (36)

While there is much to appeal to writing specialists in this argument, it also seems clear that Berlin's concern is with professors the fate of whose careers primarily depends on the *self*-reproduction of academic scholarship rather than—as is the case with elementary, secondary, or non-professorial college teachers—what and how well their *students* can produce. In his utopian project, the English professors of composition and rhetoric get to join the other "bankers," to have a say about where the treasure of "cultural capital" is to be located and how it is to be allocated. There is no suggestion of concern here with the "bank tellers" of whom Feldman writes and their struggles even to "own" the conditions of their employment.

We might not, of course, expect a direct concern for elementary or secondary teaching in an essay appearing in a book on postsecondary writing instruction. But it's important to note that Berlin does not take his argument a step or more further, to ask how and why "ownership" of "cultural capital" in English (even if that were to include rhetoricians) is underwritten by distributions of capital that are material rather than purely symbolic. To address those questions would require, for example, that he acknowledge how much the time and resources required to produce the "rich complexity" of a scholar's work are made possible by departmental structures that limit his teaching load by relegating most freshman writing instruction to marginalized, underpaid, mostly female part-time and adjunct instructors (as Susan Miller explains in *Textual Carnivals* [1991]) and by delegating the responsibility for training public school teachers to schools or departments of education. Like many other college-level writing professors, Berlin can take up the politics of English studies in a way divorced from the pressures of public school issues and can cast the debate in largely theoretical terms precisely because he enjoys the social and economic freedom to do so. And that freedom, in turn, is interdependent with reading and writing practices that must of necessity deny writers "ownership" of their texts, *must* define our work as reader-centered and "interpretive." Only thus can scholars "rewrite" the works of previous scholars by finding new meanings and uses for them, thereby being able to claim that they have made a further contribution to the "cultural capital" of the profession. The differences in our talk about teaching are interwoven with just such historically developed practices.

I'm not suggesting, let me add immediately, that a college or university professorial appointment precludes informed and sympathetic understanding of work situations other than our own. In fact, in English departments it has generally been the composition scholars who have cared about working in partnership with teachers in the schools. But I do suggest that if some of us who teach composing speak of producing additional "richness" from texts and others speak of achieving "ownership" over them, we need to listen to these differences of language and what they are telling us.

Composition in the 1990s: A Revisionist Project

As this essay's title is meant to suggest, we who teach and write about our professional work as teachers of literacy often do so in very different terms. And this is, I have argued, in part the consequence of different histories of the writing process movement and its ongoing interpretation and application by professionals working in different roles and contexts. While the expressivist terms and practices of much process pedagogy have remained popular among many progressive elementary and secondary teachers—indeed, have been reinforced by later developments such as the whole language movement—a number of social-epistemic scholars have established their rhetorical ascendency in college-level composition by rejecting the expressivism associated with the process movement (just as the process movement established *its* claims by appealing to teachers to reject "current-traditionalism" in the name of a "new paradigm"). On the basis primarily of evidence from published journal articles and textbooks, it has been argued that "composition theory must rewrite its notion of authors as integral, autonomous, individual selves and substitute instead the notion of collective but shifting 'subject positions' that contemporary feminist and neo-Marxist discourses adumbrate" (Crowley 1991, 193). The treatment of expressivism in this argument has been a largely theoretical one, however, located typically in analyses of published scholarly texts where theory is valued over practice rather than in, say, qualitative research that might contextualize expressivism in specific teaching situations. The practice represented by this social-epistemic critique is, in other words, often in contradiction to its own theoretical claim that discourses (including our own) are socially constructed and politically interested, shaped by specific and historically contingent material circumstances.

As the narrative of my own professional history is intended to suggest, I believe that a more useful as well as theoretically viable alternative to a merely negative critique of expressivism would be to reread its metaphors in a contextualized way that complicates and challenges the categories that have come to dominate our talk about teaching. This kind of revisionist project is already well under way from many directions in the field, but it is not my purpose here to chronicle this particular movement in our discipline's history. Instead, I want, by way of conclusion to this chapter, to note briefly several recently published analyses that indicate how scholarship can reexamine the metaphors of expressivism in light of the particular contexts in which they are employed. The works I'll mention are drawn from very different ends of the theoretical spectrum, yet each recognizes that differences of theoretical language suggest very real differences of access to power and its privileges.

What might it mean, for example, to talk about writing from one's "own" or "personal" experience in light of the writer's social and political location? In his recent book, *Fragments of Rationality: Postmodernity and the Subject of Composition*, Lester Faigley (1992) reminds us that expressivist pedagogy had its beginnings at the college level when professors such as Peter Elbow took the side of student activists in their own institutions in the 1960s and early 1970s and "emphasized in their pedagogy the values that their students cried out for—autonomy, antiauthoritarianism, and a personal voice" (57).[2] While expressivism lost much of this sense of political urgency in the following decade, its terms and practices are being debated again in college-level scholarship as new political issues and allegiances arise. The very success of the social-epistemic critique created by this scholarship as well as the effects of postmodernism on the profession are opening up "fissures" within the opposition to expressivism, as well as an ongoing reconsideration of its practices. Faigley notes in particular the role that feminism plays in this historical development. While some feminists like bell hooks discover reasons in their own histories to question an unproblematic notion of "authentic voice," others insist on retaining and re-examining the personal focus of expressive writing because they see that their individual lives are, in effect, the sites of political domination—and its opposition. Both positions, Faigley argues, are "consistent with those of postmodern theorists like Foucault and Lyotard, who insist that political resistance can be staged only at the micro level" (18).

A particularly eloquent example of just such concern with self-location and resistance is the recent essay on "Expressivism: Literacy for Personal Growth" that appears in Cy Knoblauch and Lil Brannon's 1993 book, *Critical Teaching and the Idea of Literacy*. It's a brave essay, in that the authors acknowledge that they have, thanks to many social-epistemic critics, come to see serious problems in their earlier, much more expressivist work in *Rhetorical Traditions*. "The limitation of 'personal growth' arguments, our own included," they write, "has been precisely their personalizing of circumstances that are profoundly social and political in character" (144).

Circumstances is a key term here. Rather than discuss only the theoretical shortcomings of expressivism, Knoblauch and Brannon emphasize its consequences for teachers in the political and material contexts of schooling, arguing that too often a pedagogy focussed on allowing student writers individual choice fails to understand and address "the situatedness of the individual in social orders that constitute her independence, that constrain it in the service of encompassing designs (economic and otherwise) that take precedence over personal interest, and that actively, purposefully resist local challenges to its privileged arrangements" (136). In fact, they argue, the "banking" practices that cast teachers in the roles of workers rather than professionals—"testing apparatuses that compel mechanistic teaching," mandated textbooks and curricula, teacher evaluation practices "that ensure the orthodoxy of the classroom," and "top-down" administration of the schools—need to be read as historical responses to the challenge posed by the process movement, reactions that function as "defense measures" to limit and even reverse that movement's achievements (129).

Knoblauch and Brannon's analysis of expressivism is a complex one, and it is not my purpose to try to do justice to it here. Suffice it to note that because, like Faigley, they historicize the process movement and because they make it their business to know and care about English teaching beyond the college level, they are able to look beyond our profession's current differences of pedagogical language and claim "the pedagogies of expressivism" as "the precursors of critical teaching," even though these pedagogies do not derive from the Marxist, feminist, or poststructuralist theories that have shaped social-epistemic rhetoric. They remind us, for example, that expressivist teaching had its origins not in the suburban schools where it now flourishes, but "in the working-class neighborhoods of London, the open enrollment colleges of CUNY, where Mina Shaughnessy did her pioneering work, and the reformatories of Michigan, where Dan Fader first developed the 'Hooked on Books' program" (128). By thus restoring the history of expressivism to its social, material, and political (as well as theoretical) origins, Knoblauch and Brannon can reclaim the politics of a student-centered pedagogy (the goals and assumptions behind metaphors such as "ownership") even as they critique that pedagogy for being too romantic, too politically naive, and too unwilling to challenge fundamental social and political arrangements that disenfranchise students and teachers in the public schools:

> One impulse [in expressivist pedagogy] from the beginning was to honor the linguistic resources of the individual child, regardless of native language or dialect or "skill level" or socioeconomic status,

> affirming that child's entitlement to speak by first celebrating the "natural" ability to speak. Another was to enfranchise marginalized populations of students through a pedagogy that values difference and begins with what historically oppressed learners already know, instead of presuming that the purpose of schooling is to force such students into the mold of the dominant culture while "explaining" their (likely) failure by appeal to intellectual inadequacy or laziness. These are revolutionary ambitions. If it's true to say that they haven't been realized, it's also true to say that no other contemporary project of school reform has done as much, notwithstanding the impatient condescension of more contemporary arguments sporting liberatory agendas. (128-29)

My third and final example of revisionist scholarship on expressivism comes from the recent work of Peter Elbow, himself an expressivist usually placed at the opposite theoretical pole from the current work of scholars like Faigley or Knoblauch and Brannon. Yet in many ways his recent book, *What is English?* (1990), undertakes a rereading of expressivist terms and practices in much the same historicizing spirit as their critiques. Elbow describes how teachers representing all grade levels at the English Coalition Conference were able, despite their theoretical differences, to place issues of "voice," agency, and choice in the often-constraining contexts of schooling. "The conference was, after all, full of teachers who are working in the midst of an educational system that seems monolithic and impossible to move, that seems to take away autonomy and agency and responsibility from both teachers and students" (84-85). A number of conclusions follow from this crucial point. Elbow argues, for example, that we cannot expect teachers "to take initiative and become excited and invested" in their schools unless we "improve material conditions in ways that cost money" (221). On the other hand, when those favorable conditions do exist and "students or teachers do something powerful and effective, they tend to experience it as a discovery of choice where formerly they felt they had none" (84). Agency ("choice") and active involvement ("investment") are not theoretical absolutes in this analysis but names for relative degrees of power in any given context.

Elbow's discussion ties in most closely to my own about "ownership" when he reminds us that theoretical debates about authorship mean very little, are in fact not even possible, when the making of meaning itself is not central to the business of teaching and learning. We must, he argues, be able first "to get people to *engage* a text. We can't effectively examine ways of reading until someone *has* a reading that carries some investment or moment. Otherwise there's no purchase for the act of reflecting or calling into question" (20). That point about reading, I might add, could be just as easily extended to composition. Does debating whether we refer to the "self" or the "subject" in discourse have much point if students are not actually writing? Can we, in fact, imagine a subjectivity more constructed by existing powerful discourses, more "always already written," than that of the typical elementary student whose "reading" and "writing" consist of reciting from a basal reader or filling in the blanks in a workbook? Or the secondary student who demonstrates "comprehension" by checking the correct box on a multiple choice exam? Or the college freshman who cobbles together quotations and paraphrases from lectures and reference books and is taught to call this "research"?

The fact that some critics of Elbow's book objected to the way his language "carried the weight of the free, autonomous subject" (82) suggests that our debates over terms such as "ownership" or similar metaphors (for example, Elbow's "purchase" and "investment") will undoubtedly continue; there is no reason to think that theoretical unity will result from any revisionist projects or that it needs to. One conclusion, then, would be to call for more occasions where the issues can be openly discussed and, perhaps, negotiated for the sake of cooperation. But genuine negotiation only happens when all parties involved feel that their voices are heard and taken seriously because they have real power over the process and a shared stake in the outcome. This is the crucial point, as I take it, of the metaphor that Lucy Calkins foregrounds in her book, *Lessons from a Child* (1983). In the following passage, Calkins reflects on what happened to the teacher, Mrs. Howard, in the classroom where Calkins had been a participant observer. She writes:

> By highlighting the importance of Mrs. Howard's teaching, the research project helped her regain the sense of personal mission which had led her into the teaching profession nine years before. It had eroded over the years, but now the NIE study had rekindled in her the belief that she had a unique contribution she could make to her students.
>
> When our study was completed, Dr. Bob Walshe of Australia asked Graves, "What is the essential message of your study?" Graves replied, "When people own a place, they look after it. When it belongs to someone else, they couldn't care less." Graves was referring to children and their ownership of a piece of writing, but his words apply also to teachers and their ownership of their teaching. When Mrs. Howard began to feel responsibility and ownership for her classroom, she began to look after it, to invest herself in it. (23)

In one important sense here Graves's metaphor is open to objection: not owning one's place of residence does not necessarily mean that one "couldn't care less" about it (any more, I would guess, than

Graves means to say that teachers working under severe constraints of curriculum and supervision cannot care about their work).[3] Certainly the issues of class and power raised by "ownership" or any of our other economic metaphors for agency and choice have become far more complex and contested than they were for the teachers and scholars who initiated the process movement at a time before Reaganomics, reformers for whom, I suspect, the security of home-owning and the opportunities afforded by schooling, not surplus wealth and privilege, defined the "American Dream" of social and economic justice.

But this chapter is not an argument that metaphors such as "ownership" should be abandoned. I suggest instead that we read them as rhetorical ironies, strategies employed by those on the margins of power in our educational system and by their allies, that point to the gap between its ideals and its realities. The persistence of such metaphors in the language of our profession challenges our comfortable tendencies to dwell in the transcendence of pure theory and raises questions that have not lost their pertinence: Why *don't* we offer a rich and choice-filled education to all students, without exception? Why *shouldn't* all teachers find opportunities in their professional lives for choice, power, and unalienated work? And for those of us who already do enjoy such opportunities, what can *we* do to make these questions more than merely academic?

Notes

1. Henry Giroux makes a similar argument in his essay, "Critical Literacy and Student Experience: Donald Graves' Approach to Literacy" (1987). In an appreciative reading of Graves's "language of critique," Giroux argues (as I am doing here) that we see a close connection between symbolic and material practices, between that is, pedagogical theory and the contexts of schooling: "In mainstream curriculum theory, teachers are increasingly reduced to the status of clerks carrying out the mandates of the state or merely implementing the management schemes of administrators who have graduated from schools of education that have supplied them with the newest schemes for testing and measuring knowledge, but rarely with any sense of understanding how school knowledge is produced, where it comes from, whose interest it serves, or how it might function to privelege some groups over others. For Professor Graves, as with myself, this approach to curriculum is in itself part of what I call the new illiteracy, characteristic of the ever-falling rate of critical literacy embedded in the educational management schemes that have proliferated in the age of Reagan" (16).

2. Berlin also mentions in chapter seven, "Major Rhetorical Approaches: 1960–75," of *Rhetoric and Reality* (1987) that the pedagogies of this period were responses to the social and political unrest of that period, but this

acknowledgment is generally brief; the focus remains on publications within a disciplinary field. Faigley, in contrast, gives a detailed history of the development of composition as this development interacted with political, social, and economic changes (the sixties as "the last years of America's geopolitical and economic dominance following World War II" [50], the subsequent turn to the Right in American politics). Like Knoblauch and Brannon, Faigley puts the reader in a position to understand the struggles over "ownership" by teachers as brought about by, among other things, a reaction against the progressivism of "process" teaching by middle-class parents experiencing what the title to Barbara Ehrenreich's 1989 book calls an economic "fear of falling."

3. My thanks to Anne Malone, a colleague of mine on the conference panel for which this chapter was originally composed, for urging me to think more about the social implications of this passage. Graves himself has recently acknowledged some of the objections to his economic metaphors. For example, in his more recent introduction to his article, "Let's Get Rid of the Welfare Mess in the Teaching of Writing," reprinted in *A Researcher Learns to Write* (1984), he notes: "I have been rightly criticized about the metaphor [of "the welfare mess"]. People have argued that welfare is a real assistance to people in trouble and that my usage has given it a negative connotation. I agree. Welfare is needed, but the way it is administered, it often leads to humiliation and dependency on the part of those who receive it. Children do need help with their writing, but given in such a way that their dignity and independence are maintained" (43).

Works Cited

Atwell, Nancie. 1987. *In the Middle: Writing, Reading, and Learning with Adolescents*. Portsmouth, NH: Boynton/Cook.

Bartholomae, David. 1982. "Writing Assignments: Where Writing Begins." *Fforum* 4 (Fall):35–45.

Berlin, James A. 1991. "Rhetoric, Poetic, and Culture: Contested Boundaries in English Studies." *The Politics of Writing Instruction: Postsecondary*, edited by Richard Bullock and John Trimbur. 23–38. Portsmouth, NH: Boynton/Cook.

———. 1987. *Rhetoric and Reality: Writing Instruction in American Colleges, 1900–1985*. Carbondale, IL: Southern Illinois University Press.

Berthoff, Ann E. 1981. "Method: Metaphors, Models, and Maxims." *The Making of Meaning: Metaphors, Models, and Maxims for Writing Teachers*. 3–13. Portsmouth, NH: Boynton/Cook.

Bourdieu, Pierre. 1984. *Distinction: A Social Critique of the Judgment of Taste*. Trans. Richard Nice. Cambridge: Cambridge University Press.

Calkins, Lucy McCormick. 1983. *Lessons from a Child: On the Teaching and Learning of Writing*. Portsmouth, NH: Heinemann.

Crowley, Sharon. 1991. "Reimagining the Writing Scene: Curmudgeonly Remarks about *Contending with Words*." *Contending with Words:*

Composition and Rhetoric in a Postmodern Age, edited by Patricia Harkin and John Schilb. 189–95. New York: MLA.

Ehrenreich, Barbara. 1989. *Fear of Falling: The Inner Life of the Middle Class*. New York: Pantheon.

Elbow, Peter. 1990. *What is English?* New York: MLA.

Faigley, Lester. 1992. *Fragments of Rationality: Postmodernity and the Subject of Composition*. Pittsburgh, PA: University of Pittsburgh Press.

Feldman, Lynda. 1992. "Damaged Goods: Teaching from the Heart." Unpublished manuscript.

Freire, Paulo. 1983. *Pedagogy of the Oppressed*. Trans. Myra Bergman Ramos. New York: Continuum.

Giaccobe, Mary Ellen. 1986. "Learning to Write and Writing to Learn in the Elementary School." In *The Teaching of Writing: Eighty-fifth Yearbook of the National Society for the Study of Education*, edited by Anthony R. Petrosky and David Bartholomae. Chicago, IL: University of Chicago Press.

Giroux, Henry A. 1987. "Critical Literacy and Student Experience: Donald Graves' Approach to Literacy." *Language Arts* 64 (February):175–81. Rpt. in *Becoming Political: Readings and Writings in the Politics of Literacy Education*. 1992. Ed. Patrick Shannon. 15–20. Portsmouth, NH: Heinemann.

Graves, Donald H. 1976. "Let's Get Rid of the Welfare Mess in the Teaching of Writing." *Language Arts* 53 (September):645–51. Rpt. in Graves, 1984, *A Researcher Learns to Write: Selected Articles and Monographs*. Portsmouth, NH: Heinemann.

———. 1983. *Writing: Teachers and Children at Work*. Portsmouth, NH: Heinemann.

hooks, bell. 1989. "'when i was a young soldier for the revolution': coming to voice." *Talking Back: Thinking Feminist, Thinking Black*. 10–18. Boston, MA: South End Press.

Knoblauch, C. H. and Lil Brannon. 1993. *Critical Teaching and the Idea of Literacy*. Portsmouth, NH: Boynton/Cook.

———. 1984. *Rhetorical Traditions and the Teaching of Writing*. Portsmouth, NH: Boynton/Cook.

Miller, Susan. 1991. *Textual Carnivals: The Politics of Composition*. Carbondale, IL: Southern Illinois University Press.

———. 1989. *Rescuing the Subject: A Critical Introduction to Rhetoric and the Writer*. Carbondale, IL: Southern Illinois University Press.

Newkirk, Thomas. 1989. "The First Five Minutes: Setting the Agenda in a Writing Conference." *Writing and Response: Theory, Practice, and Research*, edited by Chris A. Anson. 317–31. Urbana, IL: NCTE.

Phelps, Louise Wetherbee. 1988. *Composition as a Human Science: Contributions to the Self-Understanding of a Discipline*. New York: Oxford University Press.

Rosenblatt, Louise. 1978. *The Reader, the Text, the Poem: The Transactional Theory of the Literary Work.* Carbondale, IL: Southern Illinois University Press.

Sowers, Susan. 1982. "Reflect, Expand, Select: Three Responses in the Writing Conference." *Understanding Writing: Ways of Observing, Learning, and Teaching*, edited by Thomas Newkirk and Nancie Atwell. 76–90. Portsmouth, NH: Heinemann.

Stafford, William. 1970. "A Way of Writing." *Field* 2 (1970). Rpt. in *The Bedford Introduction to Literature*. 1990. Ed. Michael Meyer. 915–16. Boston: St. Martin's.

15

The Perils, Pleasures, and Process of Ethnographic Writing Research

Wendy Bishop
Florida State University

Ethnographic writing research borrows heavily from the anthropological model of participant-observation inquiry. Traditionally, the anthropologist "enters the field" of another (almost always distant) culture, identifies a key-informant, and begins to try to "learn" that culture, in hopes of making manifest what normally isn't manifest—cultural definitions and practices, and community understandings. While sociologists also practice naturalistic research, conducting community studies in the more familiar cultures of American cities, their work is often undertaken to support the work of social theorists: "who build broad conceptual models for others to test and modify in humble social settings. These models are supposed to predict and explain patterns of thought and action across cultural domains" (Van Maanen 1988, 20). In anthropology, on the other hand, ethnography always was—and still remains—the primary research method, resulting in books about cultures rather than tests of cultural models.

In *The Making of Knowledge in Composition*, published in 1987, Steven North offered an initial definition of ethnographic research in composition along with a fairly pessimistic discussion concerning the function, usefulness, and reliability of field practices in this area, pointing to the variability of research designs and lack of projects in general. Although there are still fewer published projects than might be expected or hoped for, there has been greatly increased interest since that time in what William Irmscher calls "a model of inquiry appropriate to our own discipline—composition as part of English studies—consistent with its values, supporting and enlightening it" (1987, 82).

Since North published his influential book, many in composition have argued that naturalistic research methods, particularly ethnography and teacher-research (ethnographic researchers study other teachers' classes while teacher-researchers study their own classes), may be a primary method for understanding the complex literacy cultures that occur in schools and communities. Many in composition claim that context-based study illuminates previously neglected areas (for example, classroom context) and produces holistic understandings of complex processes (composing, becoming a writer or a writing teacher, undertaking or resisting university literacy). Here's how Elizabeth Chiseri-Strater describes her choice of research methods:

> My initial research interest was to understand how students interpret the literacy demands made on them in academic settings; what it meant from their vantage point to be literate in a university. . . . An ethnographic design seemed most appropriate for my purposes because it is concerned with the informant's world-view. (1991, 184)

While Barbara Walvoord and Lucille P. McCarthy made a similar decision:

> Our questions, as we began the study, were broad ones about students' thinking and writing. They were the general questions that Geertz says are traditionally asked by ethnographers facing new research scenes: "What's going on here?" and "What the devil do these people think they're up to?" (1976, 224). We chose the naturalistic inquiry paradigm to ask those questions. . . . (1990, 10)

Four years ago when I began teaching a research methods class focused mainly on ethnography, there were few book-length studies to read. Now the number includes Chiseri-Strater's and Walvoord and McCarthy's, as well as those by Brooke, *Writing and Sense of Self* (1991); Brooke and Hendricks, *Audience Expectations and Teacher Demands*(1987); and my own, *Something Old, Something New* (1990); with others forthcoming from several composition presses. In the same time period, books on composition research methods have included attention to naturalistic and ethnographic methods (Kirsch and Sullivan (1992); Lauer and Ascher (1988)) and recent books on teacher-research include those by Bissex and Bullock (1987); Daiker and Morenberg (1990); and Ray (1993).

Ethnographic writing research would also appear to thrive because it accesses and acknowledges some formerly repudiated skills, those of several generations of writing specialists whose education was formed in literature departments and whose critique of those departments has been buttressed by the rise of literary theory. Personally, I am inclined towards ethnographic writing research and critical narratives as a primary way of reporting writing research, even while being struck with the similarity of what I now do as a naturalistic/ethnographic/phenomenological writing classroom researcher to what I do as I read and apply critical theory. And my students are quick to experience this similarity themselves. During the first week of our research methods class Devan notes:

> Ethnography seems to seek (in this stage of my thinking) to rebuild any experience, setting, or world, in writing—as does any written communication. I'm tempted to believe that ethnography is an artful science.

In these journal musings, Devan joins a diverse group of research methods teachers, research practitioners, post-modern anthropologists, and others who are trying to understand the limits and potentials of this type of inquiry. By her fourth week of study, Devan writes:

> Interesting how as we go along things become clearer. . . . or whether such matters only seem clearer to us because we are more immersed in our studies and not looking at theory quite so hard. Is this an example of the ongoing and productive oscillation between a project and theorizing about it, the oscillation which is in fact the process of doing ethnography? Yes, I think without the theorizing I might be doing research of some kind (all those notes and all that taping of interviews and classes must be something!), but it would not be ethnography.

After several years of "doing" and teaching ethnography, I have come to feel that it is possible that everything about ethnographic writing research is perilous. At the least, ethnography resists definition. It is difficult to learn to do, seemingly impossible to evaluate, inappropriate for publication in traditional formats, and complicated to teach. Ethnography is also intellectually and physically exhilarating, and naturalistic research, overall, is pleasurable in the way writing and reading and talking and learning are pleasurable. In that sense, the ethnographic activity is a primary one since it grows out of the materials at hand—human consciousness in everyday life. Anthropologist Harry Wolcott claims: "There is something of the perceptive ethnographer in each of us . . . each of us must succeed as an intuitive participant and observer for sheer survival in a social milieu. Each of us must figure out how to cope with the world we encounter, the unexpected as well as the expected" (1987, 45). It is natural as humans to be intuitive participants in the everyday landscape, but to become successful ethnographers, we need further training.

For me, then, doing, theorizing, and teaching ethnography remains the most engaging and frustrating process I've ever undertaken. The territory of ethnographic writing research seems so big and so complicated, yet I know it is also arrived at with a simple map because I attempted my own first project with no more than a nod from my dissertation director, a few sociology and anthropology field guides, and the understanding that this would be the only type of research I would ever find comprehensible.

In the rest of this chapter I'll explore some of the perils and pleasures of ethnographic writing research, including issues that are at stake in trying to teach the process to others. While doing this, I want to share the insights of theorists and practitioners I've consulted and students I've worked with. Meditations on their words are helping me attempt to say what it is we do and what it is we need to know. Consider these meditations, if you will, as a handful of beads of some luster that I *could* string together but prefer—maybe even need at this point—to hold together in a rough handful as I try to capture and touch upon their actual complexity.

Meditation 1: Defining Ethnography

Ethnography is difficult to define because of the sweeping concepts involved—culture, language, symbol. Ethnography is an activity most readily understood from the inside, by doing the work itself. To undertake ethnography, however, novice ethnographers must begin to make sense of their domain, and that domain ultimately is culture. "'Culture'," Harry Wolcott explains, "as an *explicit* statement of how the members of a particular social group act and believe they should act, does not exist until someone acting in the role of ethnographer puts it there" (1987, 41). Wolcott's assertion that culture is constituted contradicts the more prevalent view of research in general that knowledge—of the cultural or material world—is out there waiting to be discovered. Therefore, ethnographers, practitioners of a subjective process, have had to fight hard for prestige in academic communities that valorize the objective stance. Nancy, a student in a research methods course, registers this struggle:

> The readings and the interviews [conducted by our class] got me thinking right away. At first, in fact for quite awhile, I wasn't really sure what ethnography was. The authors that we read seemed to all have a slightly different answer to what ethnography was and what its purpose was. Several authors didn't seem to value ethnography all that much. They seemed to think that it was a good way to get thinking about a "real" research project.

Nancy rehearses major research arguments. Is ethnography "science" or "philosophy"? Is ethnography on a continuum of empirical methodologies, ranging from qualitative to quantitative? Is ethnographic work primarily pre-scientific, generating hypotheses for later, more rigorous, testing?

Some composition scholars have found it difficult or impossible to define ethnography and therefore are hesitant to sanction it as a research process. George Hillocks (1986) in his meta-analysis leaves qualitative research out of his story of writing. Stephen North (1987) in his research categories separates ethnography from hermeneutical research and from teacher-research—separations I would argue against—and ends up defining it as a practice that functions poorly, creating a research community with borders but no center.

Linda Brodkey directs our attention away from method and toward researchers' attitudes and alignments, distinguishing analytic ethnographers—who identify categories and sort data into those categories—from interpretive ethnographers whose "'themes' . . . might be described as arising out of 'breakdowns' in the ethnographer's understanding of particular phenomena . . . " (Brodkey 1987b, 31).

But inevitably, ethnography remains resistant to methodological definition by way of enumerating its constituent parts; that is, ethnographers may agree on required techniques in general—such as triangulation, field notes, participant-observation, longitudinal investigation, recursive analysis, and so on—but they rarely agree on the quantities and ordering of techniques, nor whether quantitative data is "allowable." And the pluralism versus purity arguments that arise from methodological distrust can make a novice researcher despair of getting any realistic advice about how to enter real writing cultures in order to conduct actual studies.

To end my meditation on the problems of definition, I'll share those I currently find most thought-provoking. First, Harry Wolcott suggests that the ethnographic label "should be reserved for descriptive efforts clearly ethnographic *in intent*" (1987, 43). Second, Lucy Calkins reminds us of the wholly human dimensions of research when she claims:

> [A]lthough many people still subscribe to the adage that research methods are determined by research questions, in the field of composition it is more accurate to say that research methods are created, combined, adapted, invented, and stumbled on—and that ideally they are chosen based on the researcher's personality and belief system. (1985, 126)

These definitions set aside received advice ("the trick is triangulation" or "first decide on your questions and population") and describe what is more likely to happen. For instance, I studied retraining college writing teachers and the ways they modified their teaching after enrollment in a graduate pedagogy seminar because I had taken that seminar two years earlier. I wanted to know more about such an experience. I began with a completely ethnographic intent, but knew I sometimes bungled my ethnographic practices—losing a taped interview or reading a transcript in an interested way—and learned I would need to weave fragmentary case study data into satisfying research stories. It is more honest and accurate, I believe, to admit to our creations, combinations, adaptations, and inventions since this is how we actually make knowledge.

Meditation 2: Writing It Down and Writing It Up

Despite increased production and increased interest in ethnographic writing research, we don't yet have a large number of published ethnographies available nor do we have many stories available that illuminate the research process. We are low both on canon and critical apparatus. Lucy Calkins feels this is because we "do not ask prominent researchers in our field to provide personal, honest accounts of their research processes" (1985, 126), and John Van Maanen reminds us that ethnographers "rarely read of unsuccessful field projects where the research was presumably so personally disastrous to the fieldworker that the study was dropped or failed ever to find its way to publication" (1988, 79). This nonreporting of disasters holds true for ethnographies in composition studies for obvious reasons.

Seldom discussed either is the guilt that can be generated by involvement in time-intensive, longitudinal work. It is no small investment of human interactions and paper and ink to have ten unsorted boxes of data in an office or storeroom. While data collection must take place within the studied culture—providing the researcher with classroom or workplace schedules that organize and regularize data collection—data analysis takes place in the cluttered spaces of the researcher's life. Without paid research time, teacher-researchers in particular will find themselves reading data at extraordinary times and in unlikely places or find those pleasures too often deferred to imaginary summer holidays.

Indeed, methods texts tend to become less helpful the farther they pursue the topic of ethnographic research. The novice learns how to form questions, identify informants and enter the field, but hears little about field notes—what they look like or how they are coded or analyzed—and less about time-management and manuscript preparation. Most methods texts remain mute concerning the development of stories, the choosing of tropes, or the shaping of narratives to please a community of readers. This foregrounded front-end view of ethnography—enter the scene, collect it all, write it all down and you're nearly done—is problematic for the beginner. And she may become the author of one of those disastrous, dropped, or failed publications if she doesn't receive guidance or practice in writing it up.

In writing up data, an ethnographer unites practice and theory; she is no longer dealing with actual situations that are in the process of being-invented-as-culture through the quality of her attention. Instead, she begins to examine, understand, shape, and share decontextualized texts that will be vivified by her careful analysis, using the lenses of her memory and intellect. This is a difficult task at best. One research student, Nancy, says: "The accumulation of data was both exciting and overwhelming . . . I sat in confusion with the data in front of me. How can I chart this? No ideas."

Another student, Kim, elaborates:

> So, what *is* it like to be an ethnographer? It is to deal with mountains of data and packed blue crates of information—and then make sense of them. . . . I soon discovered that I needed a system in which I could categorize my materials and have them available in a chronological sequence. . . . I moved to a three ring binder. . . . I know this might sound kind of trivial, to talk about my mini-epiphany involving notebook organization, but it really spoke to me about what it is to be an ethnographer. You have to see things in a different way. . . . Not only did I have to change the physical way I approached a class, but I had to try to see information differently—that is, instead of building on ideas I already had, I had to try to pull them back and make myself receptive to what might arise. . . . It is an interesting contradiction because the ethnographic process calls for strict organization, which is linear in nature, yet the interpretation calls for a more circular vision, which is recursive.

I quote Kim at such length because she raises all the themes touched on by theorist/anthropologists I've been reading. Kim was experiencing textualization:

> "Textualization" is Ricoeur's (1973) term for the process by which unwritten behavior, beliefs, values, rituals, oral traditions, and so forth, become fixed, atomized, and classified as data of a certain sort. Only in textualized form do data yield to analysis. The process of analysis is not dependent on the events themselves, but on a second-order, textualized, fieldworker-dependent version of the events. (Van Maanen 1988, 95)

And how we go about textualizing goes back to the definition we use for ethnographic research. Over time, I have come to see the ethnographer as the core element in textualization—situated, biased, interested, involved. Undertaking her work with ethnographic intent, the ethnographer becomes a storyteller, analyzing, coding, considering, and sharing her data. Harry Wolcott (1990) suggests this is a very practical stage. Ethnographies are never about *everything*—particularly if you believe it is the ethnographer who for one brief moment illuminates and creates an interpretation and a culture. Writing it up is a creative, critical, and very practical act. Wolcott says:

> [The] task in qualitative research is not to accumulate all the data you can, but to "can" (i.e., get rid of) most of the data you accumulate. This requires constant winnowing. The trick is to discover essences and then to reveal those essences with sufficient context, yet not become mired trying to include everything that might possibly be described. (1990, 35)

Since most methods texts foreground finding a question and entering a culture and collecting data, the difficulties of "canning" all that data can be surprising and then discouraging because they are so rarely discussed. And usually within a research methods classroom we never get around to experimenting with writing it up.

What does textualization look and feel like? Well, my first ethnographic report aped the cool clinical style I assumed researchers needed to maintain (or that dissertation writers needed to observe). Turning dissertation to book, I tried to improve my prose and achieved a reportorial voice that sounded like this:

> When she entered the graduate program in rhetoric, Peg had completed six years of community college teaching at a branch campus within the Florida community college system, and she was the only full-time English instructor at her branch. Having taught intensively for the last six years (five classes per semester, mainly composition), Peg commenced her graduate studies hoping to revitalize her commitment to composition instruction. Without such revitalization, she seriously believed she might need to stop teaching and look for work as a technical or business writer (or, less seriously, as a lawyer). (1990, 62).

This chapter introduction certainly gets the work done and honors the data, but it doesn't begin to hint at the complex interactions that took place between researcher and teacher. I situate myself outside of the picture. Apparently, I am *simply* presenting facts as they were collected.

Four years later, my ethnographic reporting voice is quite different. The following is the opening to a second study (only now I am considering new teachers of writing rather than retraining teachers of writing), with data collected in a similar manner through interviews and class participant-observation. Intentionally, I've moved toward impressionistic reporting, a move that also turns me from author into character:

> Two years after I first meet her, one year after I finish collecting data for a study of new teachers of college writing, Rose walks into my office.
>
> "Thank you," she says.
>
> "For what?"
>
> "I won the nonfiction essay contest."
>
> "You did that, not me," I say, realizing she had composed the essay in a class I taught.
>
> Four days later, I'm still thinking about Rose as her prize is announced at the English Department Awards ceremony. She has just completed her MA degree, and I know that for her—and for me—there is real triumph in this moment.
>
> Rose entered our program to write a thesis of nonfiction essays; found teaching first-year writing as a graduate assistant so traumatic she became the first TA in current memory to ask to be taken out of the classroom; decided and re-decided her academic future—choosing not to pursue a Ph.D. just three weeks before this ceremony—earned a 4.O GPA through all her indecision; and took M.A. exams in literature because they were doable, not because they particularly met her career goals or the dream she had of writing a book.
>
> At the awards ceremony, however, Rose is fully present, confident, just for a moment, just as she is leaving. (draft, *Composing*)

There is more pleasure for me than problem in considering myself as these two different "writers"—and, indeed, I'd still question why I don't yet add the physical details of what Rose and I looked like, where we were, and what we were doing. In studying these textual styles, I consider cans, contents, and canning methods, and I want students of ethnography to have opportunities for doing the same. Turning data into stories teaches us about ethnographic texts from the inside out, and ethnographic research gives us textualized data that is worth writing about as we ask where we stand, in relation to whom, and for what purposes.

Meditation 3: The Possible Pleasures of Postmodern "Faction" Research and Writing.

Linda Flowers (1989) tells a "story" in which John R. Hayes explains that examining write-aloud protocols is similar to finding patterns in clouds. This admission can seem astonishing, a potential betrayal of an empirical research agenda and the reports that filled composition journals throughout the 1980s. These researchers, who began their work within a positivistic tradition, are currently becoming more pluralistic, broadening their research attention to consider context; in doing so, they are participating in a critique of the rhetoric of science that many feel is long overdue.

All research reports convince us of their veracity not merely through an accumulation of facts but through the power of the author's rhetoric, and all research is reported for some community in the manner sanctioned by that community. Carl Herndl explains,

> Ethnographies persuade readers not by the power of factual description but by employing the narrative structures, textual tropes, and argumentative topoi developed by the ethnographic genre. Geertz's own notion of "thick description" is a case in point. It is a highly stylized form of verisimilitude that has become a standard in discussions of ethnographic method and functions as a textual strategy authorizing attempts at ethnographic realism. (321)

We can see thick description more clearly as a trope when we look back at Wolcott's suggestion that we're trying to "can" all the data possible, for thick description gives us the satisfying illusion of a can crammed full. When doing this, narratives are probably our most powerful reporting technique. Thomas Newkirk reminds us that "narratives are embedded in all academic discourse—even the most austere; each has conventions for telling that indicate to the writer what should be attended to and what should be ignored" (1991, 132).

It's the breadth of our gaze—creating a culture or a cultural moment—that causes ethnographers so many writing-it-up-and-sharing-it-widely difficulties: thick description literally is thick, resulting in research reports of unwieldy proportions. When those reports are trimmed to fit current journal requirements of fifteen to twenty-five pages, rhetorical power is lost since our narratives and stories are trimmed first. Current publication forums favor the scientific report that is equally trope-filled, equally stylized, but using different rhetorical strategies. "Faced with the dilemma of having more to pack than a suitcase can possibly hold," suggests Harry Wolcott, "the novice traveler has three possibilities: rearrange so as to get more in, remove nonessentials, or find a larger suitcase. Qualitative researchers have comparable [writing] options" (1990, 62). In essence, the "cool" rhetorical models of science offer only a straitjacket for our warmer ethnographic fullness. Additionally, who we are affects what we write, too; our reports are full of ourselves and others. Jennifer Hunt claims: "There is also little doubt that the sociological narrative is partly autobiographical, reflecting something about the researcher's personality as well as those of the subjects who enter the ethnographic dialogue." From this perspective, she believes fieldwork is, in part, "the discovery of the self through the detour of the other" (1989, 41–42).

Sometimes that detour is best taken in good company. One of the benefits of working as a research team in a methods class came from sharing multiple views on a complicated classroom reality. Two students, Nancy and Kim, worked to code data together. Kim recollects:

> As we began coding, we found that some of our categories were inadequate or not precise enough and we began to reshape them accordingly. There is something very rewarding about working with someone else in this manner. The normal discovery that is associated with writing is compounded and complicated which provides a deeper way of viewing your purposes. The more we worked, the more conscientious we got as one of us would take on one role and the other would provide the perceptions of another role to further define our meanings. As writers, we are constantly engaging in dialectic with ourselves, but when there is another perspective there to interject, the thinking becomes more full and comprehensive. I liked the struggle to arrive at meanings that spoke to both of our perspectives. I felt like our negotiations were productive and meaningful.

All in all, it is no wonder that the writing research methods class entertains questions very similar to those engaged in critical theory classes. Kim and Nancy read the data and then read each others' readings. In looking at ethnographic writing research, then, we are studying representations of self and society and language and symbol systems. Because ethnography is a thoroughly textual practice, it can be analyzed for its "literary characteristics" and by genre. Clifford Geertz has coined the term "faction," which he describes as "imaginative writing about real people in real places at real times" (1988, 141), and suggests that anthropological discourse is somewhat more like literary discourse than it is like scientific discourse, although he believes:

> This does not make us into novelists any more than constructing hypotheses or writing formulas make us, as some seem to think, into physicists. But it does suggest some family resemblances that we tend, like the North African mule who talks always of his mother's brother [sciences], the horse, but never of his father, the donkey [humanities], to suppress in favor of others, supposedly more reputable. (1988, 8)

Unlike anthropologists, I think writing researchers, because they have an English studies grounding, may tend to favor their donkey (humanist) side—finding they are constantly drawing on strengths they already have.

More often than not, though, ethnographic writing researchers, like postmodern anthropologists, will find themselves hovering between the two stances—cool physicist or warm novelist—outlined by Clifford Geertz:

> The first [stance] brings charges of insensitivity, of treating people as objects, of hearing the words but not the music, and of course, of ethnocentrism. The second [stance] brings charges of impressionism, of treating people as puppets, of hearing music that doesn't exist, and, of course, of ethnocentrism. (1988, 10)

Anyone who has entered a writing culture learns that her point of entry is interested. That is, as writing teachers we want to know about writing classrooms, writers, teachers, those who do write, and those who don't. We are already situated. Therefore, we are also predisposed to see already-familiar patterns or to reach for well-worn metaphors. Lad Tobin, for instance, studying his own writing class, found telling mismatches between his own and his writing students' metaphorical images for writing (1989). He was able to investigate the two and put himself and his students in dialogue, listening to the music that was in the classroom as well as the music he brought with him.

Writing teachers make excellent researchers because they are careful readers of classrooms and have a real interest in attending to what is going on. The writing researcher in the postmodern landscape needs to honor the subjective-objective discussions of her time and construct her cultural readings with an awareness of colonial impulses (that is, most of us study-down, looking at classrooms or communities under our control; and rarely study-up, looking at those who administer our programs, schools and/or communities). John Van Maanen finds this tough balancing-act taking place in what he calls "impressionist writing," which "tries to keep both subject and object in constant view. The epistemological aim is then to braid the knower and the known" (1988, 102).

But more is at stake than simple fairness. Both objective and subjective positions are constructed. New critical readings of culture *are* possible, as are interpretive reader-response readings. Analytical ethnography shades into interpretive ethnography. "Authors" are dead when they are no longer construed as solitary consciousness, while real authors are alive and writing from the strength of the multiple perspectives they inhabit as users of language within their culture(s). Ethnography is pleasurable because it creates a space for dialogue where ethnographers shuttle between the theoretical positions outlined here. Laurel Richardson suggests that when we adopt this hovering, shuttling, or weaving-together motion, we are adopting a progressive-postmodern position:

> Because all knowledge is partial and situated, it does not mean that there is no knowledge or that situated knowledge is bad. There is no view from "nowhere," the authorless text. There is no view from

> "everywhere," except for God. There is only a view from "somewhere," an embodied, historically and culturally situated speaker. (1990, 27)

What we are trying to do, then, in methodology classes is teach students how to create a view from "somewhere." We do that by teaching ethnography as a process for thinking and learning in the academy.

Meditation 4: Ethnography as Process

Taube, in her final project, a class meta-analysis, reflects on the ethnographic process:

> When I entered the classroom, I expected the worst. The teacher was enthusiastic enough, but she seemed to be addressing me in some alien tongue, a kind of anthropological Esperanto. Words like "triangulation," "coding," and "thick description"—words I did not understand, but wanted to learn with the most desperate urgency—a Berlitz-krieg approach to disciplinary terminology.
>
> In my profound ethnographic naiveté, I'm afraid I even consoled myself with delusions of mastery. If I could just learn the ethnographic steps, then I could "do" ethnography as if ethnographic methods were ritualized or formulaic, an Arthur Murray Approach to Research.
>
> I learned, too, that the taxonomic boundaries of ethnography were distressingly malleable. Not only was there a vociferous debate over the usefulness of ethnographic research as a practice, the practitioners couldn't even come to a consensus on what exactly it was they were doing. Late one night, in a moment of lexical desperation, I finally decided that ethnographic definitions were necessarily subject-ive—for how else could one interpret subjects within a cultural setting?
>
> Indeed, it was this subject-ivity offered by ethnographic research that I most appreciated.

In my second year of designing a graduate level rhetoric course in research methodology, I faced a continuing problem: how could I enable students who knew very little about this subject to gain field experience as well as to contextualize their learning through classroom reading and discussions? Eventually, I decided to forge our small, eight member, seminar group into a research team, using one meeting each week to discuss/analyze our data and using one meeting each week to talk about our readings in light of our ongoing research project. To start in the thick of things, I designed the project ahead of time and had it ready as we began. The project was to study a first-year writing classroom in our composition program titled "ENC

1142—Freshman Imaginative Writing" that included poetry and fiction writing with essayist writing.

By the second week of the semester, we were able to begin data collection in the classroom of a willing teacher; two pairs of participant-observers visited the class for several weeks. As we collected data, we read and discussed definitional essays; as we started to analyze our own data, we read several book-length studies; and as we ended the semester, we agreed to meet the following summer to finish our work, intending to draft an essay for publication. Because we were already "doing ethnography," the definition-laden essays we read seemed to have more utility. As we read book-length studies, we were more able to critique that research from the inside out, from researcher stances.

Students in that course wrote research meta-analyses that provided insights into their learning. In her summary, Nancy said:

> We read, we interviewed, we surveyed, we created statistics, we took field notes, we worked in teams, we discussed both readings and data, and we tried to figure out how to write our report. I feel good about this type of learning. It created meaning for me. My story doesn't really end here. Sometime this summer the story of this research class will be taken up again as we get back together to see if we can pull together a paper out of all this data. All I know is that I am fascinated by our work and if I had the summer to do what I like, I wouldn't be surprised to find myself spending a lot more time looking at more and more data. I must admit amazement at this idea. It wasn't one of my expectations when I began the course.

Earlier in the same analysis, Nancy had identified a crucial turning point in the semester, saying: "As this class continued, I really started enjoying ethnography instead of worrying about what it was." She suggests that it is through the process of doing ethnography that we learn how to research with ethnographic intent and start to theorize those intentions.

Ethnography, then, is an intention *and* a state of mind. And that state of mind is pursued for a lifetime, not just during data collection in the field. John Van Maanen points to the duration of the ethnographic journey:

> Events and conversations of the past are forever being reinterpreted in light of new understandings and continuing dialogue with the studied. . . . [Ethnography] is perhaps more akin to learning to play a musical instrument than to solving a puzzle. What the fieldworker learns is how to appreciate the world in a different key. (1988, 118)

Nancy, Kim and others in the class were sure they were starting to see writing *and* research communities in a new key because they had practiced ethnographic research together. In a similar ways, I am experimenting with the form of research reports as part of my own ethnographic education.

The next year, when I taught this research course to a larger group, I changed the design once more, asking students to conduct individual or co-authored six-week-long, mini-ethnographies and to share drafts in workgroups—thus offering research authors time to consider "writing it up" issues. Each class member also presented a "technique report," allowing us to produce a class research-methods handbook together. The course designs I've tried have perils and pleasures of their own, and choice of design certainly depends on goals (is it more important to explore aspects of the research process or to produce research products?) and on the number of participants overall (a collaborative research project is hard to do with a large class, obviously). And each class of researchers foregrounds different learning(s). For instance, during this term, when entering and exiting classrooms for mini-ethnographies, some graduate-teaching-assistants-turned-ethnographers experienced unsettling insights into their own teaching. Mark writes in his end of term class meta-analysis,

> Cut me through with a thousand spears of light and watch my insides dance around in their nakedness—that's what reading and writing ethnographies does to the teacher-self. Seeing into these other people's classrooms, hearing their methods criticized, criticizing them yourself, then walking into your own class. It's very painful. . . . I remember sitting in on a group discussing their papers and thinking, "This is frightening." Their advice was so lame, so superficial, often just plain wrong. I wanted to scream. But here they were acting the same way in my class, oh, how disheartening. Ethnography is like sitting out in the hallway and hearing someone else's students calling your colleague a jerk.

These experiences led many of my students to conclude, with the theorists they read, that the subject of ethnographic writing research was not, in Geertz' memorable phrase, simply "What the devil do these people think they're up to?" but also, "What the devil am I up to with these people?"

I was drawn to meditate on the perils, pleasures, and process of ethnographic writing research by the rapidity of the development of this part of composition studies and the allure of the activity itself. Raised in positivism, I felt somewhat guilty for moving so fully to this methodology as a teacher of methods and as a researcher. Under the sway of the dominant "hard" objective culture, I felt this movement might indicate I was going as "soft" as my methodology. However, I also started to take real pleasure in finding that the postmodern discussions I've touched upon in this chapter were central to anthropology, for these anthropological authors seemed more accessible to me than the more conceptual—yet very similar—pronouncements of critical theorists in English departments around the country. I thought that maybe I too, for the first time, had something to contribute to such conversations, premising my contributions on theorized practice rather than linguistic explication. (I'm alluding here, of course, to my distressing inability to read French discourse philosophers to any degree for any purpose.)

At the same time, I knew that my thoughts were drifting more to writing about research than being directed into the practice of research. Often, I find myself theorizing as much or more than researching—in a manner that takes me a surprising distance from the contexts and cultures that originally called me into research. In a teaching journal entry from that research methods class, I note (during the same term I'm teaching a poetry writing workshop): "I find the subject of ethnography so interesting; talking about poetry isn't ever as interesting as doing poetry, but thinking and talking about ethnography remains for me equally interesting as doing." This situation creates a problem similar to the one I experience as a creative writer. I have the interest and skills to write in literary genres *as well as* the need to understand the relationship of text to text by writing criticism or to move into classroom practice. Suddenly, one day, I realize it has been some time since I wrote a poem at all. One solution, of course, has been to reconceive writing theory and practice as indivisible, and to situate myself as a writer in the classroom. Equally, I hope to redefine ethnographic writing research in the same manner.

And even though I believe we need many more published ethnographies of all types *as well as* writings about how they were written, I worry about suggestions like the one offered by Michael Kleine:

> We must, in addition to writing traditional academic articles, allow ourselves to write even more in the first-person singular, to write personal diaries—even confessions—about our experiences as ethnographers. Perhaps these diaries should be published and shared. *Perhaps they should supplant formal academic articles for awhile.* By studying ourselves, we will come to terms with our own rhetoric. (1990, 124, my emphasis)

I agree with most of Kleine's suggestions about writing styles and authors' voices. But, I don't think we should join the critical rush to supplant research with writing-about-research anymore than "criticism" should supplant the production of "literature(s)." I think we need to understand that the process of writing research defines the researcher as both artist and critic, practitioner and theorist. In this manner we honor our scientific *and* our humanistic relatives but become co-opted by neither. Neither scientific horse, nor humanist donkey, nor hybrid mule, really, we are humans studying humans, creating cultures through careful attention and by examining our view from "somewhere." Perhaps we are discovering the "self through the detour of the other" but we are also adding to the "collective story." There have been strong arguments raised recently that rhetoric may offer a new vision for English studies, and I'd assert that *the process* of ethnographic writing research may provide a powerful way to reunite practice and theory in our everyday academic lives.

With all this in mind, I put down my chapter and return to the ten boxes of data in my office—voices, interludes, interviews, collaborations, complications—and continue to add to the story.

Works Cited

Bishop, Wendy. *Composing the New Teacher of College Writing: Ethnographic Essays and Reflections.* Manuscript in progress.

———. 1992. "I-Witnessing in Composition: Turning Ethnographic Data into Narratives." *Rhetoric Review* 11.1 (Fall):147–58.

———. 1990. *Something Old, Something New: College Writing Teachers and Classroom Change.* Carbondale, IL: Southern Illinois University Press.

Bissex, Glenda L., and Richard H. Bullock. 1987. *Seeing for Ourselves: Case-Study Research by Teachers of Writing.* Portsmouth, NH: Heinemann.

Brodkey, Linda. 1987a. "Writing Critical Ethnographic Narratives." *Anthropology & Education Quarterly* 18:67–76.

———. 1987b. "Writing Ethnographic Narratives." *Written Communication* 9:25–50.

Brooke, Robert. 1991. *Writing and Sense of Self: Identity Negotiation in Writing Workshops.* Urbana, IL: NCTE.

———. 1988. "Modeling a Writer's Identity: Reading and Imitation in the Writing Classroom." *College Composition and Communication* 39: 23–41.

Brooke, Robert and John Hendricks. 1989. *Audience Expectations and Teacher Demands.* Studies in Writing and Rhetoric Series. Carbondale, IL: Southern Illinois University Press.

Calkins, Lucy McCormick. 1985. "Forming Research Communities Among Naturalistic Researchers." *Perspectives on Research and Scholarship in Composition*, edited by Ben McClelland and Timothy R. Donovan. New York: MLA.

———. 1983. *Lessons From a Child.* Portsmouth, NH: Heinemann.

Chiseri-Strater, Elizabeth. 1991. *Academic Literacies: The Public and Private Discourse of University Students*. Portsmouth, NH: Boynton/Cook.

Daiker, Donald A. and Max Morenberg, eds. 1990. *The Writing Teacher as Researcher: Essays in the Theory and Practice of Class-Based Research*. Portsmouth, NH: Boynton/Cook.

Flower, Linda. 1989. "Cognition, Context, and Theory Building." *College Composition and Communication* 40 (October):282–311.

Geertz, Clifford. 1988. *Works and Lives: The Anthropologist as Author*. Stanford, CA: Stanford University Press.

———. 1976. "'From the Native's Point of View': On the Nature of Anthropological Understanding." In *Meaning in Anthropology,* edited by Keith H. Basso and Henry A. Selby. Albuquerque, NM: University of New Mexico Press.

Herndl, Carl G. 1991. "Writing Ethnography: Representation, Rhetoric, and Institutional Practices." *College English* 53.3 (March):320–32.

Hillocks, George. 1986. *Research on Written Composition: New Directions for Teaching*. Urbana, IL: ERIC and NCTE.

Hunt, Jennifer C. 1989. *Psychoanalytic Aspects of Fieldwork*. Qualitative Research Methods, Series 18. Newbury Park, CA: Sage.

Irmscher, William. F. 1987. "Finding a Comfortable Identity." *College Composition and Communication* 38:81–87.

Kirsch, Gesa and Patricia A. Sullivan, eds. 1992. *Methods and Methodology in Composition Research*. Carbondale, IL: Southern Illinois University Press.

Kleine, Michael. 1990. "Beyond Triangulation: Ethnography, Writing, and Rhetoric." *Journal of Advanced Composition* 10.1:117–25.

Lauer, Janice and J. William Asher. 1988. *Composition Research: Empirical Designs*. New York: Oxford University Press.

Newkirk, Thomas. 1991. "The Politics of Composition Research: The Conspiracy Against Experience." *The Politics of Writing Instruction: Post-secondary*, edited by Richard Bullock and John Trimber. Charles Schuster, general ed. Portsmouth, NH: Boynton/Cook.

North, Stephen. 1987. *The Making of Knowledge in Composition: Portrait of an Emerging Field*. Portsmouth, NH: Boynton/Cook.

Ray, Ruth E. 1993. *The Practice of Theory: Teacher Research in Composition*. Urbana, IL: NCTE.

Richardson, Laurel. 1990. *Writing Strategies: Reaching Diverse Audiences*. Qualitative Research Methods, Series 21. Newbury Park, CA: Sage.

Ricoeur, Paul. 1973. "The Model of the Text." *New Literary History* 5:91–120.

Tobin, Lad. 1989. "Bridging Gaps: Analyzing Our Students' Metaphors for Composing." *College Composition and Communication* 40 (December): 444–58.

Van Maanen, John. 1988. *Tales of the Field: On Writing Ethnography.* Chicago, IL: University of Chicago Press.

Walvoord, Barbara E. and Lucille P. McCarthy. 1990. *Thinking and Writing in College: A Naturalistic Study of Students in Four Disciplines.* Urbana, IL: NCTE.

Wolcott, Harry F. 1987. "On Ethnographic Intent." *Interpretive Ethnography of Education: At Home and Abroad,* edited by George Spindler and Louise Spindler. Hillsdale, NJ: Erlbaum.

———. 1990. *Writing Up Qualitative Research.* Qualitative Research Methods, Volume 20. Newbury Park, CA: Sage.

16

There is one story worth telling

James Britton
London, England

My title is one that many will recognize—the opening lines of a poem by Robert Graves about the nature of myth; a poem he has entitled: *To Juan at the Winter Solstice.*

> There is one story and one story only
> That will prove worth your telling,
> Whether as learned bard or gifted child;
> To it all lines or lesser gauds* belong
> That startle with their shining
> Such common stories as they stray into.

So much to justify my title. But the immediate context that forms my starting point comes from a philosopher whom I knew during my first years as a teacher. I suspect that you will never have heard of him, though you might have heard of his wife—she was a celebrated educator and writer called Susan Isaacs, a friend of Piaget's and one of the first authors who wrote sympathetically about children's early language development.

Her husband, Nathan Isaacs, was a philosopher who wrote frequent brief comments on some of the uses—and misuses—of language, and, in 1949, a book entitled *The Foundations of Common Sense*. For some reason I don't now recall, he knew some of the articles I had written about children's language and would send me

*Gauds is an old word for one of the larger beads found in a rosary.

copies of what he was writing—novel and often original notions about language development. What struck me above all was his belief in the collective responsibility we all share for keeping our uses of language—both spoken and written—true and comprehensible. Like Vygotsky (whose work he could hardly have known) he was a firm believer in the idea that word-meanings are not fixed and unchangeable, but grow as our experience enlarges, and form in fact the key to the development of intellectual abilities in the individual.

He challenges the notion that we communicate successfully through word-meanings, as though such meanings had been handed on from parents to children as stock in trade shared from generation to generation. "We assume that we communicate essentially through word-meanings and can do so successfully because these are, as it were, common social property." But he went on to suggest that we do not in fact share word-meanings, since they are as individual as one person's experience is to another's. It may well seem to us that we have good reasons for thinking that others' view of the world is closely similar to our own. "These good reasons, however, do not arise out of the way in which we first "impart" word-meanings to our children. In fact we do not "impart" them; we have no means of doing so. We repeatedly thrust sounds upon a child in certain kinds of situation or in the presence of certain kinds of occurrence and we hope the sounds will "take," in the sense that the child will learn to link them with those kinds of occurrence just as we do." We hope, then, that the image, the idea, of them will come into the child's mind when he hears the word, and if anything else brings them into his mind he will also recall the word (1958, 1–8).

It was this encouraging relationship between a child and an adult that Vygotsky gave a name to when he spoke of the child's "zone of proximal development"—an area of competence that he or she has not yet achieved but one that waits upon the opportunity to co-operate with an adult (or older child) and so internalize the ability to carry out the behavior when left to him- or herself. One can certainly suppose that Isaacs would have approved of Vygotsky's claim that "word meaning is an elementary 'cell' that cannot be further analyzed and that represents the most elementary form of the unity between thought and word" (1986, 212).

We tend to assume, Isaacs believes, that the child's experience in response to a word is very similar to our own, but this is surely to disregard the fact that the child is unable to call upon the "cumulative meaningfulness which we build up throughout our lives . . . the structured meaning-system which takes the shape in us stage by stage as our thought develops and into which we receive and integrate all subsequent experience-material." Our words, "even when [the child] has learnt to use them in the same situations as we do and to respond to them in apparently similar ways, cannot remotely mean the same thing for him as they do for us" (Op cit, p. 2.). Both responses, we must add, will be charged with meaning, but with different meanings reflecting different worlds of experience.

And this remains the level of agreement we can expect to find between any two people's interpretations of a verbal statement. We seem to be speaking the same language principally because we do not probe too deeply. But Isaacs makes the important point that we should form the deliberate habit of setting out to communicate in the simplest and most direct manner something that we have ourselves experienced—and in doing so encourage the maintenance of a direct and valid use of communication between people. "What we respond to," he writes, "with a fresh and vivid experience of our own built up of those effectively selected word-meanings" is something *authentically* experienced ("seen," "felt," "imagined") by the writer. . . . If one said that the more he concentrated on just trying faithfully to describe or express the experience in his mind, without any other claim or pretensions, the more chance there would be of his evoking a true counterpart response in the reader's mind. In fact one can hardly go wrong in . . . so describing it that the reader does get an experienced sense of it. . . . Such a principle might well be the *beginning* of authentic and effective writing" (Op cit. p. 9).

The beginning, we might say, of stories that are well worth telling.

My first visit to the American continent came some seven years later, when—in 1965—I spent six weeks teaching the summer session at The University of British Columbia. I had already read Susanne Langer's *Philosophy in a New Key*, and in the course of that six weeks I followed this up by reading *Philosophical Sketches*—an astonishing *hors d'oeuvres* of interests—and in particular her comments on the language of everyday speech. She contrasts man with the zoological creatures as man's picture of the world "hangs together, its events fit into each other: no matter how devious their connections, there always are connections, in one big framework of space and time. . . . All our experience—practical, ethical, or intellectual—is built up on an intuitively constructed logical scaffold known as common sense" (1979, 125, 128). Common sense, she believes, is a "rough-and-ready instrument that is prone to yield absurdities when its concepts are tested for all they imply" (Op cit p. 135). But it is our commonplace notions that raise the issues and may always at some point undergo correction in the terms afforded by more accurate and more systematic observations.

All this took place in the year before the month-long Anglo-American Seminar at Dartmouth University—to which, I learned later, Susanne Langer was invited either as consultant or as delegate, but was in fact prevented from coming by illness. It was some years before her three volume account, *Mind: An Essay on Human Feeling*, gave us her full conclusions regarding the role of feeling in our society and in our daily living.

Her focus in *Philosophical Sketches* is upon the role of feeling in works of art, both in the verbal arts and in the arts more generally. She approaches the topic with a consideration of the effects of music upon a listener: music, like the spoken language, occupies time-space. On the other hand, our response to a visual presentation—say, a landscape or a portrait—is a more free-ranging, even a spasmodic, experience. One's eye may wander at will, following the inclinations, familiar or novel, that have sparked one's concern. Her account begins by setting out as fully as possible what we, in using the English language, may be understood to mean by the term *feeling*. "'Feeling' in the broad sense here employed seems to be the generic basis of all mental experience—sensation, emotion, imagination, recollection, and reasoning, to mention only the major categories" (1979, 18). She goes on to distinguish aspects of feeling that are felt as action, and aspects that seem to us to be *sensation*, a state of mind that we take to be the outcome of circumstances that we do not necessarily control. It is the formation of these images that above all interest her: "In man, nervous sensitivity is so high that to respond with a muscular act to every stimulus of which he takes cognizance would keep him in a perpetual St. Vitus's dance. A great many acts, started in his brain . . . lead to the formation of images" (27). It is by means of these images that we seem to be "constantly thinking, remembering, recording, or dreaming—most often, in the waking state, all of these together" (27).

Her consideration in this work and elsewhere of the role of language sets up a broad division between *discursive symbolism*, words that embody our cognitive responses to experience, our ideas, and our speculations; and, on the other hand, works of art that have a special role, that of objectifying feeling "so that we can contemplate and understand it" (80). It is above all our apprehension of the future—experiences that have yet to be encountered—guises that life has yet to take up—that is immensely enriched by such means. It is thus we approach new experiences with some degree of familiarity brought about by the expectations that former states of mind have engendered—the configurations of previous experience. And the process—often enough—lasts a lifetime. There may be episodes—days out, weeks off—but it is more likely that the threads that sew a life together form part of a long-lived, consistent pattern of expectations. After all, they are a part of the person we have become, and are becoming, or may yet become.

The severely practical implication of all I have said so far is to underline the importance of affording opportunities in school for children and young people to tell some part of the stories of their lives. Certainly we can expect to find them interested, and often eager to do so, though not always. I remember what one eleven-year-old in a high school in Victoria wrote in response to the teacher's request, "Tell a story": "Teacher wouldn't know if you broke your arm. They just pile the work on. It gets harder every day. 3rd term is the most boringest time I know of. The days are long and boring. . . . This story is my life more than a story. Cause I didn't know what to write." We might well guess that former states of mind have left an antipathy—and perhaps a perplexity—that he won't easily break down.

But that is unusual—I think most of us tend to find ourselves and our views about life of interest, and worth talking about. We certainly have to recognize that fiction and autobiography are inextricably conflated: every account of actual events is to some degree embellished, fictionalized, just as every fiction makes direct or indirect reference to aspects of our first hand experience. Teachers have often noticed how children tell fairy stories with witches who speak in tones that remind us of mothers in a bad temper.

Some of the events in our lives are reported orally on repeated occasions: often what we make of the events will vary with our moods and our feelings toward the people we address—the frankness or the reticence—or maybe the downright dishonesty—with which we describe the events. It is all a part of the complex of expectations with which we face the future.

We are called upon to interpret our life experiences. We have on the one hand the meaningless flux of events and on the other a story—happenings, events, sequences that "hang together," with events "that fit into each other," as Langer has put it. John Dewey found that the outcome will depend on the purpose of the individual:

> For the person approaching a subject, the simple thing is his purpose—the use he desires to make of material, tool, or technical process, no matter how complicated the process of execution may be. The unity of the purpose, with the concentration upon details which it entails, confers simplicity upon the elements that have to be

> reckoned with in the course of action. It furnishes each with a single meaning according to its service in carrying out the whole enterprise. (1917)

It seems to me that we process the "flux" of events in two principal ways: first by the shaping power of our perceptions and then by the narratives we compose as we share experiences. Coleridge said of the first: "It is a gift of the imagination that in a succession of sounds we hear music"; and Martin Buber said of the second: "Experience comes to man as I, but it is by experience as we that he builds the common world in which he lives."

Susanne Langer, in her three volume series, *Mind: An Essay on Human Feeling*, goes into great detail to point out that order exists in the physical world independent of our perceptions: she notes, for example, that the form of a plant constitutes a record of the slow movement of its growth—a process infinitely ordered within and beyond what our eyes can perceive. At the biological level human beings share that order, but at the level of behavior they have escaped from the instinctive controls that govern the zoological creatures. It is Langer's belief that we shape our lives into a kind of narrative in order more fully to possess our experiences: the shape we give is "art-like," an attempt to recapture something that in the bustle of our daily lives we have lost—what might be called "a natural order"—the build-up and resolution of tension to be found in "the rhythms of every living act—the conception, gestation, birth, climax, and what Shakespeare called the 'dying fall.'" Graves again:

> "There is one story and one story only
> That will prove worth your telling—"

Shakespeare, in another context, provides a fitting conclusion. Hamlet confides to Horatio:

> Sir, in my heart there was a kind of fighting
> That would not let me sleep . . . Rashly,
> And praised be rashness for it, let us know,
> Our indiscretion sometime serves us well,
> When our deep plots do pall; and that should teach us
> There's a divinity that shapes our ends,
> Rough-hew them how we will. (V.ii. 4-10)

We join Horatio in responding: "That is most certain."

Works Cited

Dewey, John. 1966. *Democracy and Education: An Introduction to the Philosophy of Education*. New York, NY: The Free Press.

Graves, Robert. 1988. "To Juan at the Winter Solstice." *Collected Poems*. New York, NY: Oxford University Press.

Isaacs, Nathan. 1958, 1959. "Some Basic Reflections about Language." *The Bulletin* Part I:1-8. Part II:1-10.

———. 1949. *The Foundations of Common Sense*. London: Kegan Paul.

Langer, Susanne. 1979. *Philosophical Sketches*. Manchester, NH: Ayer.

———. 1967. *Mind: An Essay on Human Feeling*. Vol. 1. Baltimore, MD: Johns Hopkins Press.

———. 1957. *Philosophy in a New Key: A Study in the Symbolism of Reason, Rite and Act*. Cambridge, MA: Harvard University Press.

Shakespeare, William. *Hamlet, Prince of Denmark*, Act V, Scene 2.

Vygotsky, L. 1986. *Thought and Language*. Rev. ed. Cambridge, MA: MIT Press.